RECONSTRUCTING HONOR IN ROMAN PHILIPPI

This book examines Paul's letter to the Philippians against the social background of the colony at Philippi. After an extensive survey of Roman social values, Professor Hellerman argues that the *cursus honorum*, the formalized sequence of public offices that marked out the prescribed social pilgrimage for aspiring senatorial aristocrats in Rome (and which was replicated in miniature in municipalities and in voluntary associations), forms the background against which Paul has framed his picture of Jesus in the great Christ hymn in Philippians 2. In marked contrast to the values of the dominant culture, Paul portrays Jesus descending what the author describes as a *cursus pudorum* ("course of ignominies"). The passage has thus been intentionally framed to subvert Roman *cursus* ideology and, by extension, to redefine the manner in which honor and power were to be utilized among the Christians at Philippi.

JOSEPH H. HELLERMAN is Professor of New Testament Language and Literature at Talbot School of Theology and Co-Pastor at Oceanside Christian Fellowship in El Segundo, California.

SOCIETY FOR NEW TESTAMENT STUDIES
MONOGRAPH SERIES
General Editor: John M. Court

132

RECONSTRUCTING HONOR IN ROMAN PHILIPPI

SOCIETY FOR NEW TESTAMENT STUDIES

MONOGRAPH SERIES

Recent titles in the series

120. Belly and Body in the Pauline Epistles
 KARL OLAV SANDNES
 0 521 81535 5
121. The First Christian Historian
 DANIEL MARGUERAT
 0 521 81650 5
122. An Aramaic Approach to Q
 MAURICE CASEY
 0 521 81723 4
123. Isaiah's Christ in Matthew's Gospel
 RICHARD BEATON
 0 521 81888 5
124. God and History in the Book of Revelation
 MICHAEL GILBERTSON
 0 521 82466 4
125. Jesus' Defeat of Death
 PETER G. BOLT
 0 521 83036 2
126. From Hope to Despair in Thessalonica
 COLIN R. NICHOLL
 0 521 83142 3
127. Matthew's Trilogy of Parables
 WESLEY G. OLMSTEAD
 0 521 83154 7
128. The People of God in the Apocalypse
 STEPHEN PATTEMORE
 0 521 83698 0
129. The Exorcism Stories in Luke–Acts
 TODD KLUTZ
 0 521 83804 5
130. Jews, Gentiles and Ethnic Reconciliation
 TET-LIM N. YEE
 0 521 83831 2
131. Ancient Rhetoric and Paul's Apology
 FREDRICK J. LONG
 0 521 84233 6

Reconstructing Honor in Roman Philippi

Carmen Christi as *Cursus Pudorum*

JOSEPH H. HELLERMAN

CAMBRIDGE UNIVERSITY PRESS
Cambridge, New York, Melbourne, Madrid, Cape Town, Singapore, São Paulo

Cambridge University Press
The Edinburgh Building, Cambridge CB2 2RU, UK

Published in the United States of America by Cambridge University Press, New York

www.cambridge.org
Information on this title: www.cambridge.org/9780521849098

© Joseph H. Hellerman 2005

This book is in copyright. Subject to statutory exception
and to the provisions of relevant collective licensing agreements,
no reproduction of any part may take place without
the written permission of Cambridge University Press.

First published 2005

Printed in the United Kingdom at the University Press, Cambridge

A catalogue record for this book is available from the British Library

Library of Congress Cataloguing in Publication data
Hellerman, Joseph H., 1952–
Reconstructing honor in Roman Philippi: Carmen Christi as cursus pudorum / Joseph H. Hellerman.
   p. cm. (Society for New Testament Studies Monograph series; 132)
Includes bibliographical references and indexes.
ISBN 0-521-84909-8 (hardback)
1. Bible. N.T. Philippians – Criticism, interpretation, etc. I. Title. II. Monograph series (Society for New Testament Studies); 132.

BS2705.52.H45   2005
227'.6067 – dc22   2004057068

ISBN-13 9780521849098
ISBN-10 0521849098

Cambridge University Press has no responsibility for the persistence or accuracy of URLs for external or third-party internet websites referred to in this book, and does not guarantee that any content on such websites is, or will remain, accurate or appropriate.

CONTENTS

Acknowledgments	*page* ix
List of abbreviations	xi
Introduction	**1**
1 Roman social organization	**3**
Social stratification in the Roman world	3
Public expressions of the social hierarchy	11
Summary	32
2 Preoccupation with honor and the *cursus honorum*	**34**
Honor as a social value	34
Public office and Rome's *cursus honorum*	51
Summary	62
3 The Roman colony at Philippi	**64**
History of the colony	64
The military orientation of the colony	69
The imperial cult in Roman Philippi	80
Summary	87
4 Honor and status in Philippi	**88**
Honor and status among the colony's elite	88
Honor and status among the colony's non-elite	100
Summary: social status in Roman Philippi	108
5 Acts and Philippians	**110**
The Philippian narrative in Acts	110
Paul's letter to the Philippians	116
Summary	127
6 *Carmen Christi* as *cursus pudorum*	**129**
Philippians 2:6–8: a *cursus pudorum*	129
Philippians 2:9–11: reconstructing honor	148

7 Summary and conclusion	**157**
Summary: reconstructing honor in Philippi	157
Conclusion: reconstructing honor in early Christianity	163
Notes	167
References	214
Index of ancient sources	226
Index of modern authors	234
Subject index	235

ACKNOWLEDGMENTS

Each of us is indebted to the insights of others, and I have benefited from a number of mentors – in print and in person – at various stages in the development of this project. For the chapters dealing with the social values and cultural codes of the broader Roman world, the works of noted social historians, such as Ramsay MacMullen, Richard Saller, and Peter Garnsey, proved ever serviceable, while the more specialized studies of the function of honor in Roman life and politics by Jon Lendon and Carlin Barton particularly influenced my thinking at various points in the discussion. Most helpful for the chapters that treat social and religious life in Philippi were the monographs of Peter Pilhofer, Lukas Bormann, and, most recently, Peter Oakes. The excellent commentaries of Peter O'Brien and Gordon Fee, along with numerous related studies, were, of course, indispensable to my treatment of the biblical materials in chapters five and six. My argument finally rests, however, on evidence drawn from ancient source materials (primarily literary works for Roman social values; the Philippian inscriptions for social life in the colony), and here I owe a significant debt of gratitude to Peter Pilhofer, whose recent catalogue of inscriptions from Philippi repeatedly demonstrated its worth as a delightfully accessible resource for studying social and religious life in the colony.

A number of friends and former mentors graciously gave of their time and energy to peruse the manuscript at various stages in its development. The book began as an extended essay, written for a Biola University faculty seminar on Christology, led by Drs. Millard Erickson and Michael Wilkins. Several individuals read the completed book-length manuscript. Dr. Ronald Mellor's input was insightful and timely from the Roman side. New Testament specialists who interacted with the work included Drs. Walt Russell and Moyer Hubbard, colleagues at Talbot School of Theology, as well as Dr. S. Scott Bartchy, who served as my doctoral mentor at UCLA some years ago. Their input was invaluable. I am also greatly indebted to the sharp mind and careful eyes of my church secretary, Michelle Cutrona, whose proofreading abilities are nothing short of remarkable. Any remaining weaknesses are, of course, my own responsibility. Special thanks, finally, go to my wife Joann and to my two teenage daughters, Rebekah and Rachel. They patiently put up with a sometimes cranky husband and father, who was often preoccupied with the minutiae of Latin inscriptions and oblivious to the pressing realities of daily life. To them I dedicate this volume.

ABBREVIATIONS

ABD	*Anchor Bible Dictionary* (ed. D. N. Freedman)
ACCS	Ancient Christian Commentary on Scripture
AJP	*American Journal of Philology*
ANRW	*Aufstieg und Niedergang der römischen Welt* (ed. H. Temporini)
AP	*American Psychologist*
AS	*Ancient Society*
ASR	*American Sociological Review*
BBR	*Bulletin for Biblical Research*
BCH	*Bulletin de Correspondance Hellénique*
BDAG	Bauer, Danker, Arndt, and Gingrich, *Greek–English Lexicon*
BDF	Blass, Debrunner, and Funk, *A Greek Grammar of the New Testament*
Bib	*Biblica*
BJRL	*Bulletin of the John Rylands Library*
BTB	*Biblical Theology Bulletin*
CBQ	*Catholic Biblical Quarterly*
CJ	*The Classical Journal*
CQ	*The Classical Quarterly*
FIRA	*Fontes Iuris Romani Antejustiniani* (ed. S. Riccobono)
HTR	*Harvard Theological Review*
IDB	*Interpreter's Dictionary of the Bible* (ed. G. A. Buttrick)
JBL	*Journal of Biblical Literature*
JRS	*Journal of Roman Studies*
JSNT	*Journal for the Study of the New Testament*
JSOT	*Journal for the Study of the Old Testament*
JTS	*Journal of Theological Studies*
NKZ	*Neue kirchliche Zeitschrift*
NovT	*Novum Testamentum*
NTS	*New Testament Studies*
RB	*Revue biblique*

SE	*Studia Evangelica*
TDNT	*Theological Dictionary of the New Testament* (ed. G. Kittel)
TrinJ	*Trinity Journal*
WTJ	*Westminster Theological Journal*
ZN	*Zeitschrift für Numismatik*
ZNW	*Zeitschrift für die neutestamentliche Wissenschaft*
ZPE	*Zeitschrift für Papyrologie und Epigraphik*
ZTK	*Zeitschrift für Theologie und Kirche*

Titles of ancient sources are abbreviated according to the conventions of the *Oxford Classical Dictionary*.

INTRODUCTION

The purpose of this monograph is to situate the New Testament materials relating to Roman Philippi in their proper socio-historical setting. I have suspected for some time that the author of Philippians 2 intentionally structured his portrayal of Jesus with Roman social values and practices directly in view. I am now convinced that Rome's *cursus honorum*, the formalized sequence of public offices that marked out the prescribed social pilgrimage for aspiring senatorial aristocrats in Rome (and which was replicated in miniature in municipalities and in voluntary associations), forms the background against which Paul has framed his picture of Jesus in the great Christ hymn in Philippians 2.

The layout of my project is quite straightforward. The first two chapters survey the social landscape of the broader Roman world. Chapter one describes the various status groups in the empire, and then reviews the ways in which the Roman elite class sought intentionally to preserve their highly stratified social environment. Chapter two discusses the importance of personal and familial honor to Roman social sensibilities and proceeds to examine Rome's *cursus honorum* and the replication of *cursus* ideology in elite and non-elite settings across the empire. The second major portion of the monograph, consisting of the third and fourth chapters, seeks to situate Roman preoccupation with honor and public esteem in the colony at Philippi. I suggest that concern for honor and status, along with expressions of personal achievement presented in *cursus* form in the colony's inscriptions, characterized Philippi in ways currently unattested elsewhere in the Greek East. The military origins of the colony, the ruler cult, and the replication of Roman social values in non-elite settings in the colony receive particular attention.

The final chapters are dedicated to a reexamination of the familiar biblical materials relating to Philippi. Chapter five treats briefly the Philippian narrative in Acts 16, along with selected portions of Paul's letter to the Jesus community in the colony. Chapter six focuses solely upon the great Christological masterpiece in Philippians 2. I maintain that Paul, in his portrayal of Jesus in verses 6–8, has taken Rome's *cursus* ideology and turned it on its head, so to speak, as he presents Christ descending a *cursus pudorum* ("a succession or race of ignominies") from equality with God, to the status of a slave, to the physical and social death of public crucifixion. In stark contrast to the values of the dominant culture, moreover, Paul's Christ surrenders his status willingly, and, most astoundingly, he ultimately receives the highest of honors at the hands of God himself, who thereby legitimates Christ's decidedly anti-Roman approach to power and status (vv. 9–11). The presentation, I suggest, was intended by Paul (the likely author of the "hymn") to encourage persons in the church who possessed some degree of honor or status in the broader social world of the colony to utilize their status, after the analogy of Jesus, in the service of others.

1

ROMAN SOCIAL ORGANIZATION

Rank must be preserved.   Cicero (*Pro Plancio* 15)

The first section of this work examines social relations in the ancient world, with special attention to the social verticality that was so central to Roman sensibilities. Chapter one adopts a static, snapshot approach to Roman social organization. I will survey the various status groupings of the empire, as the ancients understood them, and then illustrate the ways in which the social hierarchy found expression in public life. The second chapter takes a more dynamic approach to the topic. Particular attention will be directed to the incessant preoccupation with the preservation and acquisition of honor characteristic of Roman elite social praxis and to the replication of these honor-related values and types of behavior at every level of society.

Social stratification in the Roman world

James Littlejohn has defined social stratification as "the name under which sociologists study inequality in society, i.e., the unequal distribution of goods and services, rights and obligations, power and prestige."[1] Gerhard Lenski, in his seminal treatment of the subject, similarly described social stratification as "the distributive process in human societies – the process by which scarce values are distributed."[2] Social stratification is inherent in the human species. The forms and degrees of inequality vary considerably, however, from one society to another. Lenski has been particularly helpful in clarifying these cultural distinctions through the construction of a fivefold typology of human societies based on ecology and technology.[3] Lenski's five types of societies are listed in the chart below, along with their corresponding degrees of social inequality.

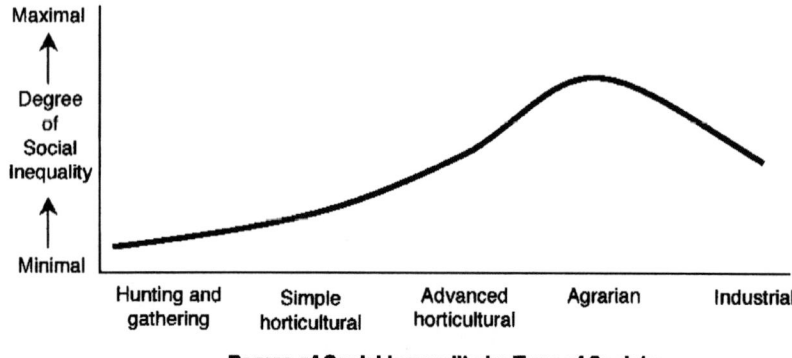

Degree of Social Inequality by Type of Society

For present purposes it is important simply to note that the Roman empire constitutes a classic example of an agrarian society – the type of society reflecting the greatest degree of social inequality in the above model. Lenski elaborates:

> One fact impresses itself on almost any observer of agrarian societies, especially on one who views them in a broadly comparative perspective. This is the fact of *marked social inequality*. Without exception, one finds pronounced differences in power, prestige, and honor associated with mature agrarian economies.[4]

Much has been written on class structure and social stratification in antiquity, and the problems associated with cross-cultural analysis undertaken across great barriers of time are well known. Fortunately for the present project, the Romans themselves were quite sensitive to the marked social inequality that characterized their relational universe, and ample source material has survived in both the literary and epigraphical records to illustrate the basic contours of Roman social organization.[5]

Before I examine Roman social life, however, some observations are in order regarding my methodology for employing ancient source material. Social historians tend to approach their sources somewhat differently than scholars who are interested in political or military history. Keith Hopkins reflects upon the preoccupation with historical reliability which has traditionally characterized historical inquiry:

> Sober historians are interested primarily, sometimes exclusively, in the truth; they therefore usually ignore untrue stories. Indeed as one reads an ancient source, there is a temptation, rooted perhaps in modern scientific rationalism, to pass over these fabrications, roughly as most readers turn over a page which contains statistical tables, with barely a glance.[6]

Hopkins, however, finds such an approach too restrictive. As a social historian, Hopkins rightly recognizes that untrue stories are often highly revealing, for such narratives speak volumes about the cultural values and social codes that inform the worldview of their authors. It is not hard to see why this is the case. Cultural values and ideals, preserved safely intact in the symbolic world of a people's collective imagination, are inevitably compromised in the complexities of daily life. As a result, although the historically accurate portions of a writer's narrative will inevitably reflect the author's cultural values, they will do so only imperfectly. When the ancient historian departs, however, from recounting the variegated realities of history and begins, instead, to increasingly embellish, fabricate, or editorialize his narrative, the details of history fade into the background somewhat, and the cultural values and social codes of the author and his contemporaries suddenly occupy a place of increasing prominence in the narrative. These values – "the perceptions and the beliefs of men," as Hopkins refers to them – will often be more evident, therefore, in non-historical source material than in more historically accurate accounts.[7] And it is the "perceptions and beliefs of men," especially where social status and honor are concerned, that I am after in the present monograph.

An illustration will suffice. In the course of a discussion of the opprobrium of slavery and servile origin in the Roman mind (chapter six), I proceed to draw, by way of example, upon Suetonius' *Life of Augustus*. Suetonius informs us that Mark Antony taunted Octavian concerning his patriline, claiming that Octavian's great-grandfather was "a freedman and a rope-maker from the country about Thurii" (*Aug.* 2). A "sober historian" (to adopt Hopkins's phrase from the above citation) would perhaps want to consider the truth value of Suetonius' narrative at two levels: (1) Was Octavian's great-grandfather really "a freedman and a rope-maker from the country about Thurii"? (2) Did Antony ever actually taunt him with such a remark? Our political historian might conclude negatively on both counts but nevertheless proceed to see behind the fabrication some kernel of historical truth, namely, an increasing rift between Antony and Octavian post-Philippi (43 BCE). Such is the general trajectory of traditional historical methodology.

In the present connection, answers to the kinds of questions framed in the previous paragraph are quite irrelevant. As a social historian I am instead interested in why, for example, a taunt like Antony's would have been offensive to a fellow-member of the Roman elite. This generates a different set of questions. Some examples: (1) How would Antony's taunt have resonated in the social world of Suetonius' readers? (2) What was the social status of a "freedman and a rope-maker"?

(3) How many generations must one be removed from a manumitted ancestor in order to escape the taint of servile origin? (Octavian is portrayed as three generations removed, and the taunt apparently still "works" in the author's narrative.) The historical accuracy of Suetonius' account is of little importance in formulating answers to these kinds of questions.

Precisely because narratives of questionable historical veracity so transparently depict the cultural values and social codes of their authors, the pages that follow are replete with citations from Roman writings that fabricate or, at least, elaborate upon the events they purport to relate. These very texts prove particularly useful for understanding the centrality of honor and social status in the symbolic universe of those who inhabited the early Roman empire.

The great divide – elite and non-elite

At the broadest level of analysis it must be emphasized that the empire had no middle class like that which constitutes the majority of the population of the United States of America. With some risk of oversimplification, it is fair to identify the ancient world as a two-class society in which the small percentage of wealthy elite (2 percent would be a generous estimate) controlled both the means of production – land, in an agrarian economy – and the legal system. The great majority of the population, in contrast, consisted of humble non-elite free persons and slaves.[8]

Ancient source materials decidedly confirm the consensus of Roman social historians reflected in the previous paragraph. Writers consistently view their social world as consisting of two basic strata. Paul's reflections in 1 Corinthians are familiar:

> Consider your own call, brothers and sisters: not many of you were wise by human standards, not many were powerful, not many were of noble birth. But God chose what is foolish in the world to shame the wise; God chose what is weak in the world to shame the strong; God chose what is low and despised in the world, things that are not, to reduce to nothing things that are, so that no one might boast in the presence of God. (1:26–29)[9]

Lucian similarly groups persons into two distinct categories. The social chasm between the poor (οἱ πένητες) and the rich (οἱ πλούσιοι) is the difference between "an ant and a camel" (*Saturnalia* 19).[10] In one of Lucian's dialogues a non-elite person complains,

Roman social organization

> We should be less distressed about [economic injustice], you may be sure, if we did not see the rich living in such bliss, who, though they have such gold, such silver in their safes, though they have all that clothing and own slaves and carriage-horses and tenements and farms, each and all in large numbers, not only have never shared them with us but never deign to notice ordinary people (τοὺς πολλούς). (*Saturnalia* 20)

Epictetus, for his part, likens the social distance between decurions (who constituted the upper stratum of the *polis*) and commoners to that between a general and a rank-and-file soldier (στρατιώτην . . . στρατηγός), or a magistrate and a private individual (ἄρχοντα . . . ἰδιώτην) (*Dissertationes* 3.24.99).

The Younger Pliny separates into two social classes those attending the races in the circus, as he bemoans the loyalty of the fans to their teams: "Such is the popularity and importance of a worthless team jersey – not just with the crowd (*vulgus*), which is worth less (*vilius*) than the jersey, but with certain serious individuals (*graves homines*)" (*Ep.* 9.6.3).[11] Tacitus, too, understands his world to consist, in the broadest sense, of "the rabble," on the one hand, and "citizens of repute," on the other (*Ann.* 3.36). Aelius Aristides argues for the preservation of this non-elite "rabble" precisely because of the service they provide in highlighting, by contrast, the social standing of Aristides' fellow-members of the elite: "Those who think that they should be superior should calculate that if they willingly destroy their inferiors, they injure their own source of pride (φιλοτιμίᾳ) – for the existence of inferiors is an advantage to superiors since they will be able to point out those over whom they are superior" (*Or.* 24.34).[12] People in most societies find themselves quite intrigued by the phenomenon of two unrelated persons sharing a family resemblance. Roman writers who comment on this topic focus most intently upon elite and non-elite persons who happen to look alike. A two-strata view of social reality surfaces, again, in their writings (italicized to emphasize the contrast):

> Vibius, of free descent, and Publicius, a freedman, bore such a resemblance to Pompeius Magnus that if they had exchanged conditions Pompey could have been greeted in their persons and they in Pompey's. Certainly, wherever Vibius or Publicius went, they drew people's eyes to themselves, as everybody noticed the appearance of the *great man* in these *nobodies* (*speciem amplissimi civis . . . personis mediocribus*). This trick of chance came to Pompey as though by inheritance. For his father too was thought to resemble Menogenes, his cook, so closely that,

> *powerful in arms and bold of spirit* as he was, he could not keep the fellow's *base name (sordidum . . . nomen)* away from himself. (Val. Max. 9.14.1–2)

Notice the manner in which the author includes both Vibius, a freeman, and Publicius, a former slave, under the single rubric "nobodies" (*personis mediocribus*). As we will see below, the strong tendencies toward inequality which so marked Roman relational sensibilities (reflected in the two-strata view of society outlined above) guaranteed a further proliferation of social distinctions *among* the elite and the non-elite, respectively. The resulting multiplication of strata generated, in turn, a profound social chasm between slave and free in the conceptual world of non-elite persons. Non-elite free persons, in particular, would have strongly resisted the lumping together of "Vibius, of free descent, and Publicius, a freedman," into a single social group. Valerius Maximus, however, writes from on high, as a member of the Roman aristocracy, among whom all non-elite persons – slave or free – are simply regarded as "nobodies" when contrasted with the author's fellow-members of the elite, such as Pompey and his father. Such was the power of the two-strata view of the social hierarchy in the conceptual universe of the Roman elite class.

Similar bifurcation into two social groups is to be found among Jewish writers. Sirach warns his readers,

> Do not lift a weight beyond your strength, nor associate with a man mightier and richer than you. How can the clay pot associate with the iron kettle? The pot will strike against it, and will itself be broken. A rich man does wrong and he even adds reproaches; a poor man suffers wrong, and he must add apologies.
> (Sir. 13:2–3; cf. 8:1–2)

For Josephus, the fundamental groups of Jewish society are the king or royal house and priests, on the one hand, and the people as a whole (λαός) or, especially, the simple person (ἰδιώτης), on the other. The former are characterized as "rich" (πλούσιος) and "powerful" (δυνατός), the latter as "weak" (ἀδύνατος/ἀσθενής) and "poor" (ἄπορος/ἐνδεής).[13]

It is important to recognize that our understanding of the ancient world is inevitably compromised by the fact that the great majority of our literary sources have been penned by elite males. Tacitus' description of his peers as "citizens of repute," along with his corresponding dismissal of the masses as "rabble," could thus be interpreted as patently self-serving elite propaganda. Derogatory terms aside, however, the two-strata perspective on social reality reflected above clearly transcended the boundaries of social class. The non-elite writings we do possess similarly divide the empire's population into two major groups:

> Also [the beast] causes all, both small and great, both rich and poor, both free and slave, to be marked on the right hand or the forehead. (Rev. 13:16)

> Listen, my beloved brothers and sisters. Has not God chosen the poor in the world to be rich in faith and to be heirs of the kingdom that he has promised to those who love him? But you have dishonored the poor. Is it not the rich who oppress you? Is it not they who drag you into court? Is it not they who blaspheme the excellent name that was invoked over you? (Jas. 2:5–6)

The author of James regrets the preferential treatment accorded to elites in early Christian communities (Jas. 2:1–4). By assigning elites places of honor in community meetings the poor are being "dishonored." Even as he challenges the values of the dominant culture, however, our author, like his pagan contemporaries, intuitively draws upon a two-strata view of social relations in order to frame his critique. As we shall see below, moreover, the deference to social status which James so vehemently denounces constituted standard social praxis wherever Rome ruled.

The Stegemanns conclude the following concerning this twofold orientation of the ancient Mediterranean world:

> At the top of the societies of the Roman empire there was apparently a small elite group that was distinguished in the consciousness of ancient authors by their noble origin, leadership in public office, wealth, and esteem. Thus this elite is to be understood as both a political (the powerful) and economic (the rich) elite and a prestige (the most esteemed) elite. Over against them are the masses of the population, who are defined by the lack of the social traits that mark the elite.[14]

Further stratification among the Roman elite

The pronounced verticality which characterized Roman social relations generated further stratification *among* elite and non-elite persons respectively. Non-elite distinctions between slave (including freedpersons) and free and, among the latter, citizen and non-citizen held sway. I will address these non-elite social groupings later in some detail. A brief look at further social stratification within the Roman elite will prove most useful in the present context.

The elite class subdivided into three aristocratic orders: senators, equestrians, and local municipal decurions.[15] Six hundred aristocrats filled the senate during the early imperial period. Each had to meet a minimum property qualification of one million sesterces, but the wealth of many senators far exceeded that amount. Senators who somehow lost their wealth could be removed from the order. At one point Claudius gave a speech "commending all who voluntarily renounced senatorial rank (*ordine senatorio*) owing to straitened circumstances (they no longer possessed 1,000,000 sesterces): those who, by remaining, added impudence to poverty were removed" (Tac. *Ann.* 12.52).[16] Equestrians were required to possess individual wealth amounting to at least 400,000 sesterces (*equites* literally means "knights" – originally a military class consisting of individuals rich enough to own a horse for a military campaign). Scholars estimate that the equestrian order boasted some twenty thousand members. The final elite order was the *ordo decurionum*, constituting the leading citizens of cities in the Roman provinces. Some 150,000–200,000 decurions occupied magistracies and priesthoods in local municipalities and assumed a significant degree of financial responsibility for civic events and local construction projects.[17] The presupposed minimum income for these town councilors varied, with Comum's standard of 100,000 sesterces probably representing the upper limit (Pliny, *Ep.* 1.19).

The assumption on the part of ancient observers that the members of all three Roman orders formed a single social stratum, vis-à-vis non-elite "rabble," has been amply demonstrated from the texts cited above. Within the elite group itself, however, a marked social cleavage existed between the dominant orders, which became painfully obvious at times. Horace relates the engaging story of a magistrate of Fundi, Aufidius Luscus, who turned out in all his regalia to greet an important entourage traveling past his town to Brundisium. As one of the most distinguished citizens of an important town – probably the largest fish in Fundi's significant social pond – Aufidius presumably anticipated a degree of respect in the broader elite world as well. The esteemed entourage, which included a person of consular rank, apparently thought otherwise, for they howled with laughter as they passed the now humiliated civic father (Hor. *Sat.* 1.5.34–36).

Each of the three elite orders further subdivided into its own characteristic social hierarchy. Among senators, those who could claim consular ancestry, designated *nobiles*, stood out from newcomers to the senatorial class and consistently flaunted their social superiority. Cicero, for example, was a son of an equestrian and lacked a senatorial lineage. He nevertheless became a highly influential Roman consul and senator. Yet as a "new man" Cicero continually struggled to establish himself as a social equal in the senate, painfully enduring an air of superiority on the part of the *nobiles*, and often experiencing aloofness and outright rudeness at the hands of his senatorial colleagues. Newcomers like Cicero, however, were not without their own strategies for ameliorating the effect of the social stigma they experienced at the hands of their social betters. Cicero would at times ignore the *nobile*–newcomer distinction and, instead, divide the senate of his day into social groups that were more functional in nature. In concert with recent tendencies in Roman social relations, Cicero portrayed the senatorial aristocracy as consisting of (1) the *optimates*, that is, the "best" men, whose policies and tactics were also noble and honorable, and (2) the *populares*, the dishonorable, who courted the masses in favor of legislation which threatened the social status quo (Cic. *Sest.* 45.96–97).

Equestrians, for their part, also subdivided into separate ranks, roughly translated "excellent" (*egregius*), "most accomplished" (*perfectissimus*), and "most renowned" (*eminentissimus*).[18] Under Claudius, a group of equestrian stewards (*procuratores*) served as the emperor's agents, performing various administrative duties throughout the empire. These officials, too, were further ranked, this time on the basis of their annual stipend, as *trecenarii, ducenarii, centenarii*, and *sexagenarii*, receiving respectively 300,000, 200,000, 100,000, and 60,000 sesterces (Suet. *Claud.* 24). Common to all of the above is the ubiquitous tendency in the Roman world to divide and subdivide into groups and subgroups, in order to clearly define the social pecking order.

Public expressions of the social hierarchy

Elite males in Roman society engaged in a relentless quest for the acquisition and preservation of personal and familial honor.[19] These concerns, in turn, generated a consuming passion to identify persons publicly according to social status, a characteristic of Roman society which found expression wherever two or more were gathered in the ancient world. I will examine in some detail the dynamics of honor-seeking in the following chapter. Here I will identify and illustrate five aspects of life through which the various social strata were carefully delineated in the public arena:

a. Attire
b. Occupation
c. Seating at public events
d. Seating at banquets
e. The legal system.

Attire

Clothing functioned as a constant reminder of rank on all social levels.[20] Most basic was the citizen toga (*toga virilis*), which young men began to wear at fourteen to sixteen years of age.[21] Boys who had not yet come of age were clothed instead with a boyhood garment (*toga praetexta*), which was white with a purple border. Consider Anthony Everitt's engaging description of the Roman toga:

> The toga, a remarkably incommodious garment, was a large length of unbleached woolen cloth, cut in a rough circle as much as three meters in diameter. Putting it on was an art and the rich employed a trained slave to arrange its complicated folds. It was draped over the body in such a way that the right arm was free but the left covered. Drafty in winter and stickily hot in summer, it had few practical advantages to recommend it and took continual care and attention to keep it in place. But, however uncomfortable, *the toga was a Roman's uniform and a powerful visual symbol of citizenship.*[22]

Manumitted slaves enthusiastically capitalized on the function of the toga as a "powerful visual symbol of citizenship." Numerous wealthy freedmen, for example, publicly proclaimed their recently acquired freedom and corresponding entrée into citizen status by portraying themselves dressed in the citizen toga, surrounded by family members, in framed reliefs carved onto ostentatious tomb monuments lining the main thoroughfares that led out of Augustan Rome.[23]

For those born into citizen families, adopting the toga constituted a central rite of passage during which a young man dedicated his boyhood toga to the household gods, put on the *toga virilis*, and proceeded, escorted by family and friends, to the forum, where he was formally enrolled in his family's citizen tribe. The donning of the toga marked the transition to adulthood in much the same way that marriage did for women. Thus, Spurius Ligustinus, a republican soldier (171 BCE), identifies his children as follows: "We have six sons, and two daughters, both of whom are now married. Four of our sons have assumed the toga of manhood (*togas viriles*), two wear the boys' stripe (*duo praetextati sunt*)" (Livy 42.34).

The symbolic significance of the *toga virilis* surfaces in a variety of contexts in Roman literature. The citizen toga figured prominently among a series of reforms instituted by Augustus.[24] The emperor, we are informed,

> desired also to revive the ancient fashion of dress, and once when he saw in an assembly a throng of men in dark cloaks [the *toga virilis* was white], he cried out indignantly, "Behold them, Romans, lords of the world, the nation clad in the toga" [sarcastically quoting Virgil, *Aen.* 1.282], and he directed the aediles never again to allow anyone to appear in the Forum or its neighbourhood except in the toga without a cloak.
>
> (Suet. *Aug.* 40)[25]

Augustus' own assumption of the toga of manhood was surrounded by anomalous portents but proved particularly symbolic for that very reason:

> When Augustus was assuming the gown of manhood, his senatorial tunic was ripped apart on both sides and fell at his feet, which some interpreted as a sure sign that the order of which the tunic was the badge would one day be brought to his feet.
>
> (Suet. *Aug.* 94)

Some years later, during the reign of Claudius, a legal debacle erupted which later provided Suetonius with a colorful opportunity to highlight the practical wisdom of the emperor. At issue in the trial was the defendant's alleged Roman citizenship. Suetonius relates,

> In a case involving citizenship a fruitless dispute arose among the advocates as to whether the defendant ought to make his appearance in the toga or in a Greek mantle, and the emperor, with the idea of showing absolute impartiality, made him change his garb several times, according as he was accused or defended.
>
> (*Claud.* 15)

The distinction between the citizen toga and the Greek mantle (*pallium*) also figures in Suetonius' *Life of Tiberius*, where he mentions the "contempt and aversion" shown to the future emperor when, while sojourning at Rhodes, Tiberius had exchanged "the garb of his country" (*patrio habitu*) for the distinctive Greek attire of mantle (*pallium*) and slippers (*Tib.* 13). Suetonius described Caligula in similarly negative terms: "In his clothing, his shoes, and the rest of his attire, he did not follow the usage of his country or his fellow-citizens (*neque patrio neque civili*)" (*Calig.* 52).

Among those entitled to wear the *toga virilis*, further distinctions in dress prevailed. Only the senatorial class could wear the toga with a broad purple stripe (*latus clavus*). Equestrians donned the toga with a narrow stripe and enjoyed the right to wear gold rings on their fingers to mark their place in the pecking order. So closely was the ring associated with the equestrian order in the minds of Roman writers, that accession to the order could simply be described as receiving "the honour of the gold ring" (Suet. *Galb.* 14; see also *Iul.* 39). On one occasion the powerful symbolism of the ring as a sign of equestrian status created a potentially troublesome situation for Julius Caesar, as he pleaded for the faithfulness of his troops at a defining moment in his rise to power:

> It is even thought that he promised every man a knight's estate, but that came of a misunderstanding; for since he often pointed to the finger of his left hand as he addressed them and urged them on, declaring that to satisfy all those who helped him to defend his honour he would gladly tear his very ring from his hand, those on the edge of the assembly, who could see him better than they could hear his words, assumed that he said what his gesture seemed to mean; and so the report went about that he had promised them the right of the ring (*ius anulorum*) and four hundred thousand sesterces [necessary to qualify for the order] as well. (Suet. *Iul.* 33)

Petronius' parody of the antics of the wealthy freedman Trimalchio also probably draws upon the *topos* of the equestrian ring, along with that of the *latus clavus* of the senatorial order. Trimalchio is carried into a feast on pillows, dressed as follows:

> he had put on a napkin with a broad stripe (*laticlavem*) and fringes hanging from it all around. On the little finger of his left hand he had an enormous gilt ring and on the top joint of the next finger a smaller ring which appeared to me to be entirely gold, but was really set all round with iron cut out in little stars. (*Sat.* 32.1–3)

Real-life persons in the empire did well not to emulate the behavior of the legendary Trimalchio. Attempts on the part of the non-elite, for example, early in the principate, to usurp elite privilege by wearing gold rings in public encountered firm resistance on the part of imperial authorities (Pliny, *HN* 33.32; the reign of Tiberius).[26] At other times, compromise prevailed. Among Augustus' reforms was a reorganization of the senate, a house-cleaning of sorts through which the emperor sought to restore the order to its former honor.[27] Augustus removed the unworthy but, interestingly enough, permitted them to retain a number of the order's social privileges, including their senatorial attire and privileged seats at the games:

> Since the number of the senators was swelled by a low-born and ill-assorted rabble he restored it to its former limits and distinction by two enrolments [sic], one according to the choice of the members themselves, each man naming one other, and a second made by Agrippa and himself . . . Some he shamed into resigning, but he allowed even these to retain their distinctive dress, as well as the privilege of viewing the games from the orchestra and taking part in the public banquets of the order.
> (Suet. *Aug.* 35)

At the same time, however, Augustus subtly reinforced the importance of the *latus clavus* as attire reserved for the senatorial class alone by enacting new legislation for the offspring of those who remained in his recently reconstituted senate: "To enable senators' sons to gain an earlier acquaintance with public business, he allowed them to assume the broad purple stripe immediately after the gown of manhood and to attend meetings of the senate" (Suet. *Aug.* 38).

Varying attire was even prescribed for a victorious general, depending upon whether he was celebrating his first or second triumph. Suetonius describes a triumph led by the emperor Claudius:

> His wife Messalina followed his chariot in a carriage, as did also those who had won the triumphal regalia in the same war; the rest marched on foot in purple-bordered togas, except Marcus Crassus Frugi, who rode a caparisoned horse and wore a tunic embroidered with palms, because he was receiving the honour for the second time. (*Claud.* 17)

The importance of the attire of a Roman magistrate as symbolic of social status and function surfaced as a key consideration for several tribunes who found themselves adjudicating a farcical legal dispute between a prostitute and a Roman aedile:

> Aulus Hostilius Mancinus was a curule aedile. He brought suit before the people against a courtesan called Manilia, because he said that he had been struck with a stone thrown from her

apartment by night, and he exhibited the wound made by the stone. Manilia appealed to the tribunes of the commons. Before them she declared that Mancinus had come to her house in the garb of a reveller; that it would not have been to her advantage to admit him, and that when he tried to break in by force, he had been driven off with stones. The tribunes decided that the aedile had rightly been refused admission to a place to which it had not been seemly for him to go with a garland on his head; therefore they forbade the aedile to bring an action before the people.

(Aul. Gell. *NA* 4.14)

The point here is that Mancinus, "in the garb of a reveller . . . with a garland on his head," was coming from a drinking party, dressed for a night on the town rather than in his magistrate's robes. As an aedile, he had the right to undertake an official inspection visit to a brothel, and Manilia would have had to admit him – only, however, if Mancinus had been arrayed in his formal attire.

Nowhere was the association of attire with social status more apparent than at funerals of members of the Roman elite. In an informative discussion, Polybius describes the typical proceedings that occur when "someone from the ranks of the illustrious dies." Notice the emphasis upon dressing those who represent the deceased with clothing appropriate to their respective magistracies:

when any distinguished member of the family dies they [surviving family members] take them [ancestor masks "reproducing with remarkable fidelity both the features and complexion of the deceased"] to the funeral, putting them on men who seem to them to bear the closest resemblance to the original in stature and carriage. These representatives wear togas, with a purple border if the deceased was a consul or praetor, whole purple if he was a censor, and embroidered with gold if he had collected a triumph or achieved anything similar.

(Polyb. 6.53)

Polybius proceeds to describe the ensuing public procession of the funeral party to the rostra, a ceremony which visibly proclaimed the social status of the deceased and his family to all who were present. The purpose of all the fanfare, according to yet another elite observer, was to "enable the spectators to distinguish from the portrayal how far each [family member] had advanced in the *cursus honorum* and had had a part in the dignities of the state" (Diod. Sic. 31.25.2).[28]

Central to the funeral procession were the ancestral masks (*imagines*) mentioned by Polybius, above. Harriet Flower's fine treatment of Roman *imagines* underscores the uniqueness of the practice among ancient peoples and emphasizes the function of the masks in preserving Rome's traditional values and social hierarchy. Although Flower prefers to avoid the loaded term "propaganda" in her treatment of the *imagines*, she nevertheless acknowledges that the *imagines* "fit quite nicely into the category of 'integration propaganda' as analysed by sociologists... The success of 'integration propaganda' comes from its support of the status quo, which can make it hard to recognize for those closely involved with the culture itself."[29] The status quo that Flower has in view includes Rome's pronounced social hierarchy, as well as the emphasis upon honor and shame so central to Roman public life. The aristocratic funeral, which centered around the use of the ancestor masks,

> acted as a powerful verification of traditional values and especially of the success and prestige of the families represented. The public part of an aristocratic funeral, which comprised the procession of ancestors and the funeral eulogy in the Forum, was reserved for families of office-holders and set them apart from ordinary citizens in a conspicuous way.[30]

The use of the masks at Roman funerals thus contributed, in Flower's view, "to the creation of a society of overt praise and blame, in which honour was considered the measure of a man's status and the greatest reward for merit."[31]

In concert with the ubiquitous replication of Roman social values and practices at every level of society, lower-ranking members of the elite in the provinces also donned attire appropriate to their rank. Apuleius narrates an encounter, in Thessaly, between his protagonist Lucius (before he was turned into an ass) and one of Lucius' old acquaintances. After Lucius is questioned concerning his well-being, he responds, "But what about you? I'm glad you have achieved success. I see, for example, that you have attendants and fasces and clothing which befits a magistrate." "Yes," the man replies, "I'm in charge of the market here; I hold the position of aedile, and if you want to buy something for dinner, I'll be happy to help you" (Apul. *Met.* 1.24–25).[32]

Certain non-elite groups also had socially appropriate attire. Just as the gold ring marked entry into the equestrian class, so also a "cap of liberty" symbolized the freedom gained by a slave at manumission. The term *pilleus*, used to describe a close-fitting felt cap shaped like half an egg, could (like the term "ring" for the equestrian class, above) serve as a synecdoche for the whole idea of a slave acquiring his freedom. Thus, Seneca utilizes the phrase "don the freedman's cap" (*vocare ad pilleum*) to refer to manumission. In similar fashion, both L. Saturninus and Sulla alternately "summoned the slaves to arms showing them a cap of liberty" (Val. Max. 8.6.2).

In the section immediately following, we will gain an appreciation of the relationship between the social hierarchy and various occupations in which persons engaged in the Roman world. In anticipation of this topic, consider the following excerpt from the writings of Dio Chrysostom, who identifies specific clothing as appropriate for occupations with which he is familiar:

> Why on earth is it that, whenever men see somebody wearing a tunic and nothing more, they neither notice him nor make sport of him? Possibly because they reason that the fellow is a sailor and that there is no occasion to mock him on this account. Similarly, if they should spy someone wearing the garb of a farmer or of a shepherd – that is, wearing an exomis or wrapped in a hide or muffled in a kosymba – they are not irritated, nay, they do not even notice it to begin with, feeling that the garb is appropriate to the man who follows such a calling. Take our tavern-keepers, too; though people day after day see them in front of their taverns with their tunics belted high, they never jeer at them but, on the contrary, they would make fun of them if they were not so attired, considering that their appearance is peculiarly suited to their occupation. (*Or.* 72.1–2)

Dio proceeds to identify "someone in a cloak but not a tunic, with flowing hair and beard" as a typically attired philosopher, and he laments the fact that, unlike persons who ply the trades outlined above, philosophers are harassed at every turn.

As Paul of Tarsus pursued his calling to establish communities of followers of Jesus throughout the eastern empire, a thoughtful contemporary in Rome took issue with the manner in which clothing was utilized to publicly proclaim and reinforce the social hierarchy. Seneca wrote, "As he is a fool who, when purchasing a horse, does not consider the animal's points, but merely his saddle and bridle; so he is doubly a fool who values a man from his clothes or from his rank, which indeed is only a robe that clothes us" (*Ep.* 47.16). The widespread association of clothing with social status placed Seneca in the distinct minority of persons who took issue with the dominant values of majority opinion. Indeed, among the empire's residents only Seneca's fellow-philosophers and Christian contemporaries shared his convictions in this regard. And one senses from Christian writings that church leaders who sought to socialize their followers to resist the values of the dominant culture often found themselves on the losing side of the battle against clothing as a symbol of social status:

> My brothers and sisters, do you with your acts of favoritism really believe in our glorious Lord Jesus Christ? For if a person with gold rings and in fine clothes comes into your assembly, and if a poor person in dirty clothes also comes in, and if you take notice of the one wearing the fine clothes and say, "Have a seat here, please," while to the one who is poor you say, "Stand there," or, "Sit at my feet," have you not made distinctions among yourselves, and become judges with evil thoughts?
> (Jas. 2:1–4)

Occupation

The basic division of the empire's population into two social strata, consisting of elite and non-elite, provided Cicero with a framework within which to discuss the stratification of Roman society according to "trades and occupations, with regard to which are suitable for gentlemen and which are vulgar." Cicero includes among those jobs wholly unsuitable for a gentleman "tax collecting and usury," "the occupations of all hired workmen whom we pay for their labor," "retail merchants" ("for they would not make a profit unless they lied a lot"), and "craftsmen." The most "shameful occupations" cater to the five senses: "fish sellers, butchers, cooks, poultry raisers, and fishermen . . . perfume makers, dancers, and all of vaudeville." Note carefully the subtle stylistic shifts in Cicero's prose in the above quotations. So "proper," in Cicero's view, are the various occupations "for men whose social position they suit," that Cicero feels free to alternate between references to "shameful occupations," on the one hand, and references to the persons who engage in them, on the other: "Least respectable of all are those trades (*Minimeque artes eae probandae*) which cater for sensual pleasures: fishmongers, butchers, cooks, poulterers, and fishermen" (*Cetarii . . . piscatores*). Cicero's grammar thus provides forceful testimony to the close connection between occupation and social status in the Roman mind.

Cicero proceeds to discuss medicine, architecture, teaching, and trade. His comments on trade are particularly illuminating, since they patently reflect his own social location. As mentioned above, Cicero came from equestrian stock, and many equestrians accumulated wealth through empire-wide trading ventures. Now, however, Cicero has advanced to the senatorial class, where trade was frowned upon, at least in public discourse. The following evaluation of trade as an occupation can thus be read as somewhat of a metaphor for Cicero's own rise to the senatorial class:

> Trade, however, if it is small scale, must be considered vulgar; but if it is large scale, and involves importing many different items from throughout the world, and bringing many things to many people without lying or misrepresentation, it should not be greatly censured. Indeed, it appears that large-scale trade could even be praised under the most stringent law of respectability if a man engaging in it, once he was tired of it, or rather once he felt satisfied that he had achieved his goals, then moved himself from the harbor to a country estate.

For our Roman equestrian-become-consul, a move "from the harbor to a country estate" was inevitable, since, according to the senatorial class to which Cicero now belonged, "of all the occupations from which profit is accrued, none is better than agriculture . . . none more suitable to the free man" (Cic. *Off.* 1.42). Later in the same work, Cicero quotes Cato in this regard:

> When Cato was asked what was the most profitable aspect of property ownership, he replied, "Raising livestock with great success." And then? "Raising livestock with some success." And after that? "Raising livestock with little success." And fourth? "Raising crops." And when the person asking questions said, "What about moneylending?" Cato replied, "What about murder?" (Cic. *Off.* 2.25)[33]

When Cicero and Cato refer in such glowing terms to the ideals of rural life, we must keep in mind that the Roman elite class did not personally raise livestock or crops. Rather, they lived off the backs of their slaves or poor free persons whom they hired to tend their estates.

The general disdain with which the elite viewed all paid work – especially manual labor – finds graphic expression in the writings of Plautus. A certain character in one of Plautus' plays disdainfully laments the incessant arrival at his villa of "tradesmen and craftsmen" who "come around to collect payment." Included are the clothes cleaner, the clothes dyer, the goldsmith, the wool weaver, the man who sells lace and the man who sells underwear, makers of veils, sellers of purple dye, sellers of yellow dye, makers of muffs, and shoemakers who add balsam scent to their shoes, linen retailers, bootmakers, squatting cobblers, slipper makers, sandalmakers, and fabric stainers ... purse makers, weavers, fringe makers, manufacturers of jewelry cases – all cluttering up your atrium.

Just when you think you have paid them all, the narrator continues, "into your atrium come more dyers ... and any other wretched gallows-bird who wants some money" (Plaut. *Aulularia* 505–22). Notice the description of the person who engages in such occupations as a "wretched gallows-bird," literally, *crux*, "one destined for crucifixion" (522).[34] I will later demonstrate that crucifixion constituted the most shameful, status-degrading experience a person could undergo in the Roman world. The facile association here of such socially shameful imagery with Plautus' extensive list of lower-class occupations sharply reveals the connection, in the Roman elite mind, between certain occupations and their corresponding place along the social hierarchy.[35]

Seating at public events

During the reign of Nero, two Frisian ambassadors named Verritus and Malorix traveled to Rome to appeal a recent command to withdraw from land recently settled by their tribes. While awaiting an audience with the emperor, the visitors wandered around viewing "the usual places shown to barbarians" and, finally, entering the theater of Pompey. With his characteristic disdain Tacitus assures us that the Frisians "had not sufficient knowledge to be amused by the play." Rather, they found themselves wholly preoccupied with that other most obvious aspect of a theater performance in the Roman world, namely, the social stratification of the population as reflected in the assigned seating in the *cavea* – or, as Tacitus terms it "the distinctions between the orders" (*discrimina ordinum*).[36]

After the Frisians had taken the initiative to question several members of the audience – "which were the knights? – where was the senate?" – they noticed a few men in non-Roman attire seated among the senators, and they began to inquire as to their identity.[37] What happened next had the potential to develop into a highly volatile sociopolitical debacle, and a public one, at that, for the drama in the *cavea* suddenly became more engaging than activities upon the theater stage itself. Tacitus relates,

> on hearing that this [permission for foreigners to sit among the senate] was a compliment paid to the envoys of nations distinguished for their courage and for friendship to Rome, [the Frisian visitors] exclaimed that no people in the world ranked before Germans in arms or loyalty, went down, and took their seats among the Fathers.

By taking the initiative to cross social boundaries and sit among the senatorial order, the Frisians had violated an important aspect of Roman social protocol that had been encoded in legislation for generations. The ambassadors were foreigners, however – "barbarians," as Tacitus puts it – and this proved to be their saving grace, for the people found themselves quite amused by the gesture: "The action was taken in good part by the onlookers, as a trait of primitive impetuosity and generous rivalry." Nero, hardly able to resist the momentum of the masses, joined in, as well, awarding both of the German visitors Roman citizenship before sending them on their way (*Ann.* 13.54).[38]

For those who knew better, expectations were altogether different. At an exhibition of games early in Augustus' reign, the emperor noticed a common soldier seated among the fourteen rows reserved for the equestrian class. He immediately had the soldier ejected by an attendant (Suet. *Aug.* 14). Even equestrians themselves "whose property was diminished during the civil wars" (and who, therefore, no longer qualified for the order) "did not venture to view the games from the fourteen rows through fear of the penalty of the law" (Suet. *Aug.* 40).[39] Knights who did have the right to sit in the fourteen rows carefully guarded their privilege. One incident particularly highlights this reality. Augustus apparently made a practice of doing his drinking outside the theater. On one occasion he reprimanded an equestrian whom he caught drinking in his seat. The quick-witted knight replied that the *Princeps* did not need to fear losing his seat – he, on the other hand, did (Quint. *Inst.* 6.3.63).

Although reflecting a different kind of social hierarchy than that of Rome (where an emperor and senators occupied the best seats), provincial populations proved equally resourceful when it came to enforcing public expressions of their respective hierarchies. In Urso, Spain, for example, the fine for sitting out of *ordo* in the theater amounted to 5,000 sesterces. As Garnsey and Saller appropriately note in this regard, "something more was at stake than getting a good seat to watch the show."[40] That "something," of course, was social status.

Literary and epigraphic sources richly detail the allocation of seating at public events according to social status in both Rome and the provinces.

As early as 67 BCE the *lex Roscia theatralis* had designated the first fourteen rows of the theater in Rome for the equestrian class, with two more rows set apart for ex-tribunes.[41] The orchestra was reserved for the senate. During the early imperial period, a rigid system segregated persons into four distinct groups: senators, equestrians, urban citizen commoners, and others (non-citizens, women, and slaves).[42] Suetonius provides us with the classic commentary on the practice under Augustus. Augustus found himself exasperated by an incident in a crowded amphitheater at Puteoli, where locals refused to give up a seat to a Roman senator.

> In consequence of this the senate decreed that, whenever any public show was given anywhere, the first row of seats should be reserved for senators; and at Rome he would not allow the envoys of the free and allied nations to sit in the orchestra, since he was informed that even freedmen were sometimes appointed. He separated the soldiery from the people. He assigned special seats to the married men of the commons, to boys under age their own section and the adjoining one to their preceptors; and he decreed that no one wearing a dark cloak should sit in the middle of the house. (*Aug.* 44)

Chariot races may, however, have been excluded from the above legislation. According to Suetonius it was Claudius who later extended the practice of assigned seating for senators to the races at the Circus Maximus (*Claud.* 21). Nero did the same for the knights (*Nero* 11).[43]

The importance of preferential seating at public events for the personal dignity of individual members of the Roman elite at times generated lively debate among the senators themselves. In 21 CE, a certain Domitius Corbulo, who had been a praetor, found himself publicly humiliated when a young aristocrat, Lucius Sulla, refused to give him his seat at a gladiatorial show. In Corbulo's favor were "age, national custom, and the partialities of older men." Sulla, for his part, rallied the likes of Mamercus Scaurus and Lucius Arruntius to his side. Tacitus informs us that there was "a sharp exchange of speeches, with references to the example of our ancestors, who had censured youthful irreverence in grave decrees" (*Ann.* 3.31).[44]

The power to dispense the honors associated with special seating at public festivals was jealously guarded. During the reign of Tiberius, a senator attempted to usurp this privilege, which had apparently become the emperor's alone (cf. Suet. *Aug.* 44, above).[45] Tacitus writes,

Junius Gallio, who had moved that the Praetorians, on finishing their service, should acquire the right to a seat in the Fourteen Rows [those reserved for knights], drew down a fierce rebuke: – "What," demanded Tiberius, as if addressing him to his face, "had *he* to do with the soldiers, who had no right to take any but their master's orders or any but their master's rewards? He had certainly hit upon something not taken into consideration by the deified Augustus. Or was it a minion of Sejanus, fostering disaffection and sedition, in order by a nominal compliment to drive simple souls into a breach of discipline?"

For his gesture, Gallio was rewarded with ejection from the senate, exile to Lesbos and, later, private custody in Rome (*Ann.* 6.3).

A most important principle that will inform the study of Roman Philippi in a later section of this book is the ubiquitous replication of Roman social verticality, and its associated public expressions, throughout the provinces. No practice is more widely attested in this regard than the assigning of seating, based on social status, at public events. Inscriptions on surviving portions of structures throughout the empire outline the various arrangements for seating in amphitheaters and theaters.[46] Our most impressive example of such testimony comes from Spain, in the *lex coloniae Genetivae Iuliae (lex Ursonensis)* (c. first century CE).[47] The legislation treats the games (*ludi*) and theatrical performances separately. At the games, preferential seating is awarded to decurions, municipal magistrates (future decurions), and to certain others who were allowed to sit *in decurionum loco* (para. 125). The last group listed may have been persons who had received the *ornamenta decurionalia*.[48]

Seating at the theater receives even more attention in the inscription (paras. 126–27). In the orchestra sat decurions, along with any Roman senators and their sons who happened to be present in the province. To differentiate publicly between these two groups the orchestra was subdivided into two sections. Senators and Roman magistrates occupied the first row, with local decurions taking their places in the row immediately behind them (cf. Suet. *Aug.* 44, above). Evidence exists for a similar arrangement in the orchestra section of theaters across the empire.[49] Seating outside the orchestra was also carefully regulated. According to a decree of the decurion body (one-half of the members had to be present to vote), seats were assigned, respectively, to *coloni coloniae* (full citizens of the colony), *incolae* (persons living on territory belonging to the colony), *hospites* (certain influential persons with whom the town sought good relations), and, finally, *adventores*. The latter were generally travelers or inhabitants of nearby towns.[50]

Persons from these adjacent settlements found themselves at a distinct disadvantage in the colony, since, regardless of their social status in their own city, they were relegated to the less desirable seats when attending the theater in Urso. The treatment was reciprocated, however, when the citizens of Urso visited other towns. Kolendo suggests that the manner in which towns dealt with citizens of other cities at public events provided strong incentive for each town to erect its own local theater and amphitheater.[51] The result: "In the Empire there were close to a thousand cities, and although many of these had relatively small populations of under 15,000 inhabitants, by the end of the first century AD frequently even the smallest towns had acquired a collection of monumental buildings, including a theater."[52] Each of these theaters provided a public setting in which to display the distinctions between the orders, so that, in every case, the social verticality of Roman life was replicated in miniature at the municipal level for all to see.

Seating at private banquets

Social historians and other students of antiquity have given much attention in recent decades to table fellowship in Mediterranean society, and the varying degrees of honor associated with different positions around the dining table. The theme is a familiar one to readers of the New Testament. Recall the story of the two sons of Zebedee, who sought for themselves the places of honor at the eschatological banquet:

> James and John, the sons of Zebedee, came forward to [Jesus] and said to him, "Teacher, we want you to do for us whatever we ask of you." And he said to them, "What is it you want me to do for you?" And they said to him, "Grant us to sit, one at your right hand and one at your left, in your glory."
> (Mark 10:35–37)

This brief text-segment reflects two important assumptions concerning banquets in the ancient world: (1) Some seats (those closest to the host) are more honorable than others ("at your right hand and . . . at your left"), and (2) The host is the one who assigns seats, and he does so according to social status. Both realities surface again and again in literature produced in the Roman world, along with the assignment of different qualities of food, and even different tables, to different social classes. In Richard Saller's opinion, members of the elite orders invited persons of inferior status to dine in their homes for the specific purpose of highlighting their own social status:

> Throughout the ages dining has served as a context for the advertisement of status, but in recent times this has more often been accomplished by the exclusion of unworthies; in Rome humble men were invited, even paid, to attend so that they might pay deference or (from the viewpoint of the jaundiced observer) suffer as victims of displays of *superbia* by their hosts.[53]

Pliny's description of a banquet he attended during the early second century is, perhaps, most familiar:

> It would take too long to go into the details (which anyway don't matter) of how I happened to be dining with a man – though no particular friend of his – whose elegant economy, as he called it, seemed to me a sort of stingy extravagance. The best dishes were set in front of the host and a select few, and cheap scraps of food before the rest of the company. He had even put the wine into tiny little flasks, divided into three categories, not with the idea of giving his guests the opportunity of choosing, but to make it impossible for them to refuse what they were given. One lot was intended for himself and for us, another for his lesser friends (for all his friends are graded) and the third for his freedmen.
> (*Ep.* 2.6)

The host's behavior appears to have impressed Pliny as rather eccentric, but the experience may have been more common than the description seems to suggest. Martial, for example, relates the following complaint that a guest directed to his less-than-gracious host: "While you are drinking pints of deep purple wine, Cotta, and guzzling rich dark Opimian, you set before me Sabine wine which has just been made. And then you ask me, 'Do you want a gold wine goblet?' Who wants a gold goblet for lead wines?" (10.49).[54] Dishonored lower-status diners like Cotta's guest might complain, but, as Plutarch warned, much worse could happen if places were not properly assigned: the eminent might fail to occupy places appropriate to their honor and the resulting dishonor would then accrue to the host (*Quaest. conv.* 616b–c).

Clients, in particular, were often shortchanged in the distribution of food at mealtime. Juvenal's instructions to a client provide us with a rare glimpse of how things might have appeared from the perspective of those seated at the less honorable end of the table:

> First of all, remember this: when you are invited to dinner, you are being repaid in full for all your earlier services. Food is your payment for serving as a client to the great. Your master, I mean patron, records these infrequent dinner invitations under "debts discharged." And thus every two months or so, when he feels like using a normally neglected client to fill up an empty spot on the lowest couch, he says: "Come and join us." Your greatest wish is fulfilled! What more can you ask for? . . . Ah, and what a dinner you get! The wine is so bad that even new wool won't absorb it . . . The bread is so hard you can barely break it, a mouldy crust of petrified dough that you can't bite into without cracking your teeth. Of course, the master of the house is served soft, white bread made from the finest flour.
>
> (5.12–22, 24, 25, 67–71)[55]

Concern to preserve the social hierarchy at mealtime extended to all levels of society. When in the provinces, Julius Caesar "gave banquets constantly in two dining-halls, in one of which his officers or Greek companions, in the other Roman civilians and the more distinguished of the provincials reclined at table" (Suet. *Iul.* 48). Augustus took similar measures:

> He gave dinner parties constantly and always formally, with great regard to the rank and personality of his guests. Valerius Messala writes that he never invited a freedman to dinner with the exception of Menas, and then only when he had been enrolled among the freeborn after betraying the fleet of Sextus Pompey.
> (Suet. *Aug.* 74)

At the opposite extreme of the empire's geography and social hierarchy, Jewish settlers at Qumran also strictly seated themselves at mealtime according to social status. Though the attributes and qualities which contributed toward a person's honor rating were conceived quite differently in the Dead Sea community than in Rome, the manner in which the social hierarchy found expression at table proves remarkably similar to the Roman behavior illustrated above:

> Each man shall sit in his place: the Priests shall sit first, and the elders second, and all the rest of the people according to their rank . . . No man shall interrupt a companion before his speech has ended, nor speak before a man of higher rank; each man shall speak in his turn. (1QS 6.9–10)[56]

So widespread was the manifestation of the hierarchy at dinner parties that it could serve as a metaphor for the social inequalities that characterized life itself. The following excerpt describes the creation of the human race and the distinctions which were established when the "king of the gods" first ordered the social universe:

> Into his universe comes mankind to hold high festival, having been invited by the king of the gods to a most splendid feast and banquet that they may enjoy all blessings. They recline in different places, just as at a dinner, some getting better and others inferior positions ... And different persons have different things in greater abundance according to the tables at which they have severally reclined. (Dio Chrys. *Or.* 30.29–30)

The cultural script outlined earlier (see the comments on Mark 10:35–37) naturally encourages the reader to assume that the "king of the gods," who hosts the feast, is also the one who assigns the guests their "different places" at the dinner. According to the analogy, then, the social stratification that characterized the author's world – and the social inequities that often resulted ("different persons have different things in greater abundance") – are relegated to the divine order established at creation. We might expect the elite class to attempt to legitimate social inequality through appeal to the will of the gods. The person whose sentiments are expressed in the above citation is introduced, however, as non-elite, a "peasant," whose poignant reflections had been immortalized in a deathbed speech of Charidemus (*Or.* 30.29–30). If Dio can be trusted on this point, we find ourselves in possession of a tantalizing piece of evidence suggesting that the principle of a highly stratified social world, though at times strongly resented by those in the lower strata of society, embedded itself deeply in the consciousness of elite and non-elite alike. Perhaps non-elite peasants in Dio's social world took some comfort in assigning to divine providence the intractable social inequities and injustices they undoubtedly experienced in their daily lives.[57]

The legal system

One day in the Roman forum a trial was underway at which certain witnesses had just begun to testify against the defendant. During the proceedings an esteemed member of the Roman elite, P. Servilius, "ex-Consul and ex-Censor, triumphator, who added the surname of Isauricus to the titles of his ancestors," happened to pass within earshot, and he listened intently to the witnesses. To the surprise of the advocates, both prosecuting and defending, Servilius suddenly took the stand himself, as a witness against the defendant. The outcome of the trial speaks volumes about the relationship between social status and legal privilege in the Roman world. P. Servilius proceeded to address the jury from the witness stand:

> "Gentlemen of the jury, I don't know where this man on trial comes from or what life he has led or how rightly or wrongly he stands accused: I know only this much, that when he met me as I was travelling on the Laurentine Way in a pretty narrow passage, he refused to get off his horse. Whether that concerns you as a jury, you will judge. I thought I ought not to keep it back."

The anonymous defendant was immediately found guilty – "almost," our narrator informs us, "without hearing the other witnesses." The reason:

> They were impressed by Servilius's eminence and his grave indignation at the neglect of his dignity [the translator has attempted to capture in English a play on words in the original: *gravis neglectae dignitatis eius indignatio*] and believed that someone who did not know how to respect our leading men would rush into any villainy. (Val. Max. 8.5.6)

A witness from the other end of the social spectrum could have precisely the opposite effect upon legal proceedings. I suspect that readers of this book will universally reject P. Servilius' testimony as irrelevant to the court case outlined above, since Servilius openly admits that he possesses no evidence relating directly to the specific charges against the defendant. Conversely, evidence that we would regard as wholly admissible and relevant to a court trial might be summarily dismissed, if that evidence was acquired from a socially dishonorable source. In 119 BCE, for example, L. Crassus launched a prosecution against Cn. Carbo "in a spirit of hostility, for Carbo was his bitter enemy." During the proceedings, one of Carbo's slaves secretly brought to Crassus "a briefcase of Carbo's containing a quantity of material with which he could easily have been brought down." Instead of taking advantage of these materials to win his case, Crassus instead "returned it to [Carbo] sealed as it was along with the slave in chains" (Val. Max. 6.5.6).

The discussion in this section is not intended to imply that the Romans were blind to the realities of evidence and counter-evidence in the courtroom. The point here is that more than evidence was expected to be taken into consideration. As Cicero enjoins on behalf of a protégé, "make it your business to enable him to conclude his negotiation . . . in a manner befitting the justice of his case *and his own position (pro causae veritate et pro sua dignitate)*" (*Fam.* 13.57.2, my italics). Priorities prevailed, however, and, as Peter Garnsey aptly notes, "The *principal* criterion of legal privilege in the eyes of the Romans was *dignitas*, or honor derived from power, style of life, and wealth."[58] It is hardly anomalous, then, that *dignitas* handily trumps *veritas* in both of the court cases outlined above.

Among the public expressions of social verticality surveyed in these pages, the legitimation of social stratification through the justice system will strike modern observers as least familiar and, likely, as most offensive.[59] No wonder, for this is precisely the point at which social scientists draw the sharpest and most basic distinction between stratification in modern industrial and post-industrial societies, on the one hand, and stratification in advanced agragrian societies like that of ancient Rome, on the other. Social verticality characterizes all human societies. In cultures like the modern West, however, the different strata in society result from an interplay of numerous factors and institutions, in a social world where it is asserted that all persons are created equal.[60] Systems like ancient Rome, in contrast, express the differences between one stratum and another

> in terms of *legal* rights or of established customs which have the essential binding character of law. In its extreme form such a system divides society into a number of distinct, hereditary human species – patricians, plebeians, serfs, slaves and so forth. Stratification is, as it were, an *institution* in its own right, and the whole structure has the quality of a plan in the sense that it is endowed with meaning and purpose.[61]

Central to the above description is the intentional institutionalization of social inequality (resulting in "a number of distinct, hereditary human species") by means of the justice system. The legal system thus served to formally legitimate and strongly reinforce social stratification in the Roman world.

The connection between justice and social status played itself out in a number of ways in the empire, as different standards of justice were variously applied to persons according to their social standing.[62] Thus Fronto, a member of the second-century consular class, exhorted a Roman governor, "Treat the provincials according to their honour" (*Ep. ad Amicos* 1.20).[63] Legal distinctions, originating in Rome, were replicated in various ways in municipal settings. In the first century, Philo observed, of his own Alexandria,

There are differences between scourges used in the city, and these differences are regulated by the social standing of the persons to be beaten. The Egyptians are scourged with a different kind of lash and by a different set of people, the Alexandrians with a flat blade, and the persons who wield it are also Alexandrians.

(In Flacc. 78)

The legal distinction between citizen and non-citizen, which will prove important for my interpretation of the biblical materials in a later chapter, sharply underscores the inequities of Roman judicial practice. In the early empire only those with citizen status enjoyed legal protection against flogging, torture, and certain kinds of execution (crucifixion, for example). Non-citizens were not so fortunate. In 17 CE, for example, when astrology was banned in Rome, citizens were exiled while foreigners were put to death. Pliny executed non-citizen Christians but sent to Rome those citizens who belonged to the Jesus movement (*Ep.* 10.96). A later pogrom found the governor of Lyons sending non-citizen Christians to the beasts but decapitating Roman citizens who confessed Christ (Eusebius, *Hist. eccl.* 5.1.47).[64]

By the early second century the distinction between citizens and non-citizens had evolved into a legal demarcation between elite (*honestiores*) and non-elite persons (*humiliores*), and cruel penalties once limited to slaves now applied to the humble free. Here is a representative example of specific legislation:

Those who break into a temple at night in order to pillage or plunder it are thrown to wild animals. But if they steal some minor object from the temple during the day, if they are *honestiores* they are exiled; if they are *humiliores* they are condemned to the mines. In the case of people accused of violating sepulchers, if they actually drag out the bodies or remove the bones, if they are *humiliores* they are punished with the ultimate torture; if they are *honestiores* they are exiled to an island. For other violations, *honestiores* are expelled and *humiliores* are condemned to the mines.   (*FIRA* 2, p. 405 [Paulus, *Opinions* 5.19–19a])[65]

As James Littlejohn maintains, a specific view of human personhood typically serves to legitimate practices like those described above: "Societies exhibiting [this type] of stratification are characterized by their acceptance of *a general norm of inequality.* People do not subscribe to the proposition that all men are equal, or at least not to the extent of ensuring that all are equally placed with regard to the law."[66] Pliny, an esteemed senator of the early second century CE, reflects Rome's unquestioning acceptance of "a general norm of inequality" when he challenges a provincial governor in Spain to take the utmost care to preserve "the distinction of orders and dignity" in legal hearings, because, Pliny unequivocally asserts, "if these distinctions are confused, nothing is more unequal than equality itself" (*Ep.* 9.5).[67] As Pascal so pointedly expressed it some centuries later, "Not being able to make that which is just strong, man has made that which is strong just."[68] These sentiments, so offensive to the modern mind, appeared perfectly reasonable to the elite classes in agrarian societies like Pliny's Rome or Pascal's early modern Europe.[69] As Valerius Maximus acknowledges, reflecting on his social world,

> how neatly Anacharsis used to compare laws to spiders' webs! He used to say that just as they kept the weaker animals but let the stronger ones through, so the laws tied up the humble and the poor (*humiles et pauperes*), but did not bind the rich and the powerful (*divites et praepotentes*). (7.2. ext. 14)

Summary

The Romans were remarkably creative in devising ways to publicly proclaim and reinforce the social hierarchy. Clothing, occupations, seating at spectacles and banquets, and the legal system all served to remind the empire's residents of their respective positions in the pecking order of society. And the list of ways in which the hierarchy was expressed could be expanded even more.[70] Rome hosted an annual parade, for example, which highlighted the prestige of the equestrian class (Suet. *Aug.* 38.3; Dio Cass. 55.31.2). Public banquets and food distribution in the provinces were administrated in such a way as to insure that resources were doled out according to rank, not according to need.[71] All such practices served the ultimate design of reinforcing the values of elite society. Garnsey and Saller summarize as follows:

> Putting everyone in his proper place was a visual affirmation of the dominance of the imperial social structure, and one calculated to impress the bulk of the population of the empire . . . The impoverished may have resented this principle, even as public event after public event imprinted it in the communal consciousness.[72]

The degree to which non-elite persons resented the values of the dominant culture must remain somewhat of a mystery, since the voices of elite males predominate in our source material. What is clear, however, is that these widespread public reminders of the social order so "imprinted . . . in the communal consciousness" the notions of rank and status that even those who were not members of the elite class ultimately embraced, rather than rejected, the marked verticality of Roman society. This is quite evident from the fact that those of lower status simply replicated the hierarchical nature of the culture as a whole in their own social groups and voluntary associations. It is to this replication of social verticality, and the incessant quest for honors at every level of society, that we now turn.

2

PREOCCUPATION WITH HONOR AND THE *CURSUS HONORUM*

> To be equal to others in liberty, and first in honour.
> Cicero (*Phil.* 1.34)

"The man who gains fair renown departs laden with blessings" (*Or.* 29.21); so wrote Dio Chrysostom of a non-elite boxer who had become quite famous for his skill in the ring but who died at an unfortunately young age. Jon Lendon, two millennia removed from Dio's world, but properly sensitive to Roman social values, paints a remarkably similar picture of relational priorities at the opposite end of the social hierarchy: "Aristocratic life often appears to us as a ceaseless, restless quest for distinction in the eyes of one's peers and of posterity."[1]

The present chapter focuses upon the insatiable desire for public esteem and recognition which characterized the social lives of males in every stratum of Roman society. I will first consider the place of honor in the hierarchy of values and briefly delineate the elements of honor as understood by the ancients. The balance of the chapter examines Rome's *cursus honorum*, or "sequence of offices," which functioned as the standard political and social career for the Roman senatorial elite. Special attention will be given to the replication of the *cursus* in non-elite settings throughout the empire. As we shall see, at every turn "the struggle for reputation" (ὁ περὶ τῆς δόξης ἀγών), as Dio graphically expressed it, served as a primary source of social energy for public service and office-seeking in Rome and in the provinces (*Or.* 66.18).

Honor as a social value

The final quarter of the twentieth century was characterized by the employment of a variety of new methodologies for the study of ancient societies. Among New Testament scholars, models imported from the fields of sociology and cultural anthropology have proven particularly fruitful for gaining a better understanding of the social world of the early Christians. The centrality of honor as a social good has attracted special attention, and almost every introductory textbook dealing with the cultural background of the New Testament now contains a chapter addressing Mediterranean sensibilities concerning honor and shame. Students of ancient Rome, as well, increasingly emphasize the explanatory power of cultural factors for a better understanding of their subject matter, and Roman historians have recently produced two important monographs addressing the role of honor and shame in the dynamics of Roman government and elite social life.[2]

Ideas about honor and shame can be found in virtually all societies. Scholars highlight two crucial characteristics, however, which serve to mark out the ancient Mediterranean world as distinct from contemporary Euro-American culture in this regard:

1. *The centrality of honor as a cultural value* – in the Mediterranean world, honor was not a secondary value (less important, for example, than wealth), as is the case in the modern West. Honor was a pivotal cultural value.
2. *Honor as a preeminently public commodity* – in the collectivist culture of antiquity, one's honor was almost exclusively dependent upon the affirmation of the claim to honor by the larger social group to which the individual belonged.

It will prove most useful to offer some reflections on each of these important characteristics.

The centrality of honor

"By nature we yearn and hunger for honor, and once we have glimpsed, as it were, some part of its radiance, there is nothing we are not prepared to bear and suffer in order to secure it" – so Cicero observed, late in life, as he reflected upon events surrounding the fall of the republic (*Tusc.* 2.24.58).[3] Scholars who study ancient social codes consistently identify honor as a "dominant" or "paramount" value in Mediterranean culture – in some cases, *the* most important value.[4] Halvor Moxnes maintains that understanding honor and shame is crucial for gaining any meaningful appreciation of the social environment of early Christianity. He elaborates:

it is possible to fathom the Mediterranean kinship system only if one understands that family honor is on the line in every public interaction. Similarly, one can understand the division between public and private space, a separation that often occurs along gender lines, only by recognizing the special roles of men and women in the honor system. Patronage, slavery, economic practices, purity rules, meal practices, and even the peculiar Mediterranean sense of identity that derives from group membership must likewise be understood in terms of honor and shame.[5]

Lendon's perspective as a Roman historian is similar. He finds honor ascribed not only to individuals in the Roman world but to cities and institutions as well. Lendon summarizes,

> Honour was a filter through which the whole world was viewed, a deep structure of the Graeco-Roman mind, perhaps the ruling metaphor of ancient society. To us value is a consequence of price; the Greeks, needing a word for "price," borrowed τιμή from the realm of honour. Every thing, every person, could be valued in terms of honour, and every group of persons: the honour of the Roman senate, of the equestrian order, or of a court of law, waxed and waned according to who its members were and their conduct.[6]

Moxnes and Lendon are only paraphrasing the convictions of the ancients themselves. Consider Pliny's musings about the greatest source of human happiness:

> Opinions differ, but my idea of the truly happy man (*beatissimum*) is of one who enjoys the anticipation of a good and lasting reputation (*famae*), and, confident in the verdict of posterity, lives in the knowledge of the fame (*gloria*) that is to come. (*Ep.* 9.3)

Dio, whose philosophical leanings left him with a certain disdain for honor-seeking, nevertheless acknowledged that honor "stood at the root of human motivation and human institutions."[7] Dio here addresses the residents of Rhodes on the subject of honor:

> For you will find that there is nothing else (besides honor), at least in the case of the great majority, that incites every man to despise danger, to endure toils, and to scorn the life of pleasure and ease. (*Or.* 31.17)

> However, this much is clear, that neither you nor any others, whether Greeks or barbarians, who are thought to have become great, advanced to glory and power for any other reason than because fortune gave to each in succession men who were jealous of honour (φιλοτίμων) and regarded their fame (εὐφημίαν) in after times as more precious than life. (*Or.* 31.20)

For Quintilian and Cicero, appeal to honorable behavior constituted the central component of effective deliberative oratory:

> If it should be necessary to assign one single aim to deliberative (oratory) I should prefer Cicero's view that this kind of oratory is primarily concerned with what is honourable.
> (Quint. *Inst.* 3.8.1)

It would be overly simplistic, of course, to suggest that honor served as the sole force energizing social relations in the ancient world. Human societies are much too complex to support such reductionism, for other dynamics often come into play. It is fair to assert, however, that in the solar system of ancient goods and values, honor occupied the place of the sun around which other priorities orbited. To remove honor and honor-seeking from the heart of an analysis of the ancient world would therefore be to render impossible a nuanced understanding of Roman social life.[8]

A most helpful way to grasp the importance of honor in the Roman mind is to consider the relationship between public esteem and personal wealth. In his ground-breaking study of social values, Lenski distinguishes between (a) goals valued in their own right and (b) other goals "sought largely or entirely for their *instrumental* value."[9] Among the former Lenski lists physical health and social status. These goals are sought as ends in themselves. Wealth, in contrast, Lenski categorizes as an instrument value, sought solely because it facilitates the attainment of more basic goals like health and prestige. Our sources suggest that precisely this hierarchy of values obtained in the Roman mind. Seneca, for example clearly situates honor among Lenski's non-instrumental goods: "The one fixed principle from which we proceed to the proof of other points is that the honourable is cherished for no other reason than because it is honourable" (*Ben.* 4.16.2). In the course of a treatise on the subject of pain, Dio Chrysostom lists, presumably in descending order of severity, various misfortunes which one may encounter in the course of life:

> For instance, either the death of a relative, or the illness of one of them, or of oneself, may occur and besides these, loss of reputation (ἀδοξία), a financial reverse, complete or partial

failure in some undertaking, pressure of affairs, danger, and all the countless other misfortunes which occur in life. (*Or.* 16.3)

In concert with Lenski's model, Dio views the loss of life or health as the most regrettable circumstance. It is interesting to note, moreover, that among the misfortunes which follow, "loss of reputation" precedes "financial reverse." Loss of honor was apparently a more grievous calamity than loss of wealth in Dio's world. Ramsay MacMullen expresses it as follows: "The Romans indeed acknowledged a goddess called Money (*Pecunia*); but . . . her cult was tributary to another, Status (*Philotimia*)."[10]

The above priorities find transparent expression in the utilitarian employment of wealth in the quest for social status on the part of the Roman elite. In the previous chapter I noted a connection between wealth and honor in the monetary requirements for admission to the elite orders. A central purpose for these qualifications was to insure that members of the elite possessed the financial resources necessary to fulfill their role as public benefactors. For their generosity as public servants, moreover, the wealthy were rewarded, in turn, with various public honors. Thus, for the elite in the Roman empire, wealth served both (a) as a *qualification* for the honor of belonging to an elite order – and thereby becoming eligible for the honor of public office, and (b) as the *vehicle* for the acquisition of further honor by means of public benefaction. In summary, ancient elites saw wealth as something to be utilized to acquire a much more treasured good: public honor. Persons who hoarded their wealth were, in fact, dishonorable.[11] Those who spent it on elaborate municipal edifices, such as temples and public baths, or bread and circuses for the masses, were accorded great honor for their benefactions.[12]

The relationship between public reputation and elite wealth reveals itself most vividly in the institution of urban patronage. The elite class engaged in building projects and public works throughout the empire, not, primarily, in order to alleviate the suffering of the poor by providing better facilities for daily life among those of lower rank but, rather, in order to enhance their own honor in the public square. Dio Chrysostom identifies desire for repute (δόξα) and honor (τιμή) as the key motivating factors for public benefactions, and the term translated "love of honor" (φιλοτιμία) finally becomes synonymous with public munificence.[13] The point to note here is that members of the elite such as Dio used their positions of power and influence – and particularly their wealth – not directly in the service of others but, rather, to enhance their own honor in public life. Although the masses often benefited significantly from urban patronage, we should be under no illusion that elite generosity was motivated, to any great degree, by the plight of the less privileged.

Notice the manner in which Pliny utilizes an inheritance recently bequeathed to him:

> I have lately purchased with a legacy that was left to me a statue of Corinthian bronze [prized by Roman connoisseurs] . . . But I did so, not with any intent of placing it in my own house . . . but with a design of fixing it in some conspicuous place in my native province, preferably in the temple of Jupiter; for it is a present well worthy of a temple and a god. Pray, then, undertake this, as readily as you do all my commissions, and give immediate orders for a pedestal to be made. I leave the choice of marble to you, *but let my name be engraved upon it, and, if you think proper, my titles.* (*Ep.* 3.6, my italics)

Pliny's final request is central – the names and titles of the Roman elite, engraved on statues, temples, amphitheaters, baths, and other public works, survive in the form of inscriptions unearthed throughout the realm that Rome once ruled. Inscriptions like the following, from Spoleto, Italy, could be multiplied a thousandfold:

> Gaius Torasius Severus son of Gaius, of the Horatian tribe, quattuorvir with judicial power, augur, built this [probably the public baths] in his own name and in the name of his son, Publius Meclonius Proculus Torasianus, pontiff, on his own land and at his own expense. He likewise gave the community for celebrating the birthday of his son 250,000 sesterces, out of the income from which on August 30 annually the decurions are to hold a public banquet and the townspeople who are present receive eight sesterces apiece. Likewise he gave to the board of six priests of Augustus and the priests of the Lares of Augustus and the block captains 120,000 sesterces, so that out of the income from this sum they might have a public repast on the same day. Because of his services to the municipality the council of decurions adopted him as patron of the municipality.
> (*CIL* 9.4815)

For the Roman elite orders, then, wealth was not an end in itself. It was a means to a more glorious end – the public assertion and augmentation of personal and civic honor. As Plutarch remarked, "Most people think that to be deprived of the chance to display their wealth is to be deprived of wealth itself" (*Cat. Mai.* 18.4).[14] For some, indeed, the former insured the latter. Dio laments,

> does not the seeker after fame find it necessary to buy a lot of food and wine? And he must collect flute-players and mimes and harpists and jugglers and, more than that, pugilists and pancratiasts and wrestlers and runners and all that tribe – at least unless he intends to entertain the mob in a cheap and beggarly manner. (*Or.* 66.8)

Catering to the tastes of "the mob" in this fashion, however, could severely test the extent of one's resources:

> by official act virtually all states have devised lures of every kind for the simpletons – crowns and front seats and public proclamations. Accordingly, in some instances men who craved these things have actually been made wretched and reduced to beggary, although the states held before them nothing great or wonderful at all, but in some cases led their victims about with a sprig of green, as men lead cattle, or clapped upon their heads a crown or a ribbon. Therefore, while a fool like that, if he so desired, might have for the asking any number of crowns, not merely of olive or of oak, but even of ivy or of myrtle, often he sells his house and his lands and thereafter goes about hungry and clad in a shabby little cloak. Ah but, says he, his name is publicly proclaimed by his fellow citizens – just as is that of a runaway slave! (*Or.* 66.2)

As Ramsay MacMullen has observed, "It was the thirst for honor, the contest for applause, that worked so powerfully to impoverish the rich."[15] Lenski's assumption, then, that in certain societies wealth functions preeminently as an instrumental commodity employed in the quest for a more central social good, namely, honor, is amply attested in the Roman world.

Honor as a public commodity

"For the Romans, being was being seen." Thus remarks Carlin Barton concerning the public orientation of Roman social life.[16] Dio, who understood not only the centrality of honor in his world but also the nature of honor as a decidedly public commodity, would have heartily concurred with Barton's assertion:

> For all men set great store by the outward tokens of high achievement, and not one man in a thousand is willing to agree that what he regards as a noble deed shall have been done for himself alone and that no other man shall have knowledge of it. (*Or.* 31.22)

Public behavior was, therefore, specifically framed with the eye of the public in view.

> Clearly, therefore, if a person is going to be exceedingly anxious to win the praise of the crowd as well, believing that its praise or censure has more weight than his own judgement, his every act and wish will be aimed to show himself the sort of person that the crowd expects. (*Or.* 77/78.24)

Building on the classic work of J. Pitt-Rivers, Bruce Malina and Jerome Neyrey define honor as "the positive value of a person in his or her own eyes plus the positive appreciation of that person in the eyes of his or her social group." As they proceed to elaborate, "In this perspective honor is a claim to positive worth along with the social acknowledgment of that worth by others."[17] Our understanding of the role of honor in the Greco-Roman world is being continually refined, and it is the second component of the above definition which is increasingly emphasized in the literature. As Halvor Moxnes maintains, "Honor is fundamentally the *public* recognition of one's social standing."[18] The collectivist nature of ancient society in fact guarantees that one's personal claim to honor is ultimately inconsequential apart from group affirmation. Moxnes proceeds to explain:

> Since the group is so important for the identity of a Mediterranean person, it is critical to recognize that honor status comes primarily from *group* recognition. While honor may sometimes be an inner quality, the value of a person in his or her own eyes, it depends ultimately on recognition from significant others in society. It is a public matter. When someone's claim to honor is recognized by the group, honor is confirmed, and the result is a new social status.[19]

Conversely, as Bruce Malina and Richard Rohrbaugh pointedly assert, "To claim honor that the community does not recognize is to play the fool."[20]

Focusing more narrowly on the public nature of honor among members of the Roman elite, Lendon affirms, "A man's honour was a public verdict on his qualities and standing, established publicly... life was lived under the constant, withering gaze of opinion, everyone constantly reckoning up the honour of others . . . for the court of prestige met many times a day, wherever men gathered, in the baths or where wine flowed."[21] Apparently Dio was particularly sensitive to this public court of honor. His comments warrant extended citation:

> Is not the trial concerning reputation always in progress wherever there are men – that is, foolish men – not merely once a day but many times, and not before a definite panel of judges, but before all men without distinction, and, moreover, men not bound by oath, men without regard for either witnesses or evidence? For they sit in judgement without either having knowledge of the case or listening to testimony or having been chosen by lot, and it makes no difference to them if they cast their vote at a drinking bout or at the bath and, most outrageous of all, he who to-day is acquitted to-morrow is condemned. Accordingly, whoever is the victim of this malady of courting popularity is bound to be subject to criticism as he walks about, to pay heed to everyone, and to fear lest wittingly or unwittingly he give offence to somebody, but particularly to one of those who are bold and of ready wit. For if he should have the misfortune to have offended somebody ever so little, as often happens, straightway the offended person lets fly a harsh word; and if with that word he perhaps misses his mark, nevertheless he causes dismay, while if he should hit the vital spot he has destroyed his victim forthwith. For the fact is, many are so constituted that they are overwhelmed and made to waste away by anything. (*Or.* 66.18–19)

Dio's philosophical leanings render him less than sympathetic to those who are victims of "this malady of courting popularity." Such persons are, in his view, "foolish men." The passion, however, with which Dio laments this characteristic behavior only serves to emphasize the ubiquitous presence and compelling influence of honor and shame in the public arena of the author's social world.

The values surface often in Roman literature. Apuleius' Lucius, for example, having been utterly humiliated by the people of Hyptata in a formal court setting, had then to face the informal court of public censure on his way to the town baths. His reaction is quintessentially Roman:

> Milo took me by the hand and led me towards the next bath; but by the way I went crouching under him to hide myself from the sight of men, because I had ministered such an occasion of

laughter. And when I had washed and wiped myself and returned home again, I never remembered any such thing, so greatly was I ashamed (*rubor*) at the nodding and pointing of every person.
(*Met.* 3.12)

Lucius found himself on the receiving end of what Barton has pointedly labeled "Visual Assassination."[22]

The power of public opinion to influence the Roman elite's behavior finds colorful expression in a story that Plutarch relates about the struggle for land reform during the time of the Gracchi (133 BCE). Tiberius Gracchus crafted an agrarian reform bill that was opposed by the senate but embraced by the Roman plebs for whom it was written. Tiberius attempted to get the bill before the people but found his efforts blocked by the veto of Octavius, a fellow tribune. In order to overcome Octavius' veto, Tiberius hatched a clever scheme: he would utilize his popularity with the masses to get Octavius deposed from his tribunate.

The citizen tribes began to cast their votes for Octavius' dismissal in a tumultuous scene in the center of Rome. Tension mounted as seventeen of the thirty-five tribes all voted in favor of deposing Tiberius' opponent. An affirming vote from the eighteenth tribe would have won the day for Tiberius and relegated Octavius to the status of a private citizen. Suddenly, however, at this very moment in the proceedings,

> Tiberius called a halt in the voting, and again entreated Octavius, embracing and kissing him in the sight of the people, and fervently begging him not to allow himself to be dishonoured, and not to attach to a friend responsibility for a measure so grievous and severe. (Plut. *Ti. Gracch.* 12)

Initially, Octavius softened, and it appeared he would relent and go along with the agrarian reform bill – until, that is, he noticed his elite peers prominently situated among the crowd:

> But when he turned his gaze towards the men of wealth and substance who were standing in a body together, his awe of them, as it would seem, and his fear of *ill repute among them* (παρ' ἐκείνοις ἀδοξίαν), led him to take every risk with boldness and bid Tiberius do what he pleased.
> (*Ti. Gracch.* 12, my italics)

Octavius apparently could not bear the opprobrium of elite consensus which would have inevitably resulted from his support of a land reform bill. As Cicero would write some decades later, "There is no one so wild as not to be greatly moved . . . by fear of reproach and dishonor" (*Part. or.* 26.91–92).[23]

Members of the elite were not alone in deferring to the opinions of those who had the power to honor or dishonor them. As we will see below, the non-elite, like their social betters, preoccupied themselves with honor-seeking. And, as Dio relates, they were apparently quite sensitive to the public nature of honor, as well. After discussing the manner in which the elite are honored ("these, as if endowed with wings, are all but carried to the stars"), Dio turns his attention to those who lack a noble pedigree or qualifying wealth but who, nevertheless, are "victims of the same malady," namely the lust for glory:

> each goes about living life with his eye on somebody else and concerned about what people are saying of him, and if people speak well of him, as he imagines, he is a happy man, cheerful of countenance, but otherwise he is depressed and downcast and considers himself to be the sort of man they say he is.
> (*Or.* 66.12)

In the words of Horace, "Glory drags along the obscure no less than the nobly born bound to her shining chariot" (*Sat.* 1.6.23–24).[24]

Even philosophers were not exempt. However Dio and his peers might dismiss as fools those who found themselves bound to the chariot of glory, philosophers themselves could hardly escape honor's pale. Ironically enough, the only way in which admirers knew to recognize a philosopher's virtue, free speech, or freedom from convention was to grant him conventional honors in the form of civic tributes like statues (Lucian, *Demon.* 11, 58, 63; *De mort. Peregr.* 18). And Dio and his fellow wise men seldom declined such honors. Assuming as much, Cicero advises persons to choose their philosophers accordingly: "If there should be any who may be moved by the distinction of philosophers, then let them briefly pay attention and listen to those whose distinction and glory are the greatest among learned men" (*Rep.* 1.12).[25] Elsewhere Cicero draws upon the example of the philosophers in order to encourage his readers to surrender to the unavoidable passion for honor so characteristic of Roman elite life:

> Ambition is a universal factor of life, and the nobler a man is, the more susceptible is he to the sweets of fame. We should not disclaim this human weakness, which indeed is patent to all; we should rather admit it unabashed. Why, upon the very books in which they bid us scorn ambition (*gloria*) philosophers

inscribe their names! They seek advertisement and publicity for themselves on the very page whereon they pour contempt upon the advertisement and publicity. (*Arch.* 26)[26]

And so they did. The Epicurean Lucretius, for example, longs for praise for his work and then turns around and scorns glory-seeking in the same volume (compare 1.922–23; 4.4 with 3.59–78; 5.1120–35). Lendon explains:

> As much as philosophers might reject the personal pursuit of honour, they no more than any other members of their society could reject honour as a deep structure by which to conceive, understand, and interact with their world. They had no alternative paradigm to honour to offer their contemporaries, not even a compelling alternative rhetoric of admiration for their own ideas and way of life. Philosophers were doomed to be honoured for their scorn of honour.[27]

As Tacitus observes in his narrative about the Stoic philosopher Helvidius Priscus, "the passion for glory (*cupido gloriae*) is that from which even philosophers last divest themselves" (*Hist.* 4.6).[28]

Elements of honor

It may seem odd to discuss the centrality of honor, and honor as a public good, before attempting to delineate those qualities that rendered a person honorable in the Roman mind, namely, the elements of honor. My approach, in this regard, has been by design. Honor/shame societies strike many moderns as quite foreign, so that it generally proves helpful to consider the importance and function of honor in the eyes of the ancients (above), before tackling the nature of honor in a more analytical fashion. As I now attempt the latter, a few preliminary remarks are in order about potential distinctions in social values among the various people-groups of the empire.

Honor functioned as a central social value throughout the ancient Mediterranean world. The elements of honor differed somewhat from culture to culture, however, while still retaining many commonalities. Manual labor, for example, dishonorable among elite Romans, continued to find affirmation among the empire's Judeans. On the other hand, both Romans and Judeans agreed in identifying wealth and natal lineage as important attributes for persons seeking public esteem. Non-Judean Romans and Greeks shared even more in this regard, particularly during the imperial period. As Lendon aptly notes, "within the world of Rome and the Romanized, the Hellenic and the Hellenized, standards of honour converged over time; the long centuries of the empire were a quiet solvent of aristocratic particularism."[29] Lendon cites several examples of increasingly shared values. Among Romans, "a proper smattering of literature" came, through Greek influence, to become part of what it meant to be a well-bred aristocrat.[30] On the Greek side, elites in the eastern cities increasingly adapted the Roman practice of *salutatio*, so that by the second century CE some Greeks had adopted retinues; by the fourth century a nobleman on the streets of Antioch *without* a group of followers had become an anomaly. Earlier, in contrast, large retinues of slaves, clients, and other hangers-on were viewed as patently offensive in elite Greek circles.[31]

As we might imagine, in any given setting the relative influence of Greek and Roman social values upon one another will vary, depending primarily upon the cultural identity of the local elite stratum of the population. In the early decades of the colony at Philippi, civic authority and power were solely in Roman hands. According to the principle of value replication, whereby non-elite persons tend to emulate the practices of their social superiors, it was inevitable that Roman influence upon Greek social values predominated in the colony. The empire-wide influence of Roman values and behavior relating to social status, along with the particular "Romanness" of Philippi (see chapter three), guaranteed that all residents of the colony, Roman and Greek alike, shared the concerns for personal and familial honor outlined in this and the previous chapter. The elements of honor, then, discussed below, will prove important for situating Paul's letter to the Christians at Philippi in its proper social setting in the final chapters of this monograph.

Any attempt to delineate the elements of honor must immediately come to grips with the fact that honor in the ancient world related most basically to one's natal origin, the family (and town) of one's birth.[32] Almost without exception, Roman imperial biographers such as Plutarch and Suetonius begin their works by laying out the ancestral lineage of the notables whose lives they narrate, for it is natal origin, first and foremost, that determines a person's value and social status in the Roman mind (compare Suet. *Aug.* 1–6; *Tib.* 1–4; *Calig.* 1; *Claud.* 1–2; Plut. *Ages.* 1; *Pel.* 3; *Dion* 3–4). The practice of emphasizing an individual's family background as a primary indicator of social rank was hardly limited to the writing of biography. Pliny, for example, who had been asked to find a spouse for a friend's charge, begins his description of the chosen groom by identifying his birthplace (Brixia) and highlighting the rank of his father, Minicius Macrinus, whom Pliny identifies as "a leading member of the order of knights" (*Ep.* 1.14.5).[33] Among the Romans a person's social status was determined, first and foremost, by the status of his or her father and other male figures in the ancestral bloodline.

The importance of family origin for a person's place in society explains why disinheritance by one's father was viewed with such horror in the Roman world. A Roman father technically had the right of life or death over his offspring. In actuality, however, *abdicatio* or *exheredatio*, expulsion from the father's house, was generally the worst punishment a recalcitrant child could expect.[34] It may as well have been death itself. In 140 BCE Decimus Junius Silanus was denounced by his own father for extortion during his provincial command. The father, Titus Manlius Torquatus, disowned his son as follows: "I judge you unworthy of the Republic and of my house; I order you to depart far from my sight." Silanus, his social identity utterly effaced by his father's banishment, estimated physical death to be an appropriate corollary to the social death he had experienced and proceeded to hang himself the following day (Val. Max. 5.8.3).

The anomalous few who achieved highly honorific posts without the advantage of an illustrious family background were ever suspect in the eyes of their senatorial peers. Tacitus describes in some detail the social and military career of a certain Curtius Rufus, who ascended the *cursus honorum* to become finally proconsul of Africa. Our author begins, in vintage Tacitean form, by casting aspersions upon his subject's unsavory natal origin: "As to the origin of Curtius Rufus, whom some have described as the son of a gladiator, I would not promulgate a falsehood and I am ashamed to investigate the truth" (*Ann.* 11.21). Tacitus then proceeds to outline Rufus' progress through the *cursus*, which included receiving the insignia of a triumph at the hand of the emperor – all this, Tacitus notes, "in spite of patrician competitors." As Tacitus concludes his narrative, he again returns to the issue of Rufus' lineage:

> Tiberius had covered the disgrace of his birth (*dedecus natalium*) by the remark: "Curtius Rufus I regard as the creation of himself." [That is, his accomplishments are enough of a lineage.] Afterwards, long of life and sullenly cringing to his betters, arrogant to his inferiors, unaccommodating among his equals, he held consular office, the insignia of triumph, and finally Africa.
> (*Ann.* 11.21)

One suspects that Tacitus was more than a little uncomfortable sharing consular honors with the likes of Curtius Rufus, even if separated by some three generations.

The great majority of the non-elite were less fortunate than Curtius Rufus, since social mobility between social strata was the exception in the Roman world. In order to circumvent this reality some persons tried to enhance their honor by daring to claim membership in a family to which they did not belong. The practice was apparently rather widespread, for Valerius Maximus' *Memorable Doings and Sayings* contains a whole section entitled, "Of Persons Born in the Lowest Station (*infimo loco nati*) Who Tried by Falsehood to Thrust Themselves into Illustrious Families (*familiis clarissimis*)" (9.15). One such individual sought to align himself with a consular family:

> Herophilus, a horse doctor, claimed C. Marius, seven times Consul, as his grandfather and so puffed himself up that a number of colonies of veterans and distinguished municipalities and almost all the clubs adopted him as their patron. What is more, when C. Caesar, after crushing Cn. Pompeius the younger in Spain, admitted the public in his suburban estate, the pretender was greeted on the other side of the column with almost equal enthusiasm by the throng. (9.15.1)

Caesar and those who survived him soon ascertained our horse doctor's true identity and banished the imposter from Italy. Herophilus was finally "put to death in prison by order of the Fathers" (9.15.1).[35]

Sufficiently evident in all of the above is the importance of an illustrious family for esteem in the public square. After noble family connections, wealth (assuming it was from landed estates and not less honorable means), legal status (senator, equestrian, or at least a citizen; no servile background), position in the *cursus* (the consulate was a greater honor than a priesthood or the office of aedile), a procession of slaves and clients, fine clothing and housing (at Rome and in the country), and a proper rhetorical education all contributed toward a positive verdict in the public court of honor.[36]

But there was more. Pierre Bourdieu, in his study of the Berber Kabyle of Algeria, found the social status of his subjects "embedded in the agents' very bodies . . . in the form of bodily postures and stances, ways of standing, sitting, looking, speaking or walking."[37] For the Romans too these attributes constituted honor's "more subtle qualities . . . the proper accent, words, posture, bearing – in short elegance."[38] Pliny thus proceeds to describe the prospective bridegroom he is recommending to a friend (see above) as one whose "general good looks have a natural nobility and the dignified bearing of a senator" (*Ep.* 1.14.8). As Lendon notes,

"Two aristocrats never needed to enquire of genealogies to realize that they were both gentlemen; all they needed was a glance."[39]

A final element of honor, namely, moral virtue, deserves some comment.[40] Sallust's description of Cato the Younger, whom he compares with Julius Caesar, emphasizes the honor that accrued to Cato's account as a result of his moral excellence:

> Cato, on the contrary, cultivated self-control, propriety, but above all austerity. He did not vie with the rich in riches nor in intrigue with the intriguer, but with the active in good works, with the self-restrained in moderation, with the blameless in integrity. He preferred to be, rather than to seem, virtuous; hence the less he sought fame (*gloriam*), the more it pursued him.
> (*Cat.* 54)

Dio would later concur with Sallust that moral excellence formed an important element of prestige: being "renowned among all Greeks and barbarians" means "being preeminent in virtue (ἀρετή) and reputation and wealth and in almost every kind of power" (*Or.* 12.11). Similarly, according to Quintilian, "the industry of Scipio Africanus brought him virtue, his virtue brought him glory" (*Inst.* 9.3.56).

Morality, however, is differently conceived in strong-group societies like ancient Rome than in individualistic cultures like those of Western Europe and America today. Non-individualistic cultures tend to produce anti-introspective, non-psychologically oriented persons, and here is where the public nature of honor intersects moral virtue (a desired component of that honor) in the world of Mediterranean antiquity. Bruce Malina observes,

> Given the anti-introspective bent of Mediterranean persons, what counts above all is what other people say, how other people assess the situation. Individuals are always playing to an audience from which they expect approval. Approval results in a feeling of honor; disapproval results in a profound sense of shame. People generally do not have to face the social sanction of internalized guilt, which is not a feature of the anti-introspective, collectivist personality.[41]

The result is that the Roman elite, and most others in the ancient world, were motivated to behave in a virtuous manner not, primarily, by internal guilt but, rather, by the desire to avoid shame and receive honor from persons and groups external to themselves.

Any categorical distinction between ancient Rome as an "honor culture" and the modern West as a "guilt culture" must, of course, be carefully qualified. The ancients were hardly immune to feelings of guilt; nor are we moderns wholly insulated from the sanctions of shame.[42] Nevertheless, the manner in which ancient writers sought to motivate their readers suggests that the general tenor of Malina's description of Mediterranean society as "anti-introspective" is on the mark (see above). Isocrates, for example, in his collection of admonitions to a certain Demonicus (*Ad Demonicum*), repeatedly enjoins "it is disgraceful" or "it is noble," instead of appealing, as we might today, to the "rightness" or "wrongness" of a given behavior or activity.[43] Aristotle claimed, "there are many things which they either do or do not do owing to the feelings of shame which these men [the ever-observing public] inspire" (*Rh.* 2.6.26). Consider, as well, the kind of behaviorial motivation Cicero envisioned for his ideal republic:

> the best men seek praise and glory, and avoid disgrace and dishonour. Nor indeed are they deterred from crime so much by the fear of the penalties ordained by law as by the sense of shame which Nature has given to man in the form of a certain fear of justified censure . . . so that shame deters the citizens from crime no less effectively than fear. And the same remarks apply, indeed, to the love of praise.
>
> (*Rep.* 5.4, Loeb, slightly adapted)

Lendon summarizes:

> It would be perverse to deny that ancient aristocrats felt the pangs of conscience, but the fact that moral reputation was numbered among the qualities for which aristocratic opinion conferred honour ensured that Graeco-Roman society was to a great degree a shame culture, that concern for reputation could be considered the main bulwark of morality, for "to scorn fame is to scorn virtue."[44]

In the words of Pliny, "Very few people are as scrupulously honest in secret as in public, and many are influenced by public opinion (*famam*) but scarcely anyone by conscience (*conscientiam*)" (*Ep.* 3.20.8–9). Pliny, of course, feels the need to broadcast publicly his own concern to be "scrupulously honest in secret" in a letter intended for the eyes and ears of his aristocratic peers.[45]

Public office and Rome's *cursus honorum*

Being chosen for public office constituted one of the most important honors a person could receive from his peers in the Roman world, but public office functioned quite differently in antiquity than it does in contemporary western society. Two illustrations from our sources will make this immediately clear. During the second century an esteemed consular named Marcus Cornelius Fronto penned a letter to Antoninus Pius requesting a procuratorship to "enhance the dignity" of a fellow-member of the elite who was advancing in years. Fronto assures the emperor that the office will be declined – the elderly man simply wants the honor of having the procuratorship granted, not the associated responsibilities (*Ep. ad Pium* 1.10). One suspects that our aged aristocrat had begun seriously to reflect upon – and desired to augment – the inscribed list of honors that would soon adorn his burial monument.

Several decades earlier, Pliny had atempted, in similar fashion, to broker an office for a friend, an equestrian named Maturus Arrianus. He makes it clear that his only intention is to enhance the man's honor. Pliny does not care what position his friend is awarded, except that "it must be a distinction (*splendidum*)" and it should not demand much work (*nec molestum*) (*Ep.* 3.2.6). Romans such as Fronto and Pliny obviously viewed public office in a manner quite different from the way in which such positions are conceived in modern bureaucracies. The difference can be simply summarized: honor – not function – was central to officeholding in the Roman world.

The honorific nature of public office manifests itself most basically in the area of lexical semantics. In both classical languages, honor words provide the most common terms for public office: *honor* or *dignitas* in Latin; τιμή in Greek. As Lendon notes, moreover, "these are not dead metaphors, technical expressions devoid of their original flavour: honour, prestige, lies absolutely at the heart of office holding."[46] I will first consider the phenomenon of honorific office as it finds expression in Rome's *cursus honorum*. The chapter will conclude with an examination of honor in the provinces, where Rome's *cursus honorum* was replicated in miniature at nearly every stratum of society.

The *cursus* in Rome

The *cursus honorum*, or "Honors Race," was a sequence of offices that marked the standard career for the Roman senatorial class, and which had been in place since the middle of the fourth century BCE.[47] The basic track to glory involved, in ascending order, the offices of quaestor, aedile, praetor, consul, and censor.[48] Notice the order in which Tacitus outlines the *cursus:* "It was counted among the portents that each of the magistracies found its numbers diminished, since a quaestor, an aedile, and a tribune, together with a praetor and a consul, had died within a few months" (*Ann.* 12.64).[49] Each office had its own responsibilities. Quaestors took care of the receipt of taxes and various payments to the Roman treasury. Aediles personally underwrote various civic projects, including the upkeep of public buildings and the staging of games for the populace. Praetors, the first rank in the *cursus* to hold *imperium*, exercised authority as judges in the courts at Rome or as magistrates in the provinces. During the republic, two consuls stood at the top of the *cursus* hierarchy. At the height of the republic specific limits were placed upon (a) the age at which a person could hold a magistracy, (b) the number of persons holding an office at a given time, and (c) the length of time a position could be occupied by an individual.[50] All of these regulations were officially altered – and unofficially compromised – on numerous occasions.

The transition to empire brought significant changes in honors and their function but served, if anything, to enhance the ceremonial nature of the posts. New offices, like the city prefect, appeared, and the emperor viewed it as his prerogative to bend the age requirements, as well as the order of the magistracies, in order to reward the loyal among the senatorial class.[51] More importantly, the increasing centralization of authority under the emperor saw the powers associated with the various magistracies gradually eclipsed, so that honor became even more central to the positions in the *cursus*.

Jona Lendering summarizes the various honorific offices as follows:[52]

REPUBLIC	Minimum age	EMPIRE	Minimum age
		Vigintivir	18
Military service		Military tribune	20
Quaestor	30	Quaestor	25
Aedile or Tribune	37	Aedile or Tribune	27
Praetor	40	Praetor	30
		Prefect Propraetor Proconsul Commander of a legion	
Consul	43	Consul	32
Censor		Praefectus urbi Propraetor Proconsul	

Preoccupation with honor and the cursus honorum

We gain significant insight into the importance of the *cursus* as a hierarchy of honors when we consider the pervasive preoccupation with various violations of the *cursus* tradition in Roman historical narratives. Ancient historians commonly lament two ways in which social standards reflected in the *cursus* were compromised. At times senators were granted certain magistracies in violation of the requirements of age and order of magistracies outlined in the chart above. These breaks in tradition occurred within the ranks of the senatorial class. More serious was a second category of violation, namely, the admission to the *cursus*, or the senate, of persons whose natal origin and corresponding social status rendered them undeserving of such honors. Both of these compromises can be seen in the activities of Julius Caesar.

After extolling Caesar's positive accomplishments, Suetonius attempts to show how Caesar "abused his power," in order to demonstrate that Caesar was "justly slain." Suetonius' explanation of Caesar's demise can be summarized as a single offense: he himself accepted – and granted to others – inappropriate honors. According to Suetonius' narrative, Caesar received

> excessive honours (*honores modo nimios*), such as an interrupted consulship, the dictatorship for life, and the censorship of public morals, as well as the forename Imperator, the surname of Father of his Country, a statue among those of the kings, and a raised couch in the orchestra. (*Iul.* 76)

Violation of the traditions associated with the *cursus honorum* and the senatorial *ordo* became equally pronounced in the honors Caesar gave to others:

> When one of the consuls suddenly died the day before the Kalends of January [the day before the new consuls took office], he gave the vacant office for a few hours to a man who asked for it. With the same disregard for law and precedent he named magistrates for several years to come, bestowed the emblems of consular rank (*consularia ornamenta*) on ten ex-praetors.
> (*Iul.* 76)[53]

The bestowal of "the emblems of consular rank" upon persons not actually occupying the office of consul is informative. Lendon elaborates:

> One key to understanding the hierarchy that Romans thought was most important among aristocratic officials lies in noting the significance of the Roman practice of granting the insignia of

political offices – the robes and tokens, both on the municipal and imperial level – to persons who had not held those offices, for use either from day to day, or on special occasions. This only makes sense when it is understood that offices were social distinctions, and that the hierarchy that was marked to contemporaries was not any official hierarchy, in our sense, but a social hierarchy – a hierarchy of prestige and standing – in which official rank was a vital criterion of ranking.[54]

Even more problematic than the above infractions, which, at least, involved only the senatorial elite, was the granting of honors by Caesar to persons whose social status was wholly inappropriate to such dignity to begin with. Caesar admitted newly minted citizens to the senate, as well as "half-civilised Gauls." He assigned three legions in Egypt to the command of "a favourite of his called Rufio, son of one of his freedmen" (76).[55]

The reaction in Rome was swift and creative. Suetonius speaks of an anonymously posted placard that purported to offer instructions to persons who might encounter a lost, newly minted senator trying to locate the senate hall for the first time. The notice read, "God bless the Commonwealth! Let no one consent to point out the House to a newly made senator" (*Iul.* 80). Someone else composed a song that, Suetonius adds, was "sung everywhere [*sic*]":

> Caesar led the Gauls in triumph
> led them to the senate house
> then the Gauls put off their breeches
> and put on the laticlave (80).

The issue of Gauls in the senate would surface again on more than one occasion. Augustus reversed Caesar's policy and restored the senate to its "former limits and distinction" by ejecting "a low-born and ill-assorted rabble" (Suet. *Aug.* 35). It is unclear whether Caesar's Gauls were removed by Augustus, but Roman citizens from Gallia Comata (Northern Gaul) would later become senators, apparently for the first time, under Claudius in 48 CE. This innovation did not occur without some debate, during which the opposing camp outlined their position as follows: "Leave them by all means to enjoy the title of citizens; but the insignia of the Fathers, the glories of the magistracies – these they must not vulgarize" (Tac. *Ann.* 11.23). The emperor, of course, got his way, and the foreigners were admitted to the *ordo*. Apparently feeling the need to satisfy senators who felt their status sullied by the admission of outsiders, however, Claudius concurrently

> adopted into the body of patricians all senators of exceptionally long standing or of distinguished parentage: for by now few families remained of the Greater and Lesser Houses, as they were styled by Romulus and Lucius Brutus; and even those selected to fill the void, under the Cassian and Saenian laws, by the dictator Caesar and the emperor Augustus were exhausted. Here the censor had a popular task, and he embarked upon it with delight. (*Ann.* 11.25)

Those senators who had advised Claudius against "vulgarizing" "the insignia of the Fathers" and "the glories of the magistracies" apparently had no problem with vulgarizing the patrician class.[56]

As the above excerpts demonstrate, Roman writers were quite preoccupied with the social infractions involved in appointing the undeserving to important posts. The reason for this, I suggest, is that alongside these violations of the *cursus* tradition there persisted an overarching ideology that was largely unimpeded by historical realities – an ideology that continued to insist on an appropriate fit between the honor of an office and the social status of its occupant. So Tacitus praises Tiberius,

> In conferring offices (*honores*), he took into view the nobility of a candidate's ancestry, the distinction of his military service, and the brilliance of his civil achievements, and left it sufficiently clear that no better choice had been available . . . The imperial property was entrusted by Caesar to men of tested merit, at times to a personal stranger on the strength of his reputation (*fama*).
> (*Ann.* 4.6, Loeb, slightly adapted)

Pliny, too, looks back from his own time and recalls an era when offices were appointed in accordance with the honor of the potential candidate (*Ep.* 3.20). Indeed, he assumes the ongoing vitality of this ideology in his own efforts as a broker, since he expresses hope that Accius Sura will be granted a vacant praetorship due to "the distinction of his family (*natalium splendor*)" (*Ep.* 10.12.2).

Given the degree of social and political upheaval experienced by Rome since the institution of the *cursus honorum* in the early republic, the preservation of the *cursus* tradition out into the imperial period is actually quite remarkable. Changes were made and standards were violated, yet the honorific nature of public office remained of central importance to the Roman elite class throughout the centuries. The endurance of this social construct can be explained, in part, by the self-perpetuating nature of the whole aristocratic value system. In the final analysis, it was elite consensus that decided which specific personal and familial attributes rendered a person honorable in Roman society – "anything praised by aristocrats conferred glory."[57] Nowhere is this more clear than in the honor conferred by the various offices of the *cursus*. Consular figures, in particular, who had passed through the *cursus honorum*, thereby acquired the highest level of prestige and, thus, the ability to confer prestige on what and whom they deemed worthy (see immediately below). And, of course, members of this elite order most valued their own honorific achievements, since "it is natural for anyone to wish high honour (*quam amplissima existimari*) to a position he has once occupied." Thus, Pliny claims "special respect" for the consulship, since he himself had ascended to that apex of the imperial *cursus* (*Ep.* 4.17.3).

A final aspect of public office relates to the social status of the persons bestowing the positions. The honor associated with public office came not only from the position itself. It also came from the individual who conferred the office, particularly during the imperial period. Pliny wrote of an individual who had been appointed by a certain Corellius as the latter's assistant in buying and distributing lands. For Pliny, the honor of the post was greatly augmented by the social status of the patron: "there could be no higher honour (*qua gloria dignum est*) than to be the special choice of so great a man from such a wide field for selection" (*Ep.* 7.31.4). Lendon describes an inscription detailing the career of an equestrian, which lists him not only as a *praefectus fabrum* (a first office in the equestrian *cursus*) but, more specifically, as the *praefectus fabrum* of the emperor Claudius.[58] Since offices were often favors given by a patron to a client (*beneficia*), the honor that accrued to a person upon the bestowal of an office was thus proportional to the social status of the bestower. This will prove especially enlightening later, when we examine the exaltation of Jesus, a crucified slave, who is awarded "the name which is above every name" by God himself (Phil. 2:9–11).

Replication in the provinces

Corax (Raven) → *Nymphus* (Nymphus) → *Miles* (Soldier) → *Leo* (Lion) → *Perses* (Persian) → *Heliodromus* (Sun-Runner) → *Pater* (Father) – thus ran the *cursus* of honorific posts (in ascending order) for devotees of Mithras, a mystery cult increasingly popular among non-elite males during the second and third centuries of the common era. The hierarchy was further divided into two broad strata. Persons in the lower three ranks were "underlings" or "servitors"; those who attained the grade Lion and above became the cult's true "participants" (Porph. *Abst.* 4.16). Mithras scholars assure us, moreover, that "the grades are linked centrally to the myth of the cult, to its life and to its theology" – the *cursus* was, in a word, institutionalized in the cult's ideology.[59] Another religious cult, the collegium of Aesculapius and Hygia from Rome (153 CE) had offices that included *quinquennalis, pater, mater, immunes, curatores*, as reflected in a list of persons to whom special distributions were made on feast days (*CIL* 6.10234.10–12). Greek cult associations also contained a plethora of honorific titles including *hiereus, archiereus, archimystes* and *archithiasites* (or *thiasarches), pater, mater, presbys, tamias, grammateus, hyperetes, diakonos*, "and a host of more specialized terms."[60]

Nor was this preoccupation with honorific posts limited to the religious collegia. Burial societies, trade groups, and household associations also elected persons to various positions of honor. Several hundred surviving inscriptions, for example, document the existence of domestic collegia associated with imperial and private households. Among the honors prized by persons in such household associations were the offices of *quinquennalis, decurio, sacerdos, honoratus, curator, mater, pater*, and *scriba*.[61] What we see in each of the above examples – and these citations could be multiplied a hundredfold – is the replication of Roman elite cultural values and social practices in non-elite settings throughout the empire.

Rome's esteemed *cursus honorum* was, of course, open to only the smallest minority of persons in Roman society. Local municipalities duplicated the Roman *cursus* in their own civic honors, and further replication of social verticality and associated honors occurred in non-elite cult groups and other voluntary associations. Consider, first, the replication of Rome's *cursus* among local elites. The following is excerpted from the municipal charter of a town in Spain from the late first century CE. The specifics of the citation have to do with oaths taken by the various magistrates:

> The incumbent douvirs [*sic*] with judicial power in this municipality, likewise the aediles and quaestor now holding office . . . likewise the douvirs, aediles, or quaestors who shall henceforth be elected . . . each of them within five days next following their entrance upon the office of douvir, aedile, or quaestor, and before a meeting of the decurions . . . is held, shall in a public meeting take oath by Jupiter, by the deified Augustus, by the deified Claudius . . . (*CIL* 2.1963)[62]

Observe the emphasis here (through repetition) upon the titles of the municipal offices of the local *cursus*. Some of the honors, in fact, parrot the official titles that were used in the *cursus* in Rome (aedile, quaestor). Nor should the oaths to the emperors go unnoticed. A local *cursus*, titular mimicry, oaths to deified emperors – all of these, of course, ensured the replication of Roman social values in provincial towns and settlements.

Like magistracies in Rome, however, municipal honors were also available only to a small percentage of a town's population, for only a handful of the local aristocracy occupied positions on the town council and fewer yet became key magistrates (aediles, quaestors, and *duumviri*). The result was that stratification and honor-seeking were replicated further down the social hierarchy in local, non-elite voluntary associations (such as the religious cults and household groups referenced above). In this way these groups afforded their members the opportunity to participate in a *cursus honorum* to which they could never aspire in a broader social setting.[63] As Kloppenborg insightfully observes, "social relations and organization tended to mirror the municipal organization of the public cult of the *polis*," including a formally enrolled citizenry (termed *populus* or *demos*), a governing council (*boule* or *gerousia*), and the division of members into voting groups (*curiae* or *centuriae*).[64] Kloppenborg's comments relate specifically to the religious collegia, but the general principle of social replication applies across the board to trade groups and other voluntary associations as well.

A lengthy inscription has survived, for example, which details the rules and procedures of a second-century burial society. A portion of the text focuses upon the responsibilities and honors associated with positions of leadership in the collegium:

> Chairmen for the dinners, four at a time, selected in turn according to the membership list, ought to provide one amphora each of good wine, and bread worth two asses, proportionate to the number of club members, and four sardines, and a room for the dinner, and hot water, and a waiter ... If any member speaks abusively or insolently to the club president (*quinquennalis*) during dinner, let his fine be 20 sesterces. It was also decided that the club president, on religious holidays during his term of office, should clothe himself in white, and make offerings of incense and wine, and perform other such duties. And on the birthdays of Diana and Antinous he should provide, in the public bath building, oil for club members before they dine.
>
> (*CIL* 14.2112)[65]

Mirroring the activities of their social betters, leaders in this collegium receive honorable posts, they dress according to their social status in the group, and they serve as the community's benefactors.

The army had a *cursus* of its own. Military organizations are markedly stratified in nearly all societies, and, as we might expect, this was particularly the case in the Roman world. I will examine the military *cursus* and military honors in the following chapters, when I survey the epigraphic record from the colony at Philippi. Here I will simply illustrate a not untypical scenario that saw a military career precede the acquisition of honorific posts in a local municipality. A soldier who had risen to the post of town decurion took pains to insure that his *cursus* would find public expression in the form of a sepulcher inscription:

> C. Luccius . . . Sabinus, decurion of Beneventum, while still living made [this tomb] for himself, his wife Ofillia Parata, and his brother Luccius Verecundus, and his posterity. He served in the First Urban Cohort at the side of the tribunes, was an attendant (*secutor*), orderly (*optio*) of the hospital, orderly of the prison, aid (*singularis*), clerk (*beneficarius*) of a tribune, put in charge of the examination of witnesses by Annius Verus, Prefect of the City; he was also officer in charge of the watchword, orderly, standard-bearer, clerk of the treasury, orderly in charge of records, senior clerk of a tribune, clerk of Valerius Asiaticus, Prefect of the City. He was discharged by the emperor Hadrian when Servianus . . . and Vibius Verus were consuls [134 CE].
>
> (*ILS* 2117)[66]

Even slaves formed a social hierarchy of sorts, as they related to other slaves in their respective households. Dio assumed that slaves would wrestle with one another "over glory and precedence" (περὶ δόξης καὶ πρωτείων) (*Or.* 34.51), and Pliny recognized that "the house provides a slave with a country and a sort of citizenship" (*Ep.* 8.16.2–3). Claudian goes into a bit more detail: "There are even grades among slaves and a certain dignity; that slave who has served but one master holds a position of less infamy" (*In Eutropium* 1.29–31). Lendon summarizes:

> The slaves of farm or household thus constitute their own community of honour, although at a vast social distance from the community of the aristocracy above. And aristocratic authors, even if they grant slaves no honour in aristocratic eyes, realize that slaves grant each other slavish honor in slavish eyes.[67]

Apparently, almost everyone could find a *cursus* appropriate to his or her social location. No wonder, for in the Roman world "there is no man too humble to be affected by the sweetness of glory" (Val. Max. 8.14).[68]

The replication of the *cursus* sheds much light on the topic of social mobility in the Roman world. Recent studies suggest that Rome exhibited a rather significant degree of social mobility given its traditional cultural orientation. Senatorial families, for example, saw a 75 percent turnover per generation. This opened the doors of the senate first to the Italian provincial elite and, later, to non-Italians. The tiny fraction of senators from outside Italy during the reign of Augustus increased to some 25 percent during the Flavian era, and to well over 50 percent by the third century.[69] Such social mobility must, however, be put in perspective. The centuries required for this gradual social change, along with the minute percentage of the empire's population affected (MacMullen calculates the senate at two-thousandths of one percent of the total population of the empire), should caution us against using this phenomenon to make generalizations about opportunities for social advancement empire-wide.[70] A snapshot view of the senate (and senatorial values) at any given generation reveals a markedly conservative attitude toward the kind of "social mobility" reflected in the diachronic overview of the changing population of the senate outlined above. Finally, it is important to remember that the provincials who advanced to the senatorial *ordo* were already elite in their local settings. They were wealthy, and they already shared much of the value system of the Roman senate long before their admission to the order itself. The mobility of these local elites, then, was, in a sense, more geographical than social in nature.

Mobility between non-elite and elite strata was an altogether different issue. Garnsey and Saller explain: "Movement into the local elites ... implied an increase in wealth, and wealth was usually passed on within families."[71] Social movement of any kind was therefore rare among non-elite persons. Aelius Aristides remarks, of the static nature of various occupations,

> Those who were yesterday shoemakers and carpenters are not today infantry and cavalrymen, nor as on the stage is one transformed into a soldier who was just now a farmer. Nor, as in a poor home where the same people do the cooking and keep the house and make the beds, have you mixed your occupations.
> (*Or.* 26.71)[72]

There were always exceptions, though, and two upwardly mobile groups, in particular, can be observed in the sources: soldiers and wealthy freedmen.[73] But a provincial municipality remained, like Rome, a "very steep social pyramid," and "the number of inhabitants who counted as rich [and thereby eligible for civic posts of honor] was minute."[74] Freedmen and retired soldiers fortunate enough to gain a position of eminence on a town council thus entered the ranks of a local aristocracy that continued to constitute a small percentage of the municipality's total population.[75]

When we consider social mobility in Roman society, it is generally preferable, therefore, to think of advancement *within* the various social strata of a given town or municipality, rather than *across* the strata – that is, to think of the replication of the elite *cursus* in non-elite settings. The typical *cursus* was not a pathway of social advancement leading an army recruit or a local dockworker through a series of posts culminating in admission to the senate in Rome. A typical *cursus* rather found our soldier climbing the ranks of his local Mithras cult, or our dockworker seeking an honorary position in "The Koinon of Berytian Poseidoniastai, Merchants, Shippers and Warehousemen" on Delos.[76] It was the replication of Rome's *cursus honorum* in these local, non-elite settings that provided opportunities for social recognition and "mobility" for the great majority of the empire's population.

The conservative nature of the social phenomenon outlined above must be underlined as I conclude this discussion of the *cursus honorum* and its widespread replication. Sandra Walker-Ramisch observes the following concerning the social structure of the ancient *polis* and the replication of decurion values in non-elite settings:

> A rigid class system in which class was legally defined and hereditary meant that upward social movement was a virtual impossibility for the lower classes. The upper class ephebes received their gymnasium education and went on to become members of the *gerousia* or to take prestigious municipal posts. The lower classes joined a collegium. Within it they structured a microcosm, a society with prestigious positions and grand titles which were attainable by all members. In short, they took over the "nomenclature of officialdom" and in their social relations and organization "constituted in every detail miniature cities."[77]

Almost without exception, voluntary associations in the Roman world both reflected and reinforced the hierarchical nature of elite society, as the source materials cited above demonstrate. Readers familiar with the development of trade unions in early twentieth-century American society will likely recall the innovative, countercultural orientation of these groups vis-à-vis the dominant culture. The unions sought, as a rule, to change the social status quo of early industrial society. In contrast, Greco-Roman voluntary associations (including trade associations) did not challenge but, rather, perpetuated and reinforced the broader elite values of hierarchy, status, and public recognition.[78] Even groups like the Christian church that began with a more countercultural, relatively non-hierarchical social charter eventually accommodated themselves to the relational verticality of the dominant culture. As I will later demonstrate, Paul of Tarsus specifically challenged these very tendencies in his attempt to construct an alternative social vision for the Christian community at Philippi, a social vision based on the teachings and example of Jesus of Nazareth.

Summary

In the second century CE, Artemidorus of Daldis penned a work on the interpretation of dreams. To understand the meaning of dreams, one must take carefully into consideration the social status of the dreamer, for, according to Artemidorus, the meaning of a dream varies with the social location of the person doing the dreaming. For example, to dream that one is sleeping on a heap of dung signifies to a poor man that he will become rich. To a rich man, however, the same dream means that he will gain public office (3.52). At times, a dream with a positive prognosis for one status category will carry negative connotations for another. Thus, for the poor it is a bad omen to dream of wearing a purple robe; the same dream is good for the rich and, interestingly enough, also for slaves (2.3).[79] Apparently no aspect of life – not even the interpretation of dreams – was immune to the effects of what Lendon has labeled "the deep structure" of honor and hierarchy in the Roman world.[80]

The present survey of social stratification, honor, and office in the ancient world is now complete. A static, snapshot overview of the social organization of the empire, detailed in chapter one, revealed a foundational division of society into two strata, elite and non-elite, each of which subdivided again and again into various expressions of hierarchy and esteem. Public expressions of the hierarchy, which insured that every individual would know the other's place in the pecking order, included clothing, occupation, seating at public and private functions, and the decisions of the courts – all designed to fit one's social location. The present chapter has sought to demonstrate the centrality of honor as a social value in the Roman world, and to emphasize the importance of Rome's *cursus honorum* and the replication of *cursus* ideology and honor-seeking in non-elite settings across the empire.

I can do no better than to conclude this overview of social stratification and the quest for honors in Roman antiquity with an observation made by Meyer Reinhold a generation ago. Reinhold, in the course of an essay dealing with the history of purple as an ancient status symbol, categorically identified Roman society as "the most status-symbol-conscious culture of the ancient world."[81] And no region east of Rome was more quintessentially Roman in this regard than the colony of Philippi.

3

THE ROMAN COLONY AT PHILIPPI

> This people, in turn – how many colonies has it sent to every province! Wherever the Roman conquers, there he dwells.
> Seneca (*Helv.* 7.7)

Chapters three and four narrow the focus of the present overview of Roman social stratification and honor-seeking to an examination of the Roman colony at Philippi. I will seek to demonstrate that the settlement was deeply marked by the social verticality and concern for personal and familial honor which characterized the broader Roman world. The present chapter briefly surveys the history of Philippi as a military colony, with special emphasis upon the hierarchy of rank and the competition for honors which characterized the Roman army. A discussion of the honors associated with the imperial cult, and the function of the cult in reinforcing the social order of the colony, concludes the chapter. Chapter four will continue to draw upon epigraphic data in order to underline the marked social verticality of Philippi as reflected in burial inscriptions and in municipal honors and public recognition that the local elite received for various acts of benefaction.[1] Similar practices among non-elite cult groups will also be examined. Evidence cited for the presence of a replicated *cursus*, in both civic and religious spheres, will prove particularly important for the discussion of Paul's letter to the Christian community at Philippi, to be undertaken in the final portion of this monograph.

History of the colony

Philippi's origins can be traced to pre-Hellenistic times.[2] Originally a Thracian settlement, the area was occupied by the exiled Athenian politician Callistratus, along with others from the island of Thasos, who founded a city and named it Krenides (*c.* 360 BCE).[3] The independence of the Thasian colony was short-lived, however, and its future was sealed when residents invited Philip II of Macedonia to side with them in their ongoing battle with invading Thracians (*c.* 356 BCE).[4] Philip, seeing the strategic value of the settlement, conquered Krenides, fortified it, and renamed it Philippi. In the words of our ancient historians,

> While these things were going on, the Thasians settled the place called Crenides, which the king afterward named Philippi for himself and made a populous settlement. (Diod. Sic. 16.3.7)
>
> Philip fortified it because he considered it an excellent stronghold against the Thracians, and named it for himself, Philippi. (Appian, *BCiv.* 4.105)

Philippi's natural resources rivaled in value its strategic location. In addition to the springs after which the Thasian colony had been named, Strabo informs his contemporaries that "there are very many gold mines in Krenides, where now the city Philippi is situated, near Mount Pangaion" (Strabo 7, fr. 34). Apparently the mines had been underutilized during the Thracian period, but this was to change dramatically when the colony came under Philip's control: "turning to the gold mines in its territory, which were very scanty and insignificant, he increased their output so much by his improvements that they could bring him a revenue of more than a thousand talents" (Diod. Sic. 16.8.6–7). The Macedonian general made efficient use of his newfound wealth. Diodorus claims that Philip used the gold coins minted from the local mines to pay off Greek mercenaries hired to fight in his army (Diod. Sic. 16.8.7).[5]

After flourishing under Philip II and his son Alexander the Great, the settlement fades somewhat from the historical record until it appears again during the Roman period.[6] The Romans, under Aemilius Paulus, conquered Macedonia in 167 BCE. Philippi was located in the first of four districts into which Rome divided the region. The construction of the Via Egnatia, the main road from Rome to the East (*c.* 130 BCE), guaranteed the strategic importance of the site for decades to come. Central to present purposes is the establishment of Philippi as a Roman colony, first under Antony (42 BCE) and then under Octavian (30 BCE). The victories at Philippi of Antony and Octavian (later Augustus) over Cassius and Brutus, the murderers of Julius Caesar, guaranteed that the colony of Philippi would have a distinctly Roman flavor.[7] The reconstitution of Philippi as *Colonia Julia Philippensis*, after Augustus' victory at Actium (Augustus' name was added in 27 BCE: *Colonia Julia Augusta Philippensis*), along with the settlement of still more veterans, insured that Philippi would be closely aligned with the increasing consolidation of power under the new emperor. Finally, in the mid-40s CE, Claudius conquered Thrace and made it a Roman province, thus further solidifying local Roman control and assuring the vitality of the colony at Philippi.

The Romanness of *Colonia Julia Augusta Philippensis*

Aulus Gellius (*c.* 123–69 CE) offers the following observations about Roman colonization:

> [colonies] are as it were transplanted from the State and have all the laws and institutions of the Roman people, not those of their own choice. This condition, although it is more exposed to control and less free, is nevertheless thought preferable and superior because of the greatness and majesty of the Roman people, of which those colonies seem to be *miniatures, as it were, and in a way copies.* (*NA* 16.13.8–9, my italics)

The comments are particularly apropos for Philippi, since epigraphic data demonstrates unequivocally that the colony was administrated by Romans in a decidedly Roman fashion.[8] Latin predominates in the inscriptions, and civic honors/offices such as *duumviri* (chief magistrates), aediles (city officers), and quaestors (finance officers) are widely attested.[9] A Latin drama troupe put on Latin productions in a theater rebuilt according to Roman tastes.[10] A forum built in Roman style marked the center of the city. Residents honored Roman gods such as Jupiter, Neptune, Mercury, and Silvanus.

Scholars, in fact, consistently highlight the Romanness of Philippi, in distinction even from other colonies in the East.[11] The colonies of Pisidian Antioch and Iconium, for example, were each superimposed upon an already thriving Greek *polis*. Local citizens shared citizenship with more recent Roman colonists from Italy and elsewhere. At Philippi, in contrast, local landowners were dispossessed and relegated to non-citizen status, with the colony's social elite initially consisting primarily of high-ranking veterans from the Roman army. The inscriptions left by the veteran colonists consistently attest to their loyalty to Rome and her emperor, and also to the pride taken by these soldiers in their former positions of honor in the army. The tenacious manner in which Philippi retained its Roman orientation thus distinguished the settlement from colonies in Asia Minor, where assimilation of Hellenistic culture and values was much more pronounced. Only in Italy could one find a

The Roman colony at Philippi 67

Roman settlement even comparable to Philippi. Pilhofer appropriately concludes,

> Wer – wie Paulus – aus dem Osten nach Philippi kam, kam in eine andere Welt. Römische Kolonien konnte man auch in Kleinasien besuchen, aber keine was auch nur annähernd so "römische" wie Philippi.[12]

Augustus and the founding of Philippi

The changes brought about through the refounding of Philippi under Augustus can hardly be overemphasized. Numismatic evidence demonstrates that Antony originally undertook to establish the colony in expressly republican fashion. Rituals associated with the foundation of Roman cities harking back to Romulus and Rome find expression in coins minted *c.* 42 BCE. In contrast, evidence for the refounding of the colony a little more than a decade later explicitly identifies Philippi with the new world order established by Augustus. The change is easily explained. The loyalty that obtained between a colony and its founding general meant that, after Actium, Philippi's relationship with Antony had the potential to undermine the consolidation of power under Augustus. Augustus, therefore, acted swiftly and shrewdly to insure that Philippi would cease to serve as a reminder of the former power and honor of Antony and his supporters.[13]

The link between Philippi and Augustus can be illustrated by the association of the emperor with the goddess Victoria on coins minted in connection with the refounding of Philippi in 30 BCE. Soon after Actium, Augustus began to portray himself, contrary to historical reality, as the sole victor at Philippi, some twelve years earlier. Antony's role at Philippi, which had, in fact, been much more prominent than that of Augustus, was increasingly effaced in the public record. This is evident from Augustus' own claims (*Res gestae* 2: *Qui parentem meum [trucidaver]un[t, eo]s in exilium expuli*) and from the association of Augustus – and Augustus alone – with Victoria on coins minted post-Actium.[14] The military victory referenced on these coins is not that of Actium but Philippi, more than a decade earlier, as the imagery and text clearly show.[15] The timing of the minting of these coins, however (post-Actium, *c.* 30 BCE), connects Victoria with Augustus not simply as the founder of a colony but, now, as the initiator and overseer of a new world order. The goddess comes to symbolize more than victory on the battlefield of Philippi. Victoria now represents the new political reality summed up in the person of Augustus.[16] And Philippi is memorialized as the location at which Augustus began his career as imperator – a career which would have far-reaching implications for the whole known world.

A number of inscriptions testify to the close relationship between the colony and the Roman emperor, a relationship that was established in 30 BCE and continued for several centuries to follow. A second-century inscription dedicates a large Corinthian temple to the imperial family (*in honorem divinae domus*).[17] Another inscription honors Hadrian and his wife Sabina.[18] Antoninus Pius appears with his *cursus* titles (*pontifici maximo, tribunicia potestate, consuli designato*) in yet another second-century monument.[19] From the first century comes an inscription dedicated to *Quieti Augustae*.[20] Another, dated to 78–79 CE, shows the close relationship between members of the elite in the colony who served on the decurion council and the emperors Vespasian and Titus:

> Imp(erator) Caesar
> Vespasianus
> Augustus trib(uniciae) pot(estatis) X,
> imp(erator) Titus Caesar
> Augusti f(ilius) trib(uniciae) pot(estatis) VIII
> pub(lice) d(ecreto) d(ecurionum)[21]
>
> Imperator Caesar Vespasian Augustus, with tribunician power for the tenth time, and imperator Titus Caesar, son of Augustus, with tribunician power for the eighth time. At public cost (this monument was built) by a decree of the decurions

A first-century inscription erected by freedmen of the imperial family honors the emperor Tiberius; yet another, which may be even earlier, attests to the relationship between the colony and its founder, Augustus:[22]

> Liberis
> et nepotib(us)
> Aug(usti) felic(is)
> col(onia) Philipp(ensium)[23]
>
> For the children and grandchildren of the happy/prosperous Augustus, the colony of the Philippians (dedicates this inscription)

After Actium, Philippi thus entered into a special relationship with the emperor – a distinctly Roman colony had now taken on "einen betont *augusteischen* Charakter" – and the stage was set for a further politico-religious development, namely, the honoring of the emperor and the establishment of the imperial cult in Philippi.[24] Before examining the ruler cult, however, it will be helpful to outline the implications of Philippi's military origins for social life in the newly founded colony.

The military orientation of the colony

Roman colonization accompanied the expansion of Roman power throughout the Mediterranean and occupies an important place in Roman history. The nature of colonization changed somewhat, however, during the long transition from republic to empire. Once employed primarily as a strategy to invest landless citizens with property to farm, colonization ultimately served to reward soldiers for faithful service to military commanders like Marius, Caesar and, later, Antony and Octavian.[25] Antony and Octavian, in particular, found themselves under pressing obligation to pay their troops for services rendered at Philippi and, for Octavian, at Actium. The establishment of a colony of veteran soldiers through land allotments, forcibly appropriated from persons in the surrounding area, satisfied much of this need.

Colonizing Philippi

Victory at Philippi in 42 BCE left Antony in charge of setting things in order in the East, Octavian in the West. According to Suetonius, the latter had some difficulty in satisfying the demands of his soldiers:

> When the duties of administration were divided after the victory, Antony undertaking to restore order in the East, and Augustus to lead the veterans back to Italy and assign them lands in the municipalities, he could neither satisfy the veterans nor the landowners, since the latter complained that they were driven from their homes, and the former that they were not being treated as their services had led them to hope. (*Aug.* 13)

Antony probably found it easier to "restore order in the East," since dispossessed landowners around Philippi, lacking in both political power and legal status, would have had difficulty making known their grievances to Rome, far in the West. So, also, Augustus, who settled still more Roman veterans in Philippi after Actium.

Scholars variously assess the number of veterans settled in Philippi by Antony and Octavian. Conservative estimates assume a total of between five hundred and one thousand colonists for 42 and 31 BCE combined.[26] Others suggest a figure of two to three thousand.[27] The latter figure harmonizes better with earlier tendencies of Caesar and the Triumvirs to place two to three thousand veterans in each of their colonies.[28]

Estimates must remain somewhat speculative, but a reasonable approximation would identify the Roman colonists as approximately one-quarter of Philippi's total population.[29] Roman influence was highly disproportionate to the Roman presence, however, since the recent settlers held all the political power in the colony, as high-ranking veterans became, by virtue of their landed wealth, the colony's local elite.

As indicated in the excerpt from Suetonius, above, the suffering of local populations at the hands of veteran soldiers was standard fare for Roman colonization, and this was especially the case outside Italy. Tacitus informs us, for example, that veterans settling the colony of Camulodunum "were acting as though they had received a free gift of the entire country, driving the natives from their homes, ejecting them from their lands – they styled them 'captives' and 'slaves'" (*Ann.* 14.31). These retired soldiers were, moreover, "abetted in their fury by the [still active] troops, with their similar mode of life and their hopes of equal indulgence" (*Ann.* 14.31).[30] Indigenous people-groups were, of course, powerless to resist. During the civil war, in 42 BCE, this kind of disregard for the local population appears to have been the norm. After Cassius' army had been routed in the first battle of the war, Brutus

> promised [his soldiers] that if they now fought well, he would turn over to them two cities for plunder and booty, Thessalonica and Lacedaemon . . . Antony and Octavius practised far greater cruelty than this in rewarding their soldiers, and drove her ancient inhabitants out of almost the whole of Italy, in order that their followers might get land and cities to which they had no right.
> (Plut. *Brut.* 46)

E. T. Salmon claims that the Triumvirs "enriched their supporters, took vengeance on their enemies, and victimised the innocent," and he suggests that such practices continued post-30 BCE. Of Octavian, in particular, Salmon observes,

> Presumably he was also just as unscrupulous as his triumviral colleagues in obtaining land for colonies. The *Eclogues* of Vergil make it clear that he did not hesitate to confiscate it, and the later insistence of his official autobiography that he was the first to buy land for distribution to settlers, a claim that has reference in the main to the period after Actium, suggests that, as Augustus, he had considerable difficulty living down the misdeeds he had perpetrated as Octavian.[31]

Bormann suggests that Philippi may have been spared some of the harsher practices that accompanied colonization, since he assumes that the area was relatively uninhabited at the time of the battle of Philippi.[32] Peter Oakes, however, charges Bormann with underestimating the significance of pre-colonial Philippi, citing evidence for a thriving population devoted to agriculture. He concludes that Roman colonization would have involved "large-scale dispossession of Greeks."[33] In either case, we can be assured, with Bormann, that the allocation of land to veterans during the founding of the colony necessarily involved the dispossession of *all* local landowners.[34]

Two results of Roman colonization will prove important for study of the social orientation of the colony and the social setting of Paul's letter to the Philippians. First, Greeks who lost their land generally stayed in the area, and the majority of them are likely to have moved into the town itself. As Susan Alcock has demonstrated, increased nucleation – movements of dispossessed farmers to urban centers – characterized Roman colonization in Greece during the period.[35] As a result, Oakes estimates that 60 percent of Philippi's population were Greeks during the first century CE.[36] Thus, the facile identification of the colony as a Roman military settlement, characteristic of much secondary literature, demands some qualification. Romans would have been in the minority in Philippi during the time of Paul's ministry in Macedonia, and they would have been in the minority in the Jesus community that Paul established. The common assumption that the church was populated primarily by the descendants of Roman veterans is, therefore, no longer tenable. This is one of the most valuable insights of Oakes's study.

A second result of colonization, however, must also be factored in. Though a numerical minority, the Romans remained an ideological majority, particularly where issues of honor, status, and social values were concerned, since the dispossession of local landholders by Roman veterans ultimately determined not only the social hierarchy, but also the social values, of the reconstituted settlement. After Actium, only persons who possessed sufficient landed wealth would qualify to hold office in the newly founded colony, and these persons were almost exclusively Roman. The result was an influence upon the social orientation of Philippi which was markedly disproportionate to the raw percentage of the Roman population. As Pilhofer notes, "Gewiss waren die Römer zahlenmässig nicht in der Mehrheit, wie es das römische Gepräge der Stadt vermuten lassen könnte, aber *das Lebensgefühl war durch und durch römisch.*"[37] As will be amply illustrated in the following chapter, the principle of social replication, whereby cultural values and social codes tend to "trickle down" from elites to lower-status groups who, in turn, mimic the practices of their social betters, guaranteed that the Roman elite who occupied positions of power and prestige in Philippi would continue to influence the social values and behavior of the colonists, Roman and Greek alike, well into the second century CE.[38] Thus, Roman military imagery and metaphors occur quite often in Paul's letter to the Philippians, a letter written in Greek to a predominantly non-Roman, non-elite congregation.[39] It is not the number of veterans settled at Philippi, then, but, rather, their disproportionate social influence in the colony that demands some consideration of honor and status in the Roman military.

Social stratification in the Roman army

The military is by nature a stratified, alternative society. In Rome this was especially the case. The army, of course, had its own system of ranks and titles, its own *cursus*.[40] Polybius divides the Roman army of his day into several groups: *velites* (youngest soldiers), *hastati* (next in age), *principes*, and *triarii*. They wore different clothes, were armed differently, and received various compensation, all according to social status:

> The common soldiers wear in addition a breastplate of brass a span square, which they place in front of the heart and call a heart-protector . . . but those who have a property value of more than ten thousand drachmas wear instead of this a coat of chain-mail.　　　　(Polyb. 6.23, Loeb, slightly adapted)

> As pay the foot-soldier receives two obols a day [obol = about 1/6 denarius]; a centurion twice as much [about a denarius], and a cavalry-soldier a drachma.　　　　(Polyb. 6.39)

Augustus' consolidation of power included careful attention to military remuneration:

> Furthermore, he restricted all the soldiery everywhere to a fixed scale of pay and allowances, designating the duration of their service and the rewards on its completion *according to each man's rank*, in order to keep them from being tempted to revolution after their discharge either by age or poverty. To have funds ready at all times without difficulty for maintaining the soldiers and paying the rewards due to them, he established a military treasury, supported by new taxes.　　(Suet. *Aug.* 49, my italics)

Accurate figures for imperial Rome are increasingly accessible, and they demonstrate that social verticality in the army was reinforced by a steeply stratified pay scale, and that it was further demarcated by the uneven manner in which booty was distributed according to military rank. Under Augustus, the legion was paid annually (in sesterces), as follows:

miles legionis	900
eques legionis	1,050
centurio legionis	13,500
primus ordo	27,000
primuspilus	54,000[41]

As M. Alexander Speidel appropriately concludes, "to a simple legionary soldier the salary of the *primuspilus* must have been a staggering sum."[42] Augustus' measures were necessary but not completely successful, for soldiers at times remained dissatisfied with the differences in rank and pay. The establishment of an elite cohort of well-paid troops as the emperor's personal bodyguards at Rome seemed to fuel resentment among the outlying legions, for at the top of the list of demands presented to Tiberius by mutinying soldiers in Illyricum and Germany was the request "above all, that they should receive the same pay as the praetorians" (Suet. *Tib.* 25).

The army hierarchy found other ways to express itself. The physical layout of a legionary fortress, for example, spoke volumes about the various differences in rank among its occupants. The dwelling of the consular or senatorial commander (*legatus*) consumed some 75,000 square feet of the encampment, boasting rich furnishings, decorated halls, and a peristyle courtyard. A typical legionnaire had to content himself, in contrast, with some 50 square feet of living space.[43] Morning in a Roman camp, moreover, replicated morning in a Roman city in a way that particularly highlighted the centrality of honor in both social settings. Mirroring the morning *salutatio* in Rome, camp soldiers attended the centurions' *salutatio*, centurions attended the tribunes', and all the officers attended the legionary commander's (Joseph. *BJ* 3.87). As this replication of the *salutatio* reveals, rank in the legions was not simply an issue of function and order. It was also highly honorific, since the military hierarchy was not only a hierarchy of responsibility and obedience but also a hierarchy of honor. In the words of a centurion who felt that he himself was being inappropriately honored by conversing with the imperator while senior officers waited outside, "It is a shame, Caesar, that you should be talking with a centurion while the prefects stand outside" (Dio Cass. 69.19.1).

The disproportionate distribution of booty and land according to rank should also be noted. Consider the division of spoils at Pompey's triumph:

To his staff officers	c. 800,000 denarii each
To his legionary tribunes	c. 180,000 denarii each
To his legionary centurions	c. 30,000 denarii each
To his legionary privates	c. 15,000 denarii each[44]

Land allotments, as well as monetary payments, would differ according to an individual's position (*pro portione office*) and the meritorious nature of his service (*pro merito*). As mentioned above, such practices, in turn, become defining for the social orientation of a fledgling colony like Philippi, since high-ranking veterans who had received the largest allotments of land would now have the prerequisite wealth to enjoy the honor of public office as decurions, magistrates, and priests in the civic cults.

Initially, land allotments, as well as magistracies, priesthoods, and decurion status were assigned to high-ranking settlers by the founder of a colony. In 42 BCE it appears that Antony delegated the responsibility of establishing the colony at Philippi to a legate, as the reverse side of a coin minted at the founding of the settlement indicates:

> Q(uintus) Paqui(us) Ruf(us) leg(atus) c(oloniae) d(educendae)[45]
> Quintus Paquius Rufus, Legate for the founding of the colony

The responsibility for the distribution of Philippi's landed resources, which fell to Quintus Paquius Rufus, was publicly exercised in a scripted, highly traditional ritual. In preparation for the ceremony, officials known as *agrimensores* measured the land and partitioned it into large square parcels (*centuriae*). The parcels were then subdivided into smaller portions (*sortes, acceptae*). Next, the colonists were separated into groups to determine the order in which they would draw lots for the available land. The colony's founder (here Rufus, as *legatus coloniae deducendae*) took in hand the formal record of the above proceedings and then presided over the distribution of the land; he sat on a ceremonial chair called the *sella curulis* with a vase containing the lots (*sorticulae, pittacia*) at his feet. A brief ritual enacted by the legate led immediately to the drawing of lots and the assigning of land to the colonists.[46]

Most colonists came, of course, from the legions' rank-and-file soldiers.[47] In the case of Philippi we can identify the particular legion in which one veteran had served. His gravestone reads as follows:

Sex(to) Volcasio
L(uci) f(ilio) Vol(tinia) leg(ionis)
XXVIII domo
Pisis.[48]

To Sextus Volcasius, son of Lucius, from the tribe Voltinia, 28th Legion, from Pisa

Numismatic data informs us that, along with legionnaires, a praetorian cohort was also settled at Philippi by Octavian in 30 BCE.[49] Praetorians received one-and-a-half to two times the pay of a legionnaire, and we can expect similarly disproportionate distributions of land among Philippi's veteran colonists.[50] The combination at Philippi, then, of (a) high-ranking veterans who qualified for civic honors, (b) a praetorian cohort, and (c) common soldiers guaranteed that, at its founding, the social orientation of the colony would replicate the strong verticality of the Roman army, or, as Bormann more directly asserts, "Die militärische Hierarchie setzte sich nach Beendigung des Dienstes in eine soziale Hierarchie um."[51]

Competition for honors in the army

One of the more engaging family sagas of Tacitean history narrates an encounter between two German brothers who found themselves on opposing sides in a battle between the Romans and Cheruscan forces. One of the brothers, Arminius, was a notorious enemy of Rome who, after serving as a Roman auxiliary, realigned himself with his Cherusci compatriots and led his armies in the destruction of three Roman legions in 9 CE. Arminius' brother, Flavus, remained faithful to the Romans, at one point losing an eye in battle while fighting under the generalship of Tiberius. Tacitus relates a dialogue between the two brothers, as they approached one another from their respective camps on opposite sides of the River Weser:

> Walking forward, [Flavus] was greeted by Arminius; who . . . asked his brother, whence the disfigurement of his face? On being told the place and battle, he inquired what reward he had received. Flavus mentioned his increased pay, the chain, the crown, and other military decorations; Arminius scoffed at the cheap rewards of servitude. (*Ann.* 2.9)

Arminius might scoff at Roman military decorations. The Romans themselves held such honors in the highest esteem. As Cicero wrote, "the first thing to recommend to a young man in his quest for glory (*gloriam*) is that he try to win it, if he can, in a military career" (*Off.* 2.13).

Lendon aptly describes the army as "a society characterized by vehement competition for honour, and by an equally strong sense of shame."[52] Competition for military honors surfaces often in the sources. The *Digest* depicts a demoted soldier as "gnawed upon by another's honour" (*C.Theod.* 7.1.10 [367]).[53] Sallust views the desire for honor as a key explanation of the ability of a small band of Roman soldiers to overcome a large enemy force or storm a strongly fortified town: "their hardest struggle for glory was with one another; each man strove to be first to strike down the foe, to scale a wall, to be seen by all while doing such a deed. This they considered riches, this fair fame and high nobility" (*Cat.* 7.6).

Julius Caesar narrates the details of a rivalry over honor which manifested itself during his Gallic campaigns. The particular match involved a couple of centurions. "Why do you hesitate, Vorenus? What occasion for proving your bravery are you waiting for? This day will settle our rivalry!" shouted one centurion to another, as he charged into the thickest of the enemy's ranks. The centurion who was challenged responded by leaving the safety of the ramparts and charging in turn. The man was "terrified," Caesar writes, but not by the might of the enemy. The soldier's concern, rather, was "for his reputation among all." After the battle, which saw each man saving the other's life, the men returned to camp "with the greatest glory," and "it was impossible to decide which was the better man in bravery" (Caes. *BGall.* 5.44). The battleground was the kind of place where, as Caesar wrote in another connection, "nothing done well or shamefully could be concealed, and lust for praise and fear of disgrace drove both sides to bravery" (Caes. *BGall.* 7.80).[54]

An act of cowardice in the competitive arena of the battlefield could stain a soldier, and his family, with irredeemable shame, as the son of Marcus Aemilius Scaurus discovered in the late second century. After the young officer had "fled in terror to Rome" in the face of a Cimbrian attack at the river Athesis (*c.* 102 BCE), deserting his consul and commanding officer, his father Marcus promptly informed him that "he would rather come upon the bones of his son killed in action than see him in person guilty of so disgraceful a flight; therefore, if he had any remnant of shame left in his heart, he would avoid the sight of the father from whom he had degenerated." Finally, the son, no longer able to bear the opprobrium of family and peers, took his life in an act which, in the view of our narrator, restored at least some of his lost honor:

"Receiving the message, the young man was driven to use his sword more bravely against himself than he had used it against the enemy" (Val. Max. 5.8.4).

During the imperial period, it was the emperors who awarded military honors, and competition for such honors was strongly encouraged, since it reinforced the loyalty of the troops to their *princeps*.[55] Decorations were most often awarded in campaigns in which the emperor himself participated. The result was a bond of loyalty between an emperor and his troops. Velleius Paterculus relates Tiberius' troops variously exclaiming, "Is that you we see, imperator?" "I served with you in Armenia." "I in Raetia." "I was decorated by you in Vindelicia." "I in Pannonia." "I in Germany" (2.104.4).

In a similar vein, Josephus describes the honors given by Titus to those who distinguished themselves in the battle at Jerusalem (*c.* 70 CE). Note the emphasis upon competition:

> upon those who had more eminently distinguished themselves in the fight by superior energy, and had not only shed a lustre on their own lives by deeds of gallantry but rendered his campaign more famous by their achievements, [Titus] would forthwith confer their rewards and honours, and not a man who had chosen to exert himself *more than his fellows* should miss his due recompense. (*BJ* 7.11, my italics)

The ethos of competition and honor-seeking among the troops manifested itself throughout the Judean campaign. Even the construction of siegeworks was not exempt, for it became a contest in which

> not only the legions, but their component companies vied with one another: the soldier studied to please his decurion, the decurion the centurion, and he the tribune, while the emulation (φιλοτιμία) of the tribunes extended to the staff-officers, and in the rivalry between the officers Caesar himself was umpire.
> (*BJ* 5.503)

Lendon offers a trenchant commentary on the above citation: "There is more than a passing similarity between the psychology of the building of these entrenchments and that of the erection of public works in an ancient town. Everything soldiers did, in short, could become a competition."[56] I will cite evidence in the following chapter for the elite practice of benefaction by means of public works in the colony. Suffice it to say, at this point, that the transition from chief centurion in Octavian's army to *duumvir* and benefactor in Roman Philippi would have been a natural one – both settings were characterized by incessant competition for honors.

Sometimes the granting of honors by an emperor to his troops was reciprocated. Lendon discusses a practice, among veterans, of casting decorations on the funeral pyre of the emperor who had granted them, and suggests "honours for the emperor and the imperial cult [were] probably a larger part of military life than civilian."[57] The centrality of the ruler cult in the military colony at Philippi (below) probably owes much to the viability of this dynamic among the colony's high-ranking veterans.

The honorific nature of military rank is markedly underscored by the tendency of retired soldiers and their families to publicize their ranks and honors in *cursus* form. As discussed in the previous chapter, honorific inscriptions produced by the local aristocracy typically catalogued (for viewing by posterity) the various civic offices held by an individual during his lifetime. In similar fashion, those soldiers who could afford to do so left inscriptions detailing their various posts in the Roman army, their military *cursus*. Here, of course, the actual function of rank recedes completely into the background, and it is the ability of these posts to augment the honor of their occupants that is left behind for the viewing public to consider.

A number of inscriptions from Philippi detail the military careers of veterans settled in the colony. The following monument, dated before 96 CE, was financed by a group of the soldiers under the charge of the officer in view. Both the ranks occupied by Lucius Tatinius Gnosus and the decorations he received at the hands of the emperor are carefully enumerated for all to see:

> L(ucio) Tatinio
> L(uci) f(ilio) Vol(tinia) Cnoso,
> militi cohortis IIII pr(aetoriae),
> singulari et benef(iciario) trib(uni),
> optioni, benef(iciario) pr(aefecti) pr(aetorio), evoc(ato)
> Aug(usti), donis donato tor-
> quibus, armillis, phaler(is),
> corona aurea [[ab imp(eratore) Do-
> mitiano Caes(are) Aug(usto) Germ(anico)]],
> c(enturioni) cohor(tis) IV vigil(um), c(enturioni) stator(um),
> c(enturioni) cohor(tis) XI urbanae,
> veterani qui sub eo in vigilib(us)
> militaver(unt) et honesta mis-
> sione missi sunt[58]

> For Lucius Tatinius Gnosus, son of Lucius, from the tribe Voltinia, soldier of the fourth praetorian cohort, *singularis* and *beneficiarius tribuni*, adjutant, *beneficiarius praefecti praetorio*, *evocatus* of Augustus, who was given, as decorative honors, neckchains, bracelets, breastplates, and a golden wreath by the imperator Domitianus Caesar Augustus Germanicus, centurion of the fourth cohort of the watch, centurion *statorum*, centurion of the eleventh urban cohort, the veterans who had served under him in the cohort of the watch, who were dismissed with an honorable discharge (set up this inscription)

Paul himself may have seen a large monument that proclaimed the military *cursus* of an important officer from the Fifth Legion, located just outside the city walls in the eastern graveyard:

> C(aius) Vibius C(ai) filius
> Cor(nelia) Quartus, *folium*
> mil(es) leg(ionis) V Macedonic(ae)
> decur(io) alae Scubulor(um)
> praef(ectus) coh(ortis) III Cyreneic(ae)
> [tribunus militum le]g(ionis) II Au[g]u[stae . . .]
> [. . .][59]
>
> Gaius Vibius Quartus, son of Gaius, from the tribe Cornelia, soldier of the Fifth Legion Macedonica, decurion of the ala Scubulorum, prefect of the Third Cohort Cyreneica, military tribune of the Second Legion Augusta . . .

Even more remarkable is a lengthy inscription detailing the career of a veteran named Tiberius Claudius Maximus who boasts a variety of posts, and who was decorated by both Domitian and Trajan. Perhaps his greatest claim to fame: during the Dacian campaign Tiberius had brought the head of King Decebalus to Trajan (the capture of Decebalus is also portrayed on Trajan's Column), who honored the soldier by awarding him the rank of decurion in the auxiliary cohort in which he was serving.[60]

At times, moreover, the honors of military rank and public office combine to form a single *cursus*. Nowhere is the honorific nature of these army posts more apparent. In Philippi we have surviving inscriptions detailing the *cursus* of certain individuals from their humble beginnings in the military to the attainment of key civic posts later in life. Publius Mucius, for example, is publicly recognized as a centurion of the Fourth Legion *Ferrata* who later became *duumvir* of the colony.[61] This blending of military and municipal honors serves to underline, once again, the honorific nature of office and rank in both spheres of social life.

The imperial cult in Roman Philippi

The population of *Colonia Julia Augusta Philippensis*, which included Romans, Greeks, and Thracians, guaranteed that pluralism and syncretism would mark the religious life of the colony.[62] The Augustan character of the colony, and the control of Philippi by the Roman elite, however, assured the imperial cult of a position of prominence at the very center of the settlement's religious and social life. I will examine the social organization of various non-elite cult groups in the next chapter. Here I will focus on the honors associated with the ruler cult and the role of emperor worship in reinforcing the colony's social hierarchy.

The veneration of the emperor

The centrality of the imperial cult to religious life in first-century Philippi has received extensive treatment by Lukas Bormann.[63] The raw conceptual material for the development of emperor veneration in the colony had been present for centuries. A ruler cult is attested as early as the fourth century BCE, under Philip II, which was later intentionally propagated by Philip's son, Alexander the Great.[64] One would expect that the special relationship between the Philippian veterans and Augustus, along with the openness to the veneration of the ruler evidenced in the settlement's earlier history, would ensure the early establishment of the cult in the colony, and archaeological evidence confirms that this was precisely the case.[65] Bormann discusses the remains of two temples found in the forum at Philippi which were closely connected to the worship of the imperial family. Although the temples date to the second century, first-century statues of Augustus and his family have also been unearthed in the forum, and inscriptions from the second half of the first century attest to a cult of the empress Livia with its own priesthood.[66] Chaido Koukouli-Chrysantaki's conclusion about the imperial cult in first-century Philippi is quite on target:

> The cult of Augustus, as also of his adopted sons Gaius and Lucius Caesar, already existed in Philippi when Paul arrived. The cult of Livia had been introduced by Claudius in 44 CE, but the apostle may not have seen the monument with the statues of the seven priestesses in front of the temple, because it was probably not built until the second half of the first century CE.[67]

The ruler cult and social stratification

Much progress has been made in recent decades in understanding the function of the ruler cult in the social and religious world of Roman antiquity. Until relatively recently, a tendency to view ancient religion anachronistically as private in practice, and individualistic in orientation, skewed our understanding of the imperial cult, and of Roman religion in general. Due to a variety of influences, both pietistic and sociopolitical, post-Enlightenment Christianity in the West has increasingly (and regrettably) framed itself in highly individualistic and subjective terms. As a result, modern Euro-Americans tend to view religion as a private and personal enterprise, unrelated to life in the public arena. Such a conception of religion, however, poses no small obstacle to a proper understanding of the Roman ruler cult, since civic religion (*religio*), of which emperor veneration was to play an increasingly important part, was decidedly public and collective in nature. The imperial cult found its primary public expression in festivals that involved the whole populace. And these public rituals constituted much more than simply an aggregate of individuals honoring the emperor (or his family). It is interesting to note, in this regard, that thousands of bronze, stone, and marble statues of Roman emperors occupied places of prominence throughout the empire. Apparently none, however, have been found in private homes. Emperors were "public gods who protected the public good," a "public good" which, we might add, included the social hierarchy.[68]

Grasping the public and collective orientation of the ruler cult is crucial for appreciating the cult's role in reinforcing social distinctions in a setting like Roman Philippi.[69] S. R. F. Price views the veneration of the emperor as a way of "conceptualizing the world."[70] Garnsey and Saller are even more forthright: the imperial cult was "a conveyor of imperial ideology, a focus of loyalty for the many, and a mechanism for the social advancement of a few."[71] Keith Hopkins relates the ruler cult to the unity of the empire, suggesting that the Roman emperors reinforced the political system by allowing themselves to be associated with the gods. The cult embodies "an ideal king, who symbolises the fixed order of the world."[72] In the present connection, evidence from Philippi strongly suggests that the rites and honors associated with the cult served specifically to reinforce in the public arena the "fixed order" of the colony's social hierarchy, especially demarcating distinctions between the elite and the non-elite, and citizens and non-citizens, respectively.

Opportunities to participate in honoring the emperor and his family were available to persons of various social classes, but the distinction between these classes was decidedly reinforced in the process. Two central honorific offices were associated with the ruler cult in Philippi: *flamines* and *sexviri Augustales*. The local decurion senate awarded both honors but did so to two distinct classes of persons. The flaminate was reserved exclusively for Roman citizens who had possessed their citizenship from birth (*ingenui*). The title *sacerdos divae Augustae* was parallel to *flamen*, referring specifically to priestesses of the imperial cult who, in Philippi, served in the veneration of Livia, the *diva Augusta*. A number of inscriptions have survived evidencing both titles.[73] The two cited immediately below reflect the flaminate. Notice, though, that the portrayals of honors reflected in these inscriptions are hardly limited to the imperial priesthood. In each case, a *cursus honorum* of sorts is publicly portrayed for every passerby to see:

> divi Iuli flamini
> C(aio) Antonio
> M(arci) f(ilio) Volt(inia) Rufo,
> flamini divi Aug(usti)
> col(oniae) Cl(audiae) Aprens(is) et
> col(oniae) Iul(iae) Philippens(is),
> eorundum et principi
> item col(oniae) Iul(iae) Parianae,
> trib(uno) milit(um) coh(ortis) XXXII voluntarior(um) trib(uno) mil(itum) leg(ionis) XIII
> Gem(inae), praef(ecto) equit(um) alae I
> *vacat* Scubulorum *vacat* . . .[74]

For the flamen of the divine Julius, Gaius Antonius Rufus, son of Marcus, of the tribe of Voltinia, flamen of the divine Augustus in the colonies of Apri and Philippi, the chief leader of both colonies, as, likewise, of the colony of Parium, military tribune of Cohort XXXII of the volunteers, military tribune of the Thirteenth Legion, Gemina, prefect of the cavalry division I Scubulorum . . .

P(ublius) Cornelius Asper Atiarius Montanus
equo publico honoratus, item ornamentis decurionatus et IIviralicis, pontifex, flamen divi Claudi Philippis, ann(orum) XXIII h(ic) s(itus) e(st)

Publius Cornelius Asper Atiarius Montanus, honored with equestrian status, also with the decorations of a decurion and of the duumviri, priest, flamen of the divine Claudius in Philippi, 23 years old, lies buried here.[75]

The honor of serving as a *flamen* must have been greatly prized, for it was held by the highest magistrates of the colony (*duumviri*), probably for one year at a time.[76] Evidence for elite women serving as priestesses to Livia includes the following:

> Cornelia P(ublii) fil(ia) Asprilla sac(erdos) divae
> Aug(ustae) ann(orum) XXXV h(ic) s(ita) e(st)[77]
>
> Cornelia Asprilla, daughter of Publius, priestess of the divine Augusta, 35 years old, is buried here
>
> [Iu]lia[e] C(ai) f(iliae)
> Auruncinae
> sacerdoti divae
> Aug(ustae)[78]
>
> For Julia Auruncina, daughter of Gaius, priestess of the divine Augusta

The *sexviri Augustales*, in contrast, came from a different social class, that of wealthy freed persons (*libertini*).[79] Whereas the *flamines* busied themselves with offerings and cult services for both living and consecrated emperors (Augustus, Claudius, and Vespasian are attested for Philippi), the *sexviri Augustales* focused solely upon Augustus, and their primary responsibility consisted of underwriting the expenses of festival day games. This understandably endeared them to the local populace, and recent excavations have confirmed the assumptions of Collart that special seats were reserved in the theater at Philippi to honor the *sexviri Augustales* publicly among their peers.[80] Those who enjoyed the privilege of serving the imperial cult in this way also had their honors proclaimed on their tombstones:

> C(aius) Postumiu[s]
> Ianuarius
> sevir Aug(ustalis)
> an(norum) XXXV h(ic) s(itus) e(st)
> [. . .] ELA
> [mari]to[81]
>
> Gaius Postumius Ianuarius, an Augustalis, 35 years old, lies buried here . . . for her husband
>
> [V]arroniae Damalidi uxori et
> Curretiae Philippicae socrae [fe]c(it)
> IIIIII vir Aug(usti) . . .[82]

For Varronia, wife of Damalidus, and for Curretia Philippica, his mother-in-law, the Augustalis has made . . .

Public inscriptions detailing the honors of those who held the flaminate, along with inscriptions and special seating at public events for wealthy freedmen priests, only served to reinforce the social hierarchy in the colony, and intentionally so, from the perspective of those in power. For, as Andrew Clarke notes, "Roman élites *used* their religious appointments to define the boundaries between themselves and the rest of the populace."[83] Related, and equally effective in this regard, were the regular festivals celebrating the ruler cult. Surviving festal calendars, organized and kept by local decurion councils, reveal some ten annual ceremonies in honor of Augustus or his followers. Included were the birthday of Augustus, the birthdays of his sons and of the currently reigning emperor, Augustus' victory at Actium, the day on which a triumph was held, and the day of the divinization of an emperor. Public offerings and communal meals typically accompanied these great festivals, the precursor to which was a public procession to the place of celebration in which the participants processed in order of social rank. Decurions and *duumviri*, along with current *flamines* of the cult, led the way, with other lesser functionaries close behind.[84]

Elite space: the social impact of territoriality and the ruler cult

The dominance of the imperial cult in first-century Philippi has not been universally acknowledged. Two recent treatments of religion in Roman Philippi offer markedly divergent opinions on the issue. Lukas Bormann sees emperor veneration as the dominant form of religion in the colony during the first century, strongly maintaining that evidence for foreign cults, such as Isis, does not surface until the following century.[85] Peter Pilhofer, whose treatment departs most significantly from Bormann's at this very point, draws upon more recent archaeological data and maintains that Bormann has grossly underestimated the persistence of Thracian and Greek religion in the colony.[86] Both authors argue strongly for the Romanness of the colony. Pilhofer, however, generally ignores the ruler cult in his treatment of Philippi's religious background.[87]

Considerations of geography and public space suggest that a degree of common ground can be established between the divergent opinions of Bormann and Pilhofer. Pilhofer is correct to insist on the presence of Thracian influence and Thracian religion throughout the early Roman period. Inscriptions attest to the presence of Thracians in the territory of Philippi throughout the first century. Some of the surrounding *vici* appear, in fact, to have been predominantly Thracian. As Pilhofer aptly notes, however, few Thracians resided in the city of Philippi proper.[88] In distinction to the surrounding territory, for example, no name lists with Thracian names have been unearthed from the city, and hardly any gravestones with Thracian names have been found on the acropolis.[89] This is an important observation, for power and social status had a spatial component in antiquity, and it is clear that, as we move from places of little influence (surrounding *vici*) to places of power (the city itself), Thracians recede and Romans dominate.[90]

Cultural anthropologists have recently given much attention to the function of "territoriality." Robert Sack defines it as follows: "Territoriality will be defined as the attempt by an individual or group to affect, influence, or control people, phenomena, and relationships, by delimiting and asserting control over a geographic area."[91] Such attempts "to affect, influence, or control people, phenomena, and relationships" typically manifest themselves in observable ways: (1) classification of places, (2) communication of this classification, and (3) control of the places so classified. A number of patterns for classification are offered, all of which are binary in nature. Jerome H. Neyrey provides the following inventory as illustrative: public/private, sacred/profane, honorable/shameful, clean/unclean, civilization/nature, and center/periphery.[92] Much overlap will be reflected in any specific real-life setting. Communication of these socially constructed classifications, and control of the places so classified, will also manifest themselves in culturally specific ways.

A connection exists, moreover, between political geography and social status. The demarcation of social classes often accompanies the classification of geographical territory in socially stratified societies, and at times the connection is explicit. The geographical center of power in Rome, for example, was the city's forum. In chapter one, I noted Augustus' concern that citizens attire themselves in clothing appropriate to their social status, namely, the citizen toga. Augustus' decree, however, was not without a territorial qualification: "He directed the aediles never again to allow anyone to appear *in the Forum or its neighbourhood* except in the toga without a cloak" (Suet. *Aug.* 40, my italics). It is no accident that Augustus chose the forum, the geographical symbol of Rome's preeminence, as the place in which citizen and non-citizen status are to be publicly demarcated by the wearing of the citizen toga. For, in the words of Anthony Everitt, "The Forum was the city's political, commercial and legal heart . . . its spiritual center, a space even more sacred than the city itself."[93]

Roman colonies replicated in miniature the social construction of public space characteristic of the mother city, so that in Philippi the geographical center of power was the city's forum. Correspondingly, the east end of the forum served as the location for temples dedicated to the veneration of the most powerful figures in the empire, the emperor and his family. According to the above model, the geography of emperor veneration in Roman Philippi suggests that we should situate the cult squarely in the former category of each of the following overlapping classifications: sacred/profane, honorable/shameful, and center/periphery. Temples erected for the worship of the emperor and his family constituted the most sacred and honorable structures in Philippi, and they therefore occupied the colony's geographical center of power. As we proceed with this model to consider the communication and control of these socio-geographical realities, we will hardly be surprised to discover that, although the imperial cult involved the whole colony in its festive celebrations, control of the cult remained in the hands of the local elite, who also shared in the cult's highest honors (e.g. the flaminate), and whose formal meeting house, the *curia* of the colony, was situated at the west end of the forum, directly opposite the temples of the cult, at the center of civic life.[94] Elite religion and elite power are thus closely associated with what we might call elite space.

Consider, in contrast, the cult of Silvanus – a distinctly non-elite association. As Peter Dorcey has observed, Silvanus "remained unconnected with political and civic life, and continued to be of little concern to elite society."[95] Given the spatial component of power and prestige in the colony, it is not surprising, then, to find no evidence of Silvanus worship anywhere near the center of the city. Rather, venerators of Silvanus appear to have been relegated to an old stone quarry north of the forum, a location suitable for an exclusively Roman, yet conspicuously non-elite, religious association.

Non-Roman deities were also spatially marginalized in the layout of the recently founded colony. The worship of Dionysus, which has been traced well back into the Thracian period, persisted during Roman colonization. The central sanctuary of the cult, which welcomed Thracians, Greeks, and Romans, remained on top of a local mountain (*Pangaion*), well outside the city of Philippi. The main sanctuary of the Thracian Horseman, the most important Thracian god, was located in Kipia, also several miles from the walls of Philippi. It has yet to be conclusively demonstrated that the worship of either Dionysus or the Thracian Horseman had penetrated the walls of the city in the form of a permanent cult sanctuary during the first century. What is indisputable is that the worship of these two local deities found no foothold in the Philippian forum itself.[96] Most readers will be familiar, finally, with Luke's narrative in Acts, where we are informed that Paul expected Jewish worship at Philippi to occur outside the city's gates (Acts 16:13). As Witherington suggests, the location points to the Jewish assembly's "lack of social recognition in Philippi."[97]

Summary

As Charles Whittaker has recently maintained, "The relationship of religion to society and politics . . . is not so much that the former reflects the social order as that it shapes it."[98] The imperial cult clearly shaped the social world of Roman Philippi (a colony with "einen betont *augusteischen* Charakter") by reinforcing the social verticality of the dominant culture on at least two levels. Most obviously, public rites and honors associated with the veneration of the emperor – as well as the location of the cult's temple in Philippi's Roman forum – regularly reminded the colony's residents of Augustus' place as the founder of the colony and of the position of the imperial family at the top of the empire's hierarchy of power and prestige. As illustrated above, however, elite control of the cult's practices, personnel, and sacred space also served to impress upon the public consciousness the rank of Philippi's local elite at the apex of the civic hierarchy.

4

HONOR AND STATUS IN PHILIPPI

> And in these various colonies you may behold copies of the customs and the form of government which their founders enjoy.
> Dio Chrysostom (*Or.* 30.26)

The overview of the social environment of Roman Philippi continues in this chapter with a survey of further evidence for preoccupation with honor and status among both the elite and the non-elite in the colony. The previous chapter introduced the military *cursus* and examined various honors that were available through the imperial cult. We now turn our attention to the civic *cursus* and the social environment of local cult groups. I will first demonstrate that concern for honors strongly characterized the public life of Philippi's local elite (generally restricted here to the decurion class and higher). A number of surviving inscriptions detail the ascension of various colonists through a series of honorific posts, culminating with membership in the decurion council and, at times, the highest office in the colony (*duumvir*). The balance of the chapter highlights the replication of elite values in non-elite circles in Philippi. A generous epigraphic database generates much evidence for honorific posts in voluntary cult groups, such as those dedicated to the veneration of Silvanus and Dionysus, robustly attesting to the vitality of a replicated *cursus honorum* in non-elite social settings in the colony. Against this background, Paul's portrayal of Jesus' descent of what I will identify in a later chapter as a *cursus pudorum* will have special meaning for the small Christ-confessing community in Philippi.

Honor and status among the colony's elite

Dio Chrysostom, whose Stoic philosophical orientation led him to challenge prevailing social values concerning honor and shame, was nevertheless painfully aware of the underlying motivation that generated the bulk of our inscriptional evidence:

Honor and status in Philippi

> For all men set great store by the outward tokens of high achievement, and not one man in a thousand is willing to agree that what he regards as a noble deed shall have been done for himself alone and that no other man shall have knowledge of it. (*Or.* 31.22)

Surviving examples of these "outward tokens of high achievement," as Dio calls them, abound in and around Philippi to a degree unparalleled elsewhere in the eastern empire. As we proceed to examine a representative sample of the Philippian honor inscriptions, we must remind ourselves that we owe our surviving evidence solely to the incessant desire of members of the aristocracy to proclaim their social status publicly in the form of monuments erected throughout the colony: "the pillar, the inscription, and being set up in bronze are regarded as a high honour by noble men" (Dio Chrys. *Or.* 31.20).

Inscriptions from Philippi's forum and marketplace

Honor inscriptions detailing the careers and benefactions of various citizens of Philippi have been unearthed throughout the colony. The following evidence comes from the Philippian forum. In view of the discussion of territoriality and political geography in the previous chapter it will not be surprising to encounter a most extensive display of elite honors in the city's forum and immediately adjacent areas. The western fountain in the forum, for example, boasts a number of inscriptions, including one honoring Lucius Decimus Bassus, a leading citizen who contributed 30,000 sesterces for the construction of the edifice.

> [. . . L(ucius) Decimiu]s L(uci) f(ilius) Vol(tinia) Bassus aed(ilis)
> Philippis testamento sibi et
> L(ucio) Decimio L(uci)
> f(ilio) Vol(tinia)
> [q(uaestori) II vir(o) Philippis patri(?) e]t C(aio) Decimio L(uci)
> f(ilio) Vol(tinia) Maxsimo fratri fieri iussit
> HS ((I)) ((I)) ((I))[1]

Lucius Decimius Bassus, the son of Lucius, from the tribe Voltinia, aedile of Philippi, has, on the basis of his will, ordered (this fountain) to be made for himself and for Lucius Decimius, the son of Lucius, from the tribe Voltinia, the quaestor and duumvir of Philippi, his father, and for Gaius Decimius Maxsimus, the son of Lucius, out of the tribe Voltinia, his brother, at a cost of 30,000 sesterces

The location served as a fitting place to honor several of the Decimii family, and the original benefactor (above), as well as his father and brother, listed above, are each honored in other inscriptions found in close proximity to the fountain. The aedile who erected the fountain again appears as follows:

> L(ucio) Decimio L(uci) f(ilio)
> Vol(tinia) Basso, aed(ili)[2]
>
> For Lucius Decimius Bassus, son of Lucius of the tribe Voltinia, an aedile

The honors attained by our benefactor's father, who rose to the height of the civic *cursus* with the rank of *duumvir*, appear again in another nearby inscription:

> L(ucio) Decimio L(uci) f(ilio)
> Vol(tinia), q(uaestor), II vir(o)[3]
>
> For Lucius Decimius, son of Lucius, of the tribe Voltinia, quaestor, duumvir

Lucius Decimius Bassus' brother, apparently possessing no municipal honors of which to boast, nevertheless publicly proclaims his citizen status (*Voltinia*) in yet another Decimii family inscription.[4]

A different set of inscriptions, also found in the forum near the western fountain, vividly attests to the variety of honorific posts gained by two members of another elite family in the colony. Gaius Mucius Scaeva here enumerates his father's military *cursus*:

> C(aio) Mucio Q(uinti) f(ilio) Fab(ia)
> Scaevae, primopilo
> leg(ionis) VI Ferratae, praef(ecto)
> c(o)hort(is), ex testamento
> ipsius C(aius) Mucius C(ai) f(ilius) Fab(ia)
> Scaeva posuit[5]
>
> For Gaius Mucius Scaeva, son of Quintus, from the tribe Fabia, the first centurion of the Sixth Legion Ferrata, prefect of the cohort, on the basis of his own will, Gaius Mucius Scaeva, son of Gaius, has set up (this inscription)

In a nearby inscription the same Gaius outlines the career of his father's brother, a *cursus* which includes both military and civic honors:

P(ublio) Mucio Q(uinti) f(ilio) Vol(tinia)
c(enturioni) leg(ionis) VI Fer(ratae), II vir(o) i(ure) d(icundo)
Philipp(is), ex testamento
C(ai) Muci Q(uinti) f(ili) Fab(ia) Scaevae,
C(aius) Mucius C(ai) f(ilius) Scaeva posuit[6]

For Publius Mucius, son of Quintus of the tribe Voltinia, centurion of the Sixth Legion Ferrata, duumvir *iure dicundo* in Philippi, Gaius Mucius Scaeva, the son of Gaius, has set up (this inscription) on the basis of the will of Gaius Mucius Scaeva, son of Quintus, of the tribe Fabia

The two brothers had apparently set out on parallel military careers but later went in different directions. Both had been officers in the Sixth Legion Ferrata. Gaius went on to command an auxiliary cohort (*praefectus cohortis*). Publius, on the other hand, did not rise above the rank of centurion in the Roman army, but he was later awarded the colony's highest municipal honor, when he occupied the office of *duumvir iure dicundo*.

Careers like that of Publius Mucius, above, may help to shed some light upon the special pride taken in honorific posts in the colony. As observed in the previous chapter, the Roman army provided one of the few avenues of upward social mobility between the non-elite and elite strata of the population in a local municipality. Even within the army, moreover, only a minute percentage of retired officers ultimately entered the ranks of the local decurion order. Veterans like Publius who became members of the decurion council in Philippi would have taken great pride in their exceptional achievement in ascending an otherwise conservative and static social hierarchy. That "new men" like Publius, who gained access to local elite status for the first time upon retirement from the army, constituted the majority of the decurion council early in the colony's history guaranteed a particular pride in the honor of public office in Roman Philippi.[7]

Philippi's forum attests to the activities of several members of the elite who sought honor through public benefaction. A public record house, apparently destroyed in a fire, was restored by a certain Gaius Oppius:

[. . .] P[hilip]piensium C(aius) Op[pius . . .]
[. . .] incendio consum[ptum . . .]
[. . . re]stituit[8]

The Philippian, Gaius Oppius
. . . by the fire consum(ed)
. . . restored

The same individual may have financed the construction of a library as well:

> [. . .] in ho[n]orem div[i]nae do[mu]s et
> colo[niae Iul(iae)
> Aug(ustae) Philipp(ensis) . . .]
> [. . .] Iunior [. . .]S[. . .]ONI[. . .] Optatus opus
> bybl[iothecae . . .]⁹

> in honor of the divine house (the house of Caesar) and the *Colonia Iulia Augusta Philippensis* (has) Junior . . . Optatus the work of the library

A woman whose full name has not survived was honored for her contribution to the restoration of a temple:

> [. . .]ana Proba [ex v]ol[u]ntat[e . . . resti]tuit
>
> [. . . C(aius) Modius Laetus Rufi]nianus, q(uaestor) pr(o) pr(aetore)
> et curat[or r(ei) p(ublicae)
> Philipp(ensium) . . .]¹⁰

> Proba, of her own freewill, rebuilt (this temple)
>
> . . . Gaius Modius Laetus Rufinianus, quaestor, pro praetor, and curator *rei publicae* of the Philippians

According to Michel Sève, the temple which Proba had financed served the imperial cult.¹¹

Most remarkable, as far as status is concerned, are a few select witnesses to persons of senatorial rank in the colony. The first outlines the *cursus* of Gaius Modius Laetus Rufinianus, an individual also referenced in Proba's inscription, immediately above. The title *vir clarissimus* identifies him as a member of the senatorial order:

> C(aio) Modio
> Laeto Ru-
> finiano, q(uaestori)
> pr(o) pr(aetore) provinc(iae)
> Maced(oniae), cur(atori)
> r(ei) p(ublicae) Phil(ippensium), cl(arissimo) v(iro),
> L(ucius) Velleius
> Velleianus
> amico b(ene) m(erenti)¹²

Honor and status in Philippi 93

> For Gaius Modius Laetus Rufinianus, quaestor, pro praetor of the province of Macedonia, curator of the *res publica Philippensium*, the *vir clarissimus*, (for) his well-deserving friend Lucius Velleius Velleianus (has set up this inscription)

The above inscription, along with an identical one (230/L334), appear in connection with two large temples. An inscription erected by Gaius Modius Laetus Rufinianus himself confirms the important role our senator played in overseeing and financing temple construction:

> Genio colo[niae]
> Iul(iae) [Au]g(ustae) Phi[lipp(ensis)]
> [et rei] publi[cae]
> [C(aius) Modiu]s Laet[us]
> [Rufinianus q(uaestor) pr(o)]
> [pr(aetore) provinc(iae) Maced(oniae)]
> [cur(ator) r(ei) p(ublicae) Philipp(ensium)]
> [. . .]
> [. . .]
> [. . .]
> [. . .] in ha[c aede]
> [facie]ndam cur[avit][13]

> To the Genius of the *Colonia Iulia Augusta Philippensis* and to the *res publica* Gaius Modius Laetus Rufinianus, quaestor, pro praetor of the province of Macedonia, curator of the *res publica* of the Philippians, has presided over the construction in this temple

The only other senator whose honorary inscription has been found in the forum likely hailed from Philippi itself, as the name of his citizen tribe suggests:

> [C(aio)] Iul(io) C(ai) f(ilio) Vol(tinia)
> [M]aximo Muci-
> ano, viro cl(arissimo), la-
> toclavo hono-
> [r]ato a divo Pio,
> [q(uaestori)] pr(o) pr(aetore) Ponto-Bithy(niae),
> [a]ed(ili) cerial(i), praet(ori)
> desig(nato), idem dec(urioni) Phil(ippis)
> et in provinc(ia) Thra(cia),
> C(aius) Iul(ius) Teres, thra-

carc(ha), pater sena-
torum, fr(atri)
l(oco) a(dsignato) d(ecreto) d(ecurionum)[14]

For Gaius Iulius Maximus Mucianus, the son of Gaius, of the tribe Voltinia, a *vir clarissimus*, honored with the *latus clavus* by the divine (Antoninus) Pius, quaestor, pro praetor of Pontus and Bithynia, aedile of the grain supply, designated praetor, also decurion of Philippi and in the province of Thracia, (for) his brother Gaius Iulius Teres, the Thracharch, father of senators, (has set up this inscription) in the place determined by a decree of the decurions

An aristocrat like Gaius, appearing in the forum attired in his citizen toga, decorated with the broad purple senatorial stripe (*latus clavus*), would have impressed observers as a rare and notable sight in Roman Philippi. Consider, as well, the final phrase in the above inscription: *loco adsignato decreto decurionum.* The technical expression surfaces often in our sources. The involvement of the members of the decurion council, in formally assigning a place in the forum for the inscription, attests to their desire to recognize two of their own (Gaius Julius Maximus and his brother, Gaius Julius Teres, who pays for the inscription), whose careers, in different ways, had brought great honor to the colony. Gaius' sepulcher inscription, found in the eastern graveyard (also identifying him as *praetor designatus*) indicates that he had died (*annorum XXXV*; 35 years of age) before he could occupy the office of praetor.[15]

Philippi's marketplace was located between the forum and Basilica A. As elsewhere in the empire, the colony's aediles were responsible for overseeing activities in the marketplace, including the use of proper weights and measures in calculating the prices of goods bought and sold. At one point in the settlement's early history, two aediles financed the construction of a monument of some sort. The forty-four pounds of bronze used to erect the structure may have come from the melting down of improper measuring weights confiscated from dishonest merchants. The two brothers who financed the monument proudly proclaim their titles (aediles) and their names (Marcus Cornelius Niger and Publius Valerius Niger), as well as their contribution toward the monument, in the inscription.[16]

Also found in the marketplace is an inscription set up by members of the local Isis cult to honor a member of the elite who, we must assume, functioned in some way as the association's patron:

L(ucio) Valerio L(uci) fil(io)
Volt(inia) Prisco,
orn(amentis) dec(urionatus) hon(orato),
dec(urioni), irenar(chae), II vi-
r(o) iur(e) d(icundo), munera-
rio, cultores
deor(um) Serapis [et]
Isidis[17]

For Lucius Valerius Priscus, the son of Lucius, of the tribe Voltinia, honored with the decorations of a decurion, decurion, *irenarch*, duumvir *iure dicundo*, organizer of games, the devotees of the gods Serapis and Isis (set up this inscription)

After he was admitted to the decurion council (*honorato decurioni*), but before gaining the honor of *duumvir*, Lucius served the colony as *irenarch*. The *irenarch* was something of a town police chief, responsible for maintaining the peace in the territory of the colony and suppressing various forms of civil unrest. The municipal games sponsored by Lucius probably provided the occasion for the Isis association to honor its elite patron.

It was much in the interest of voluntary associations like the Isis group, above, as well as the municipal councils throughout the empire, to publicly honor their benefactors. Scholars have recently focused their attention, in this regard, upon the broader social function of such inscriptions. The honorary inscription served not only as an appropriate response on the part of a voluntary association or civic body to the generosity of an individual benefactor. Honorary inscriptions also encouraged future benefaction. Thus, Elizabeth Forbis, in the introduction to her detailed study of 482 Italian municipal honorary inscriptions, writes of "the ability of Roman honorary inscriptions... to encourage virtuous behavior with the promise of public recognition," and proceeds to assert that "the primary function of the inscriptions' honorary language was to present the honorand as an *exemplum* of virtue, rather than to express appreciation for his or her achievements."[18] Dedicators like the Isis group in the above inscription could thereby "encourage and even influence specific, desired types of behavior in other potential honorands."[19]

Remaining honor inscriptions from the Philippian marketplace include one that recognizes an elite male (whose name has not been preserved) as *duumvir* and *curator* (guardian/overseer) of the *res publica*.[20] The civic *cursus* of yet another of Philippi's noblemen has been restored as follows:

> [- Varin]io [- f(ilio)]
> [V(oltinia) M]acedo[ni],
> [aed(ili)], q(uaestori), II vir(o) i(ure) d(icundo) Ph[ilip-]
> [pis], munerari[o II].
> [pup]illae Vari[niae]
> [M]acedonia et Pro[cula]
> [p]atri ex testa(mento) eius [f(aciendum) c(uraverunt)]

> For . . . Varinius Macedo, the son of . . . from the tribe Voltinia, the aedile, quaestor, and duumvir *iure dicundo* in Philippi, who twice provided the games; the wards Varinia Macedonia and Varinia Procula have set up (this inscription) for their father on the basis of his will

Inscriptions from the eastern and western cemeteries

Honorary inscriptions adorn the tombs of persons buried in a western and an eastern graveyard in the colony. The following fragmentary inscription was found in the eastern burial site:

> [. . .] Iuli Fidei Manli Ba[sci]la et GAI[-]VR[-]Γ[. . .]
> sua paria VII pugna[ve]ru(n)t. Philipp[is . . .]
> unco (?) IIII venatio[nes] PIΛNA et crocis sparsi[t arenam?]

Although full restoration is no longer possible, we are clearly dealing here with a free-spending citizen who wishes to be remembered by passers-by for, among other things, providing seven pairs of gladiators and financing four beast-hunts for spectacles in Philippi's recently rebuilt theater.[21] The elite of the colony also left *cursus* inscriptions on gravestones in the western cemetery. Most prominent was a senator who owed his membership in the order to special intervention by the emperor Antoninus Pius:

> L(ucio) Salvio
> Secundino
> Secundi filio
> Quirina, quaest(ori)
> urbano, adlecto
> inter aedilicios ab
> imp(eratore) Antonino Aug(usto),
> practori urbano, le-
> gato pro praetore
> provinciae Asiae

> Petrusidia Augurina
> uxor faciendum curavit[22]

> For Lucius Salvius Secundinus, the son of Secundus, from the tribe Quirina, the *quaestor urbanus*, received among the aediles by Imperator Antoninus Augustus, *praetor urbanus, legatus pro praetore* of the province of Asia; Petrusidia Augurina, his wife, has arranged for (this inscription)

Others proclaimed a municipal *cursus* more narrowly associated with the colony of Philippi itself:

> P(ublius) Marius P(ubli) f(ilius) Vol(tinia) Valens or(namentis)
> dec(urionatus) hon(oratus), aed(ilis), id(em) Philipp(is),
>   decurio,
> flamen divi Antonini Pii, II vir, mun(erarius)[23]

> Publius Marius Valens, son of Publius, from the tribe Voltinia, honored with the decorations of a decurion, aedile, also decurion of Philippi, priest of the divine Antoninus Pius, duumvir, sponsor of games

The above inscription helpfully outlines a full civic *cursus*. Elite males were often honored with the decorations of decurion status (*ornamentis decurionatus honoratus*) long before they were old enough to be eligible for the office itself, sometimes while still children (see below). The office of aedile or, more likely, quaestor formally marked one's entrance to public life.[24] The aristocrat concurrently served as a member of the decurion council (*decurio*), with the goal of finally ascending to the top post in the colony, *duumvir (IIvir)*, with its municipal responsibilities and associated recognitions (here, *munerarius*). Publius Marius Valens, whose *cursus* is outlined above, also enjoyed the public honor of serving as a priest in the imperial cult (*flamen divi Antonini Pii*).

Another individual of decurion status apparently failed to ascend, like Publius, above, to the heights of the municipal *cursus*, but he wished to proclaim the honors he had achieved nonetheless:

> M(arcus) Antonius M(arci) fil(ius) Vol(tinia) Macer,
>   orn(amentis) dec(urionatus)
> hon(oratus), q(uaestor), sibi et Cassiae Valentiae filiae[25]

> Marcus Antonius Macer, son of Marcus, of the tribe Voltinia, honored with the decorations of a decurion, quaestor, (has) for himself and his daughter Cassia Valentia (set up this inscription)

It is worth pausing to remind ourselves, once again, of the basic values that encouraged the elite in local municipalities such as Roman Philippi to pursue public office. Those who held prestigious imperial priesthoods and who sought to ascend the civic *cursus* from quaestor to *duumvir* did so

> not for the sake of what [was] truly best and in the interest of their country itself, but for the sake of reputation and honours and the possession of greater power than their neighbours, in the pursuit of crowns and precedence and purple robes, fixing their gaze upon these things and staking all upon their attainment.
> (Dio Chrys. *Or.* 34.29)

Dio's cynicism where pomp and honor-seeking are concerned has, to be sure, led him to overstate his case, but one can hardly question the compelling force of "reputation and honours" as a central motivation for pursuing public office and engaging in municipal benefaction.

Other inscriptions detailing elite honors and benefactions

I focused above on inscriptions unearthed around Philippi's forum and in the colony's burial grounds. I conclude this study of elite honors with a sampling of inscriptions found elsewhere in the colony. Scattered throughout the region are inscriptions describing persons who held various posts, including patron (*patronus*) of the colony, *irenarch*, quaestor, aedile, and *duumvir*.[26] From Kavala come two early inscriptions, one of which identifies an unnamed individual as the holder of an imperial priesthood (*flamen*) and a patron (*patronus*) of the colony.[27] The second outlines the achievements of a young equestrian encountered in the discussion of the flaminate in the previous chapter. Consider now his additional honors:

> P(ublius) Cornelius Asper Atiarius Montanus
> equo publico honoratus, item ornamentis decu-
> rionatus et IIviralicis, pontifex, flamen divi Claudi Philippis,
> ann(orum) XXIII h(ic) s(itus) e(st)[28]
>
> Publius Cornelius Asper Atiarius Montanus, honored with equestrian status, also with the decorations of a decurion and of the duumviri, priest, flamen of the divine Claudius in Philippi, 23 years old, lies buried here

Though apparently qualifying for an imperial priesthood, Publius, who died at twenty-three years of age, was not old enough to take his place

Honor and status in Philippi

on the decurion council. Like a number of young men from elite families, however, Publius received the honorary decorations of both council membership and *duumvir* status early in life. How early, we are not sure, but other inscriptions inform us that elite children were decorated with municipal honors at a very young age. A child of six years of age could be honored with the decorations of decurion status:

> [An]n<i>us Agricola orn(amentis) dec(urionatus) ho(noratus) ann(orum) VI mens(ium) II h(ic) s(itus) e(st).
> L(ucius) Annius C(ai) fil(ius) Vol(tinia) Agricola et
> Flavia Atilia Augustina
> parentes[29]
>
> Annius Agricola, honored with the decorations of a decurion, six years and two months old, lies buried here. Lucius Annius Agricola, son of Gaius, of the tribe Voltinia, and Flavia Atilia Augustina, the parents (have set up this inscription)

Gaius Vibius Daphnus was decorated at an even younger age:

> C(aius) Vibius C(ai) fil(ius) Vol(tinia) Daphnus
> orn(amentis) dec(urionatus) hon(oratus) an(norum)
>   V m(ensium)
> IX h(ic) s(itus) e(st)
>
> C(aius) Vibius C(ai) fil(ius) Vol(tinia) Florus dec(urio)
> II vir et munerarius Philippis
> fil(io) kariss(imo) f(aciendum) c(uravit)[30]
>
> Gaius Vibius Daphnus, the son of Gaius, of the tribe Voltinia, honored with the decorations of a decurion, 5 years and 9 months old, lies buried here
>
> Gaius Vibius Florus, son of Gaius, of the tribe Voltinia, decurion, duumvir, sponsor of games at Philippi, has arranged for (this inscription) for his dearest son

As I observed in chapter two, the granting of the decorations associated with the posts of decurion and *duumvir* long before the recipient was eligible to assume the functions of office pointedly underlines the honorific nature of public service in the Roman world. Notice that in the second inscription cited above the father utilizes his son's tombstone to proclaim his own honors as well.

At one point in time the two *duumviri* of the colony financed the restoration of (and additions to) Philippi's public baths. Although parts of the inscription remain open to alternative readings, some kind of baths and adjoining facilities are clearly in view:

> II viri quinq(uennales) Philipp(is) AVGVR[. . .]
> Sermo Turpilius Vetidius [. . . per]
> Oppium Frontonem patrem [. . .]
> adiecta cella natator[ia thermas restituerunt][31]
>
> The *duumviri quinquennales* in Philippi, Sermo Turpilius Vetidius (and . . .) have, through Oppius Fronto, their father, [restored the baths] and added a swimming chamber

The inscription conveniently afforded the two men the opportunity to proclaim publicly both their official status (*duumviri*) and their act of beneficence on behalf of their fellow-colonists. Notice that the two benefactors are brothers. We encountered the same phenomenon above, in an inscription honoring a pair of brothers who served together as aediles for a monument they erected in the marketplace.[32] As discussed in chapter one, in any given setting in the Roman empire the elite stratum of society constituted a minute percentage of the local population. The concurrent enjoyment of key municipal honors by two brothers demonstrates the presence of just such a demographic in Roman Philippi, where a few elite families apparently controlled access to desirable positions of power and honor at any given point in time.[33]

Honor and status among the colony's non-elite

Throughout the empire, non-elite voluntary associations and cult groups tended to replicate in their own social contexts the verticality of elite society. Evidence from Philippi markedly underscores the ubiquitous nature of this tendency. Numerous religious associations at Philippi boasted official honors for the most privileged of their members, a few of which are attested only here in the ancient world. Public benefaction, along with the anticipated response of honorary recognition, also finds expression in monuments erected by non-elite persons. Here, the "public," of course, generally consisted of the fellow-members of the donor's collegium.

Non-elite cult associations

Religious associations in the colony included a group of persons describing themselves as *cultores Cupidinis*.[34] A *thiasus Maenadum* is also attested, which was associated with the Bacchus cult.[35] An official of a Cybele cult, as well as an association of those who venerated the Egyptian deities Isis and Serapis, also flourished in the colony of Roman Philippi.[36] Worshipers of Dionysus organized themselves into several local θίασοι. In the rural territory of the colony, near the mountain of Pangaion, for example, we find a group referring to themselves as μύσται Διονύσου.[37] Also outside the city walls was a συμπόσιον of the Thracian god Suregethes whose members identify themselves on the same inscription as ποσιασταὶ "Ηρωνος.[38] Little is known of the organization of these cults, although honorary titles occur in nearly all of the above inscriptions, and claims of benefaction (along with related honors) often appear as well. An association dedicated to the god Silvanus, however, is very well attested, and careful examination of the cult's inscriptions significantly informs our understanding of the manner in which non-elite cult groups replicated the values and practices of elite society.

Five inscriptions survive from the Silvanus cult, two of which are quite comprehensive.[39] The veneration of Silvanus is a distinctly Roman phenomenon, and the great majority of Silvanus cult sites are located in the western and northern provinces.[40] All five inscriptions from Philippi are in Latin. No Thracian names appear on an extensive list of association members. Silvanus worshipers were typically of non-elite status and practiced their religion without reference to local municipal administration. Peter Dorcey explains:

> [Silvanus] qualifies as popular, because his cult was restricted to the private domain, remained unconnected with political and civic life, and continued to be of little concern to elite society. Senators and equestrians were not very interested in him and failed to include him in the state calendar. The lettered aristocracy rarely mentioned the god in their writings.[41]

Dorcey's comments relate to Silvanus worship in the empire at large, and the evidence from Philippi confirms this general assessment. Members of the association (all male) included freeborn, freedmen, and slaves. No elite males are listed, decurions and *duumviri* being conspicuously absent from an extended list of sixty-nine members.

The social location of Silvanus worship, and its popular orientation as a cult group unconnected to formal municipal administration render the association somewhat analogous to the Christian *ekklesia*. Indeed, the quotation from Dorcey, cited above, could be applied without qualification to Paul's congregations in the East. A comparison between the two groups proves quite informative. The Silvanus cult, like worshipers of Jesus, ameliorated the sharp verticality of the broader society by including as members slaves, freedpersons, and freeborn, and by downplaying these social distinctions in community life. The manner, for example, in which the names of slaves and freedmen are somewhat randomly scattered throughout the extensive list of members suggests little concern on the part of Silvanus worshipers to categorize persons carefully according to natal status.[42] Also of note in this regard is the fact that the cult's central honor, the office of aedile, was awarded to a person of freedman status (see below). The early Christians, of course, also sought to challenge the social distance between slave and freeborn in their values and in their community relations. In addition, both groups included whole households among their members.[43]

So much for the similarities. The restriction of Silvanus worship to Roman males generated a *collegium* that was significantly less variegated in its membership, with respect to both gender and ethnic composition, than were the early Christ-confessing communities in the East. More important for present purposes is evidence from Philippi which demonstrates that Silvanus worshipers embraced the dominant culture's preoccupation with honor and social status in ways that early Christian leaders, like Paul of Tarsus, founder of the Jesus community at Philippi, clearly did not (see chapters five and six). The salient point here is the tendency for elite values relating to social verticality and the pursuit of honor to replicate themselves in non-elite associations. The Silvanus cult is our best attested evidence for this phenomenon at Philippi.

Members of the cult were organized into *decuriae* of which there were at least seven. A hierarchy of honors included priests (*sacerdotes*) and an *aedilis*. Those identified in the inscriptions as priests of the cult include Marcus Alfensus Aspasius, Lucius Volattius Urbanus, and Macius Bictor.[44] Apparently only one person held the office of *sacerdos* at any given time. Alongside the priest of Silvanus was the office of aedile. The office is specifically described in the inscriptions as an honor (*ob honorem aedilitatis*).[45] We may assume that *aedilis* here refers not to an aedile of the colony but, rather, to an aedile honored as such among members of the association. Just as a local municipality would adopt terms from the senatorial *cursus honorum* in Rome to designate honors occurring in its replicated civic *cursus*, so also cult groups such as Silvanus worshipers appropriated the same terms to denote honors held within the confines of their non-elite, voluntary associations. Titular mimicry is, again, indicative of the social value replication characteristic of non-elite groups in the Roman world.

The analogy extends, in the present case, to the activities of the office of aedile as well, for the individual who is identified as an aedile in

Honor and status in Philippi

the Silvanus association in Philippi, Publius Hostilius Philadelphus, also functioned as the group's benefactor. Above we saw a municipal aedile, Lucius Decimius Bassus, spend 30,000 sesterces to erect a fountain at the western end of Philippi's forum.[46] Here Lucius' activities are replicated in miniature, as Publius, the association's aedile, finances a pair of inscriptions and underwrites the construction of some kind of stairway leading up into the Silvanus cult's temple structure.[47] Yet another person is titled *pater* in the Silvanus cult group. Here, again, the term is to be interpreted in reference to the association's hierarchy, and not in its traditional sense, as referring to the patriarch of a natural family. Pilhofer suggests that the individual designated *pater* functioned as a patron of some sort for the group.[48]

In addition to the extensive list of sixty-nine members of the cult found on one inscription (identified as *cultores*), another inscription enumerates the names of seven adherents of the cult who contributed significantly toward the temple to Silvanus. The fascinating list warrants extended citation, for it graphically attests to the public recognition available to those who were willing to utilize their financial resources for an association building project:

> P(ublius) Hostilius Philadelphus
> ob honor(em) aedilit(atis) titulum polivit
> de suo et nomina sodal(ium) inscripsit eorum
> qui munera posuerunt.
> Domitius Primigenius statuam
> aeream Silvani cum aede.
> C(aius) <H>oratius Sabinus at templum tegend(um)
> tegulas CCCC tectas.
> Nutrius Valens sigilla marmuria
> dua, Herculem et Mercurium.
> Paccius Mercuriales opus cementic(ium)
> * CCL ante templum et tabula picta Olympum * XV
> Publicius Laetus at templum aedifi-
> candum donavit * L.
> item Paccius Mercuriales at templum
> aedificandum cum filis et liberto don(avit)
> * L, item sigillum marmurium Liberi * XXV
> Alfenus Aspasius sacerd(os)
> signum aer(eum) Silvani cum basi,
> item vivus * L mortis causae sui
> remisit.

> vacat
> Hostilius Philadelphus inscin-
> dentibus in templo petram excidit d(e) s(uo)[49]
>
> Publius Hostilius Philadelphus, on account of the honor (given to him) of being aedile, furnished this inscription at his own expense and inscribed the names of those members who contributed work:
>
> Domitius Primigenius, a bronze statue of Silvanus with a temple.
> Gaius Horatius Sabinus, 400 roof tiles for the covering of the temple.
> Nutrius Valens, two marble statuettes, Hercules and Mercury.
> Paccius Mercuriales, 250 denarii for concrete in front of the temple, and Olympus on a painted table for 15 denarii.
> Publicius Laetus 50 denarii for the temple building.
> Paccius Mercuriales, also, along with his sons and one of his freedmen, 50 denarii for the temple building, along with a statuette of Liber made of marble for 25 denarii.
> Alfenus Aspasius, the priest, a bronze statue of Silvanus with a base, and he also deposited during his lifetime 50 denarii for his death.
> Hostilius Philadelphus had the rock cut, at his own cost, for the stairway up to the sanctuary.

A certain perspective can be gained on the replication of municipal elite practices of benefaction in the Silvanus cult when we compare the amounts of money donated in the above inscription with elite Lucius Decimius Bassus' contribution to the fountain in the forum. At four sesterces per denarius, Lucius' donation of 30,000 sesterces to the fountain project is thirty times as large as the most generous contribution to the Silvanus temple specified above (250 denarii) and 150 times the average gift of 50 denarii. We are obviously dealing with two distinct levels of social status, with correspondingly different amounts of money available for benefaction. Nevertheless, the social values and behavior of the two status groups mirror one another in a remarkable way.

The evidence cited above paints a rather complete portrait of a non-elite association markedly influenced by the cultural values and social codes which characterized the dominant society of Philippi's decurion elite. Although the social chasm between slave and free was significantly bridged among Silvanus worshipers, the association's appropriation of the widespread preoccupation with official honors and public recognition for acts of beneficence, so characteristic of the elite of Philippi, is transparent at every turn. The association thus constitutes a classic example of the phenomenon outlined in some detail in chapter two, whereby, in the words of Ramsay MacMullen, voluntary associations "ape(d) the high-sounding terminology of larger, municipal bodies, the nomenclature of officialdom . . . and constituted in every detail miniature cities."[50]

Other associations offered similar honors. The worshipers of *Iuppiter Optimus Maximus* had a *curator*, an office once occupied by a Lucius Firmius Geminus, as well as a priest.[51] A high priest (*antistes*) serves the goddess Diana, with a priest (*sacerdos*) named Manta Zercedis, along with a whole series of *curatores*.[52] Followers of Dionysus had *subcuratores* which, of course, implies the presence of *curatores*.[53] A freedman named Marcus Velleius identifies himself as *dendophorus* of the Cybele cult.[54] Local Thracian cult associations also reflect a preoccupation with honorific offices or ranks. Interestingly enough, as Pilhofer observes, a number of the honors attested for voluntary associations in the above inscriptions are unique to Philippi. For example, only in Philippi is the honorific position of aedile attested for the Silvanus cult. Among those who honored the Thracian Horseman, a local association which persisted throughout the Roman era, only in Philippi do we find among cult functionaries a group of officials identified as *procuratores*.[55]

Benefaction, like that practiced by certain members of the Silvanus association (above), surfaces in other non-elite cult inscriptions. A woman named Scandilia Optata fulfilled a vow by dedicating to Venus a small temple (*aedicula*) and statuette (*sigilla*).[56] Rufas Zipas was honored as μυστάρχης and εὐεργέτης for his generosity in support of a Dionysius collegium.[57] Marcus Velleius Zosimus wished to be remembered publicly for setting up images of the "Unconquerable Nemesis" during his tenure as priest in the cult.[58] Valeris Severa, who identifies herself as "high-priestess of Diana Caszoria," provided for a statue of the goddess:

> Valeris
> Severa an-
> tistes Dean<a>e
> Caszoriae p[e-]
> titu a sanct[is-]
> simo ordine
> et decreto d-
> [ec(urionum)] imaginem [p(ecunia) s-]
> ua si<b>i et Atiar[i-]o
> Aem<a>eo nepot(i)
> suo l(ibens) p(osuit)[59]

> Valeris Severa, high-priestess of Diana Caszoria, at the request of the holiest order and by a decree of the decurions, has gladly set up (this) statue [of Diana?] at her own expense for herself and for her grandson Atiarius Aemaeus

The phrase "the holiest order" (*sanctissimo ordine*) probably points to the existence of a voluntary association in service of Diana. The involvement of the decurion council in the erection of the above statue suggests some connection between the donor and the elite stratum of the colony's population. It could be inaccurate to identify Valeris as elite, however, for the phrase *decreto decurionum* occurs in other inscriptions honoring persons who do not appear to belong to the decurion class. A doctor named Quintus Mofius Euhemerus, for example, built an altar and a set of benches for the Isis cult, at a place determined by a council decree (*loco adsignato decreto decurionum*).[60] A priest of Isis named Lucius Titonius Suavis provided, at his own expense (*ex suo*) for some kind of stairway to the Isis sanctuary.[61] The same man also donated a sacrificial table and pedestal to "Queen Isis."[62]

Other non-elite honors

The colony's non-elite were also concerned to publicize titles associated with responsibilities and honors they had acquired outside the religious sphere. A Greek inscription identifies Archedemos as πραγματευτὴς Βαβίου Μάγνου, "steward (or manager of the estate) of Baebius Magnus."[63] The Latin equivalent of the title, *actor*, occurs in five other inscriptions.[64] The identification of six "stewards" in the region potentially informs our understanding of the social hierarchy as it developed during the early decades of the colony. Peter Oakes argues for the increasing consolidation of land in the hands of fewer and fewer members of the Roman elite, resulting in the accentuation of social distance between the elite and the non-elite in the colony. The survival of these six inscriptions attesting to "estate managers" supports Oakes's reconstruction.[65]

Most remarkable is a first-century inscription detailing the career of a key official of Philippi's Latin theatrical troupe. As has been rightly noted, the *cursus* cited below unfolds in much the same manner as a legionary veteran might outline his ranks and the years of his campaigns:[66]

> T(itus) Uttiedius Venerianus,
> archimim(us) latinus et of<f>i-
> cialis an(nos) XXXVII, promisthota an(nos)
> XVIII, vixit an(nos) LXXV, vivos sibi et

Alfen<a>e Saturninae coniugi suae bene de se meritae.
Alfena Saturnina an(norum) LI[67]

Titus Uttiedius Venerianus, for 37 years the chief Latin mime and official (of the city of Philippi), 18 years *promisthota*, lived 75 years. (He has) during his lifetime, for himself and for his good and deserving wife, Alfena Saturnina, (erected this tomb). Alfena Saturnina, 51 years old

The identification of Titus as an *officialis* suggests a formal connection between theatrical spectacles and municipal authorities in Roman Philippi. Such an official connection would be exceptional, perhaps necessitated by the difficulty of assembling a Latin troupe on an occasional basis in the colony. The term *promisthota* identifies Titus as a contractor of sorts who served as a broker between the colony and the theater, in order to arrange for theatrical productions, including the hiring of a troupe of actors.[68]

I conclude my discussion of non-elite honors in Philippi with mention of a phenomenon that underscores, in a unique way, the concerns of persons in the colony to publicly proclaim their social status. I refer here to numerous inscriptions erected by slaves and freedpersons in the colony who, surprisingly, seem quite proud to proclaim their rank in society. A man named Eutyches, for example, refers to himself as "slave of Bullenus Venustus" (*Bulleni Venusti servus*). A freedwoman named Annia Secunda specifically identifies her husband as "freedman of Manius" (*Mani liberto*) on her daughter's burial inscription.[69] Marcus Velleius is a "freedman of Marcus" (*Marci libertus*).[70] The western cemetery contains an inscription dedicated to a freedwoman of Gaius (*Cai liberta*), named Vibia Piruzir, and another erected by a home-born slave (*verna*) named Sulpicius for his dear departed sister.[71] Elsewhere in the colony, a certain Vitalis financed an inscription identifying himself both as "slave of Gaius Lavius Faustus" (*Cai Lavi Fausti servus*) and then, more specifically, as a slave born in the house (*verna domo natus*).[72]

The phenomenon of slaves and freedpersons recording their status in inscriptions is hardly unique to Philippi. The practice is widely attested throughout the empire and has been variously explained. At one level, a title such as "slave of so and so" could simply function as a means of identification. Our understanding of Roman social values, however, leads us to suspect that more is involved here than mere identification. Dale Martin explains the phenomenon of lower-class persons proclaiming their status on burial inscriptions as follows: "slaves and freedpersons may have willingly given their status in order to emphasize their connection with someone higher up in the patronage structure of the society . . . naming oneself as a slave of an important person was a way of claiming status for oneself."[73] The evidence strongly supports Martin's observation. Scholars who have studied these inscriptions throughout the empire note that slaves and freedpersons who identify themselves as such are careful to stress on their tombstones their connections with persons further up the social scale, and this is precisely what we find in Philippi. Notice, for example, that all but one of the inscriptions cited above identify the respective slave or freedperson in connection with a (former) owner. The order of the names in the inscriptions is also informative. It is no accident that the name of the owner (or former owner, now patron), in the genitive, almost invariably precedes the title "slave," or "freedwoman" in such inscriptions.[74] This suggests that the emphasis is not simply upon "slave" or "freedperson" as such, but rather on the identity of the slave's owner. Martin summarizes: "Slaves and freedpersons did not hesitate to call themselves such. They used the term as a title and as an opportunity to link themselves to more powerful people. They seemed to feel no shame in their slavery as long as they could enjoy this status-by-association."[75] I would only add that in appealing to their "status-by-association" slaves are not comparing themselves with, or vying for honors with, freeborn persons in the surrounding society. Rather, they are vying for honors with others of their same social stratum who may or may not be able to claim a relationship with such an honorable household.

Summary: social status in Roman Philippi

Excavations at Philippi have produced the most detailed inscriptions found anywhere in the Roman empire outlining the various honors enjoyed by the residents of a local municipality. We have observed *cursus* after *cursus* replete with municipal posts, military ranks, and various decorations enjoyed by the elite in the colony. And we have seen these honors colorfully replicated in cult associations and other non-elite settings. Commenting on the army veterans in the colony, Pilhofer rightly asserts in this regard, "Ich nehme es als ein Indiz dafür, dass man in Philippi *besonders stolz* darauf war, seine Posten und Pöstchen zur Schau zu stellen."[76] As we have learned, moreover, such pride was hardly limited to the military. *Cursus* ideology permeated every level of the social hierarchy. Even Titus Uttiedius Venerianus, a lowly actor who was hardly a member of the local elite, was compelled to list in great detail on his sarcophagus the various stations of his course of life.[77] As Pilhofer notes, we might expect such parading of honors on the part of elites. At Philippi, however, everyone who could scrape together the resources necessary to erect an inscription of some kind apparently felt the need to publicly proclaim his achievements. Pilhofer rhetorically queries, "War es für Ἐνκόλπιος, der seinem *patronus* einen Sarkophag mit Inschrift anfertigen lässt, nötig, sich auf dieser Inschrift als ἀπελεύθερος zu bezeichen und diesen seinen Status auf diese Weise auch der Nachwelt zu überliefern?"[78] Whether or not we deem the action of Ἐνκόλπιος here as necessary (nötig) will depend, of course, on our cultural orientation. What is indisputable is that persons in first-century Philippi felt strongly compelled to proclaim publicly the honors they had received and their social location in the pecking order of this highly stratified Roman colony. Christians in the colony would hardly have been immune to these social pressures.

5

ACTS AND PHILIPPIANS

> These men are disturbing our city; they are Jews and are advocating customs that are not lawful for us as Romans to adopt or observe.
> Acts 16:20b–21

In this chapter I will examine the biblical texts relating to ancient Philippi, in view of the Roman cultural values and social codes that have served as the focus of the earlier portions of this book. I discuss here Paul's ministry in the colony, as narrated in the book of Acts, and also look at select passages in the letter to the Philippians, where Paul intentionally draws upon issues of status and honor for rhetorical effect. The chapter which follows (chapter six) is reserved for an exposition of the great Christological passage Philippians 2:6–11, which presents Jesus as descending a *cursus pudorum* and ultimately receiving the highest of honors for approaching his status and power in a radically countercultural way.

The Philippian narrative in Acts

The general thrust of the first four chapters of this monograph could be fairly summarized in two simple propositions: (1) Rome was the most status-conscious society in the ancient Mediterranean world, and (2) based on the evidence at hand, no settlement in the East was more Roman, in this regard, than Philippi. The narrative of Paul's ministry in Philippi in Acts 16 underscores the validity of these assertions, portraying the colony as a markedly Roman settlement boasting a population preoccupied with issues of status, honorific office, and citizenship.[1] The first indication of Luke's sensitivity to the Romanness of the region is his identification of Philippi as "a leading city of the district of Macedonia and a Roman colony" (16:12). The description stands out as exceptional when compared with the manner in which Luke introduces other cities in Acts. According to Ben Witherington, in the first portion of the description the author intends to communicate Philippi's "honor rating in that portion of Macedonia."[2] A thorny textual problem renders uncertain the reading that Witherington adopts, however, and the phrase is better translated, "a city of the first district of Macedonia."[3]

What is not in question in the Greek text of Acts 16:12 is the identification of Philippi as a "colony" (κολωνία). The term is used only here in the New Testament, and this is particularly striking in the case of Acts, since no fewer than eight other Roman colonies are mentioned in Luke's narrative, none of which the author so designates.[4] Pilhofer attributes the anomaly to an author who is simply better informed about Philippi than elsewhere. I suggest, instead, that Luke specifies the colonial identity of Philippi expressly to draw attention to the Romanness of the settlement, in order to prepare the reader for the striking charge brought against Paul by residents of the colony later in the story: "These men are disturbing our city; they are Jews and are advocating customs that are not lawful for us as Romans to adopt or observe" (16:20–21). Throughout the narratives of Paul's journeys, only in Philippi are the apostle and his co-workers explicitly charged with advocating behavior inimical to the Roman way of life, that is, with encouraging behavior that contradicts the Roman *mos maiorum* (ἔθη ἃ οὐκ ἔξεστιν ἡμῖν παραδέχεσθαι οὐδὲ ποιεῖν Ῥωμαίοις οὖσιν).[5] Luke's unique designation of Philippi as a colony and the exceptional charge against the missionaries in verse 21 therefore show that the author of Acts is highly sensitive to the Romanness of the settlement.

Luke is also attuned to the social values and practices of the colony, for the incessant concern for public honors which characterized the Roman world receives particular emphasis in the Philippian portion of the Acts narrative (16:12–40). In an earlier chapter I emphasized the honorific nature of public office in the Roman world. The honor associated with municipal posts is particularly well attested for Philippi, where, as we have seen, the titles of honorific offices appear in a great number of inscriptions (chapter four). It is hardly surprising to discover, therefore, that only for Philippi, among the various locations where Paul ministered, does Luke specifically mention the offices of οἱ στρατηγοί (16:20, 22, 35, 36, 38) and οἱ ῥαβδοῦχοι (16:35, 38), as well as the title δεσμοφύλαξ (16:23, 27, 36).

Scholarly consensus identifies the στρατηγοί as the *duumviri iure dicundo*, the top civic officers in the colony, occupying a post we have seen evidenced in a number of Philippian inscriptions.[6] The term ῥαβδοῦχοι corresponds, in turn, to the Latin *lictores*, a title for persons who proceeded before the chief magistrates bearing the *fasces*, which symbolized magisterial authority. The two official posts of στρατηγός and ῥαβδοῦχος would certainly have been in existence in other places where Paul ministered, for example in Pisidian Antioch. A comparison with the Antioch narrative is, in fact, quite informative. According to Luke's story about Paul's ministry in Pisidian Antioch, "the Jews incited the devout women of high standing and the leading men of the city, and stirred up persecution against Paul and Barnabas, and drove them out of their region" (13:50). As Pilhofer notes, we are dealing here with city officials engaged in some official action, for the expression "their region" (τῶν ὁρίων αὐτῶν) designates the formal territory of the colony, and not simply the city as such.[7] Those with the authority to take such action against the missionaries are most probably the colony's *duumviri iure dicundo*. They are not, however, specifically designated as such. Rather, Luke identifies Antioch's magistrates in general terms, as "the leading men of the city" (τοὺς πρώτους τῆς πόλεως).

Notice, in contrast, the manner in which the Philippian narrative unfolds. The local magistrates first appear on the scene when the slave-girl's owners drag the missionaries "before the authorities," where the officials are identified with a general expression, ἄρχοντες (16:19). Luke immediately becomes much more precise, however, as he drops ἄρχοντες for the balance of the narrative, referring instead to the magistrates, more specifically, as στρατηγοί (16:20, 22, 35, 36, 38; see above).[8] The fivefold repetition of στρατηγοί – a term used of Gentile magistrates nowhere else in Acts – along with specific references to ῥαβδοῦχοι and a δεσμοφύλαξ, suggest an awareness on Luke's part of the heightened sensitivity to social status and honorific titles which characterized the colony, a sensitivity we saw evidenced in the archaeological data outlined in the previous chapter. The appearance of the topic of citizen status in the verses that follow points in precisely the same direction.

Like the honorific titles discussed above, the missionaries' claim to Roman citizenship in the story stands out as exceptional among the narratives of Paul's three journeys in Acts (16:37). Peter Garnsey reminds us of the varying standards of justice that were applied to different persons in the ancient world, and he makes specific application to the legal situation of citizens versus non-citizens in a veteran colony like Philippi: "In a Roman colony it appears that arrest, beating, and imprisonment were normal for aliens, but that it was potentially dangerous to give citizens the same treatment."[9] Luke, of course, portrays Paul and Silas enduring precisely such maltreatment at the hands of the Philippian magistrates in Acts 16. A socially attuned reader would naturally assume, then, that the missionaries are *peregrini* – foreigners lacking the rights and privileges that accompanied Roman citizenship. Near the end of Luke's saga, however, when Paul and Silas are released from prison, the reader is surprised to learn that the missionaries had been Roman citizens all along:

> But Paul replied, "They have beaten us in public, uncondemned, men who are Roman citizens, and have thrown us into prison; and now are they going to discharge us in secret? Certainly not! Let them come and take us out themselves." The police reported these words to the magistrates, and they were afraid when they heard that they were Roman citizens; so they came and apologized to them. And they took them out and asked them to leave the city. (16:37–39)

Commentators variously explain the reticence of the missionaries to draw upon the privileges associated with their citizen status until after they were beaten and imprisoned.[10] Some suggest that Paul may have simply lacked opportunity to present his claims in the chaos surrounding the arrest, beating, and imprisonment.[11] This, however, fails to satisfy, and it is preferable to seek reasons in the social particulars of the Philippian situation itself. Brian Rapske suggests that

> the self-defense of an early citizenship claim would probably have been construed by the magistrates and populace as an assertion of commitment to the primacy of Roman, over against Jewish (i.e. Christian) customs. The signals sent would also have put the church at risk of dissolution if the new Philippian converts did not possess the Roman franchise. At the least there would have been uncertainty surrounding Paul's commitment to his message. Converts might wonder whether only those suitably protected (i.e. by Roman citizenship) should become believers in Christ, and they might think it disingenuous for Paul and Silas to ask others to suffer what they themselves were able to avoid.[12]

Rapske is on target to find explanation in the Romanness of the colony of Philippi, and the last sentence in the above quotation invites further elaboration.

Peter Oakes, who has done the most comprehensive work along these lines, estimates a population of 40 percent Roman citizens in the town of Philippi by the middle of the first century. His estimation for the church population at the time when Paul wrote Philippians (slanted for social accessibility) stands at 36 percent.[13] Moving back in time to Paul's ministry in Philippi, a decade or so earlier, let us assume from Oakes's figures that between one-third and one-half of the persons responding positively to the preaching of Paul and Silas possessed Roman citizenship. This would render the majority of persons responding to the gospel unable to call upon citizen privileges in the face of the kind of official persecution experienced by Paul and Silas at the hands of the municipal authorities. This is a crucial consideration, given the legal and social significance of Roman citizenship in a colony like Philippi. Consider Cicero's sentiments regarding the importance of the citizen franchise, particularly for non-elite Romans in the provinces:

> Poor men of humble birth sail across the seas to shores they have never seen before, where they find themselves among strangers, and cannot always have with them acquaintances to vouch for them. Yet such trust have they in the single fact of their citizenship that they count on being safe, not only where they find our magistrates, who are restrained by the fear of law and public opinion, and not only among their own countrymen, to whom they are bound by the ties of a common language and civic rights and much else besides: no, wherever they find themselves, they feel confident that this one fact [their citizenship] will be their defence. (*Verr.* 2.5.167)

Cicero's assertions concerning the importance of citizenship for Roman provincials find ample support among the Philippian inscriptions.

A number of the inscriptions cited in the previous chapters include the abbreviation *VOL* (*Voltinia*), indicating the individual's citizen tribe. The abbreviation, in fact, occurs on one-half of all first- and second-century inscriptions found in the city.[14] Even a child who died at two years of age had his membership in the citizen tribe Voltinia proclaimed on his tombstone:

> [. . .] f(ilius) Volt(inia) Nepos
> ann(orum) II h(ic) s(itus) e(st)[15]
>
> Nepos, son of . . . , of the tribe Voltinia, (died at) two years of age, lies buried here

One suspects from the epigraphic witness that the colony's Roman residents would have heartily concurred with Dio's assessment of the importance of Roman citizenship: "To the disenfranchised, life seems with good reason not worth living, and many choose death rather than life after losing their citizenship" (*Or.* 66.15). Some comments on this preoccupation with citizen status are in order, particularly in view of the striking manner in which the issue surfaces in the narrative in Acts 16.

Claims of citizenship were particularly important to the subjects of the honorific inscriptions in Philippi due to the settlement's origin as a Roman colony. Colonies at their founding were typically identified with one of Rome's citizen tribes. In the case of Philippi that tribe was the *tribus Voltinia*. For the citizen of Philippi, citizenship in the colony was inseparable from membership in the *tribus Voltinia*. One who belonged to the *tribus Voltinia* possessed citizenship in Philippi and was, at the same time, a full Roman citizen: *civis Philippensis* and *civis Romanus*. Under the *ius Italicum*, citizen privileges included exemption from taxes, tributes, and duties, along with the right to prosecute civil lawsuits (*vindicatio*) and acquire (*manicipatio*), own (*usucapio*), and transfer (*in iure cessio*) property.[16] For present purposes it is important to recognize that this pervasive concern to proclaim publicly one's citizen status attests to a sharply pronounced social distinction between citizens and non-citizens in a Roman colony like Philippi where, unlike Greek cities in the East, for example, the rights of city citizenship were directly related to Roman citizenship.

The status distinction between citizen and non-citizen in Philippi is reflected in another way in the colony. An inscription cited in the previous chapter portrays the senator Gaius Modius Laetus Rufinianus paying honor both to the *genius* of the *Colonia Iulia Augusta Philippensis* and to the *res publica*.[17] Fanoula Papazoglou has recently argued against interpreting the two expressions interchangeably. She prefers to distinguish between *Colonia Iulia Augusta Philippensis* and *res publica*, and she does so specifically with respect to the citizen franchise:

> le terme de *colonia* s'applique à la collectivité des citoyens à pleins droits, aux *Philippenses*, c'est-à-dire aux colons, à leurs descendants et aux autochtones naturalisés et inscrits au nombre des colons, tandis que par *res publica* on désigne le domaine communal de la colonie, dont la population était composée d'éléments qui différaient par leur statut juridique et étaient organisés dans des communautés jouissant de certaines prérogatives.[18]

If Papazoglou is correct, the manner in which the above inscription specifies both realms – *Colonia Iulia Augusta Philippensis* and *res publica* – suggests that the distinction between citizen and non-citizen was an important one for inhabitants of the colony. The ubiquitous presence of *Vol(tinia)* among the epigraphic evidence decidedly confirms this assumption.[19]

I return, now, to Acts 16, in order to reflect upon the missionaries' reluctance to call upon their citizen status until after they had been beaten and imprisoned. In a social setting in which hierarchy, status, and, especially, a profoundly felt distinction between citizen and non-citizen occupy center stage in the symbolic universe of the local population, Paul and Silas must establish at the outset the manner in which these issues will relate to the message of the gospel. The missionaries' citizen status affords them the opportunity to do just that. As Rapske observes (above), the missionaries refuse to call upon their social status in a way that might privilege them with treatment that other Christians in the colony might be unable to receive. Luke thus portrays Paul and Silas modeling behavior that Paul will later associate with Jesus of Nazareth in his letter to the Philippian Christians: the missionaries refuse to regard their status as "something to be exploited," enduring suffering, instead, for the benefit of others (see the discussion of ἁρπαγμόν, Phil. 2:6; chapter six).

If we can trust Luke's narrative in Acts 16, then, Paul has begun reconstructing honor in Philippi more than a decade before his letter to the Christians in the colony. The story concludes, moreover, with a remarkable turn of events which parallels the honor reversal experienced by Jesus at the end of the Christ hymn in Paul's epistle to the Philippians. Paul portrays Jesus willingly enduring public humiliation and ultimately receiving the highest honors for renouncing his status in the service of others (Phil. 2:6–11). Acts 16, as well, concludes with an honor reversal, whereby Paul and Silas, who had been publicly humiliated, ultimately shame the colony's magistrates, who are now "afraid" (ἐφοβήθησαν), into "apologizing" (παρεκάλεσαν) to the missionaries and personally escorting them out of prison (16:38–39).[20] Early Christian readers and listeners, steeped in the agonistic relational world of Mediterranean antiquity, would surely have been delightfully surprised and impressed to find Luke's protagonists, Paul and Silas, emerging as social victors in their honor contest with Philippi's elite *duumviri*.[21]

Paul's letter to the Philippians

An examination of Paul's letter to the Christians at Philippi continues to confirm the analysis of the colony as a highly stratified, distinctly Roman environment. The preoccupation with public honors/offices and, particularly, the pride taken in citizenship in the colony shed much light on various portions of Paul's short epistle. It is no accident, in this regard, that only in Philippians does Paul specifically address overseers and deacons in his salutation (ἐπισκόποις καὶ διακόνοις; 1:1). Only in Philippians, moreover, does Paul so carefully delineate his own social honors and achievements as a Pharisaic Jew (3:5–6). And, finally, only here does Paul substitute the term πολιτεύομαι for his more common περιπατέω, when he describes the manner in which Christians are to conduct their lives (1:27; πολίτευμα, 3:20). The πολιτεύ- imagery has been ably handled by others, so I will limit my comments below to the address to the readers in the letter's salutation and to Paul's pre-Christian *cursus* as presented in 3:5–6.[22]

Philippians 1:1 – office and honor

Paul's opening salutation in Philippians differs in several important ways from the greetings found in other letters addressed to local Christian communities and traditionally assigned to the apostle. A comparison of the parallels highlights these differences:

	Sender(s)	Recipients
Romans	Paul, a servant of Jesus Christ, called to be an apostle, set apart for the gospel of God	all God's beloved in Rome, who are called to be saints
1 Corinthians	Paul, called to be an apostle of Christ Jesus by the will of God, and our brother Sosthenes	To the church of God that is in Corinth, to those who are sanctified in Christ Jesus, called to be saints
2 Corinthians	Paul, an apostle of Christ Jesus by the will of God, and Timothy our brother	To the church of God that is in Corinth, including all the saints throughout Achaia
Galatians	Paul an apostle – sent neither by human commission nor from human authorities, but through Jesus Christ and God the Father, who raised him from the dead – and all the members of God's family who are with me	To the churches of Galatia
Ephesians	Paul, an apostle of Christ Jesus by the will of God	To the saints who are in Ephesus and are faithful in Christ Jesus

(cont.)

(*cont.*)

	Sender(s)	Recipients
Philippians	Paul and Timothy, servants of Christ Jesus	To all the saints in Christ Jesus who are in Philippi, with the bishops and deacons
Colossians	Paul, an apostle of Christ Jesus by the will of God, and Timothy our brother	To the saints and faithful brothers and sisters in Christ in Colossae
1 Thessalonians	Paul, Silvanus, and Timothy	To the church of the Thessalonians in God the Father and the Lord Jesus Christ
2 Thessalonians	Paul, Silvanus, and Timothy	To the church of the Thessalonians in God the Father and the Lord Jesus Christ

Consider first the various ways in which the sender(s) are identified in the above salutations. Paul generally refers to himself as "an apostle" in his greetings, the Thessalonian correspondence and Philippians providing the only exceptions. In only two of the nine letters, moreover, Philippians and Romans, does Paul refer to himself as a "servant" (δοῦλος). The data overlaps to leave Philippians as the only epistle traditionally assigned to Paul in which the author refers to himself solely as a δοῦλος of Christ without any parallel titles or descriptions.[23]

The manner in which the recipients are mentioned should also be noted, since Philippians stands out as exceptional here as well. Although substantial variation obtains among the letters ("God's beloved," "saints," "churches," "church," and "faithful brothers and sisters" are all used), only in Philippians does Paul single out by title church leaders among his intended recipients ("bishops and deacons," 1:1). As I will suggest below, the exceptional nature of the salutation in Paul's letter to the Philippians is to be explained by the social setting in which the congregation found itself. Paul de-emphasizes his own status as an apostle, referring instead to himself as a slave, and publicly acknowledges the honorific titles of the community's leaders, in order to model the kinds of behavior that he deems appropriate for his reconstruction of Roman cultural values relating to honor and social status, behavior which will find its archetypal expression in the humiliation of Christ in Philippians 2:6–8 (see chapter six).

I will first consider Paul's reference to himself and Timothy as "servants of Christ Jesus," and the corresponding omission of the term "apostle." The absence of "apostle" in the salutations of Philippians and 1–2 Thessalonians is generally explained in terms of Paul's relationship with the recipients. Thus, O'Brien reminds us that Paul's authority was not challenged in the Macedonian churches, where the apostle enjoyed "special bonds of affection" with both the Philippians and the Thessalonians. "Apostle," therefore, was unnecessary in the author's salutation.[24] O'Brien is certainly correct to underscore the closeness of the relational bonds between Paul and the Macedonian Christians. The correlation between the presence of "apostle" in Paul's greetings and a corresponding threat to Paul's authority, however, is not a consistent one. Certainly Paul's authority was at stake in Galatia and Corinth, and in each case Paul emphasizes his divinely appointed status as "an apostle." One would be hard-pressed to argue, however, that Paul's apostleship was particularly challenged in Rome, or in the churches around Ephesus, and yet in the salutations of Romans, Ephesians, and Colossians the author nevertheless refers to himself as "an apostle."

Fee acknowledges the close relationship between author and audience and proceeds to consider the kind of letter that such a relationship would generate. He finds explanation for the absence of "apostle" in Philippians 1:1 in his identification of the epistle as a friendship letter. He observes, "A letter primarily of friendship and exhortation, not of persuasion, does not need a reminder of Paul's apostleship; indeed, the summons to obedience in this letter is predicated altogether on the secure nature of their mutual friendship."[25] This would certainly explain why the greeting in Philippians, in distinction even from Romans, Ephesians, and Colossians, lacks the designation "apostle," since only Philippians has been formally crafted as a letter of friendship. I could be persuaded by Fee's explanation, if the absence of "apostle" in the greeting were not accompanied by the other anomalous characteristics outlined above, including the identification of the senders as "servants of Christ Jesus," without any parallel titles or qualifiers.[26] In my view, the explanation of the omission of "apostle" is to be found neither in the relationship between Paul and the recipients (O'Brien) nor in the literary form of the letter (Fee), but, rather, in the challenges posed by the social values and cultural codes that characterized relational life in Roman Philippi.

Two explanations of the phrase "servants of Christ Jesus" surface most often in the scholarly literature. The first reads the phrase in a positive sense, based on background material from the LXX. In the Greek Old Testament, δοῦλος was commonly used to designate persons whom

God used, and through whom he spoke, at turning points in Israel's history. Thus, Moses (Neh. 10:29), Joshua (Josh. 24:29), David (Ps. 88:21 [LXX]), and Jonah (2 Kings [4 Kgdms] 14:25) are each called "servant (δοῦλος) of the Lord." Although the term was also commonly used for slaves in the Old Testament, the addition of the qualifier "of the Lord" invested the term δοῦλος with all the honorific connotations associated with divinely bestowed authority. This background is then imported into Philippians 1:1, where, it is argued, the phrase "servants of Christ Jesus" is to be understood as an honorific title.[27]

The second major alternative situates δοῦλος in a Greco-Roman setting, resulting in a distinctly different connotation. Given the pervasive presence of slavery in the ancient world, Fee asserts that "no one would have thought it (δοῦλος) to refer other than to those owned by, and subservient to, the master of a household."[28] Instead of nuances of honor and divine authority (see above) the term would carry negative connotations of servility, humility, and obedience. Perhaps, as some have suggested, both connotations are present.[29] The social setting of the colony and the predominantly Gentile audience, however, argue in favor of privileging the Greco-Roman background as the key to interpreting the term δοῦλος in Philippians 1:1. So does the content of the epistle. O'Brien is surely on the mark to conclude, "In a letter that gives prominence to humility it is more likely that Paul is focusing on the word's reference to lowly service than its nuance of privileged position."[30] The dishonor associated with slavery in the Roman mind should thus be understood to constitute the key aspect of the term's semantic resonance.[31]

Preoccupation in the colony with rank and social status, therefore, sufficiently explains the exceptional nature of Paul's salutation to the Christians in Philippi. Paul, who had the legitimate right to proclaim his apostolic status, chose instead to refer to himself as a lowly δοῦλος. Those in the Christian community who felt constrained to adopt the honor-seeking practices of the colony's social value system, by living according to "selfish ambition or conceit" (ἐριθείαν . . . κενοδοξίαν, 2:3), would have been forcefully challenged by the esteemed apostle's example.[32]

We turn now to the designated recipients of the letter. The presence of "bishops and deacons" (ἐπισκόποις καὶ διακόνοις) in Paul's opening greeting has elicited scholarly dialogue for centuries, often in the service of various preconceived notions of the development and social organization of early Christian communities. While the recent application of models from sociology and cultural anthropology promises to bring some clarification to the debate, no single reconstruction of the nature and development of leadership in the early church presently commands scholarly consensus.[33] Pilhofer assumes from the singly attested presence of the title "bishops" in Philippians that, at this time, Christian leaders were called ἐπίσκοποι only at Philippi. He attributes the anomaly to "das 'römische' Klima der Kolonie."[34] In contrast to Pilhofer, I understand the position of overseer to have been relatively widespread by the early 60s CE, the term ἐπίσκοποι being interchangeable with the more familiar πρεσβύτεροι (Acts 14:23; 20:17; Titus 1:5; Jas. 5:14; 1 Pet. 5:1). Although local Christian communities did not wholly duplicate the variety of honors and offices characteristic of other voluntary associations during the mid-first century, specific leadership positions appear deeply embedded in the literature, and it is most reasonable to trace the position of πρεσβύτερος/ἐπίσκοπος back, with Luke, to the founding of these congregations (Acts 14:23). Indeed, the rather widespread use of ἐπίσκοπος in later literature (Acts 20:28; 1 Tim. 3:2; Titus 1:7) weakens Pilhofer's association of the term solely with the "römische Klima" of Philippi.

The Roman setting does inform the present inquiry, however, in a somewhat different way. The social stratification of the colony sheds light not upon the particular term in question but, rather, upon the fact that Paul specifically addresses local congregational leaders at all here. Paul's intentions become most transparent when we place the anomalous presence of "bishops and deacons" alongside the omission of "apostle" and Paul's self-designation as "servant" in the salutation. In marked antithesis to cultural norms relating to honor, office, and social status, Paul begins, at the outset of his epistle, to model a principle expressly stated, and exemplified in Jesus, later in the letter (2:5, 6–8). By refraining from calling attention to his apostolic office, and instead honoring the congregation's leaders by singling them out by title, Paul directly undermines the social values of the colony, which viewed office as a prize to be competitively sought – and, once attained, publicly proclaimed – in order to enhance the holder's social status.[35]

Philippians 3:5–6 – Paul's Jewish *cursus*

Philippians 3:5–6 is one of several autobiographical passages among Paul's letters (see also Gal. 1:13–2:14; 2 Cor. 11:23–12:12). Paul presents his Jewish background in the context of a warning passage which reads as follows:

> ² Beware of the dogs, beware of the evil workers, beware of those who mutilate the flesh! ³ For it is we who are the circumcision, who worship in the Spirit of God and boast in Christ Jesus and have no confidence in the flesh – ⁴ even though I, too, have reason for confidence in the flesh. If anyone else has reason to be confident in the flesh, I have more: ⁵ circumcised on the eighth day, a member of the people of Israel, of the tribe of Benjamin, a Hebrew born of Hebrews; as to the law, a Pharisee; ⁶ as to zeal, a persecutor of the church; as to righteousness under the law, blameless. (Phil. 3:2–7)

I am particularly interested here in the list of honors and achievements (vv. 5–6), but the list must be situated in its surrounding context for Paul's rhetorical strategy to be fully appreciated. In this regard, I make a number of assumptions with respect to the interpretation of Philippians 3:2–4, which set the stage for Paul's autobiographical comments in the verses that follow.

First of all, I take Paul's strong language to be directed against Jewish Messianists who taught the necessity of circumcision for Gentile converts to the Jesus movement.[36] This represents majority consensus and need not be argued anew. That circumcision is the main issue generating Paul's rhetoric is demonstrated by (a) the reference to "those who mutilate the flesh" (τὴν κατατομήν), (b) the counter-assertion, "For it is we who are the circumcision" (ἡμεῖς γάρ ἐσμεν ἡ περιτομή), (c) the threefold repetition of the expression "confidence/confident in the flesh" (ἐν σαρκὶ πεποιθότες ... πεποίθησιν καὶ ἐν σαρκί ... πεποιθέναι ἐν σαρκί), and, finally, (d) the fact that the first piece of autobiographical information that Paul provides is "circumcised on the eighth day" (περιτομῇ ὀκταήμερος).

Secondly, with most expositors I assume that Paul, in the ensuing context, moves beyond the issue of circumcision as a mark of membership in the people of God to that of meritorious Jewish privilege and achievement in general, that is, from the sociological to the theological, although I suspect that such distinctions would strike the apostle as somewhat imposed and artificial. The pivotal expression in this regard is "confidence in the flesh," which first appears, I suggest, primarily in reference to circumcision (v. 3) but is then used more generally in verse 4, to refer to Paul's inherited and achieved status in Judaism in general. The expansion of meaning is indicated by the fact that Paul moves far beyond "circumcision" in delineating the reasons for his "confidence in the flesh" in the autobiographical phrases that follow.[37]

Given the content of verses 5–6, many have understandably sought to limit this expanded connotation of "in the flesh" to the realm of Jewish self-confidence.[38] Others interpret "in the flesh," more generally, as "a comprehensive expression to denote all that in which human beings place their trust."[39] Fee is representative: "As before, 'in the flesh' refers first to the rite of circumcision, but now carries all the theological overtones of trying to have grounds for boasting before God on the basis of human achievement, the ultimate 'self-centered' expression of life."[40] O'Brien makes room for both perspectives by taking the expression "in the flesh" in a comprehensive sense while, at the same time, viewing verses 5–6 as a culturally specific example of what such human achievement might entail for a Jew of Paul's stature.[41]

I side with those who argue for a comprehensive meaning for "in the flesh" in Philippians 3, but I would make the case differently. The content of Paul's autobiography in verses 5–6 is quintessentially Jewish and remains so throughout the ensuing verses. Based solely on content, then, I find it difficult to postulate a broader meaning for "in the flesh" without importing the idea from other Pauline letters. Although expressions such as "whatever gains I had" (v. 7) and "everything" (v. 8) might be taken to imply that Paul has moved beyond a specifically Jewish context to consider human boasting in general, the immediate return to "righteousness . . . that comes from the law" (v. 9) suggests otherwise. Had Paul intended the content of his list of privileges to have universal connotations, moreover, we might expect him to include his Roman citizenship among his pre-Christian honors.

It is not the content, then, of the various terms and phrases in Philippians 3 which encourages a more comprehensive reading of "in the flesh" (v. 4). Rather, it is the rhetorical framework in which Paul presents his status and accomplishments that would have given the phrase "confidence in the flesh" a trans-Jewish resonance for the first Gentile hearers of the letter. The manner in which Paul outlines his inherited status and achievements in Judaism would have pointedly resonated in a Roman setting, where the display of one's honors in *cursus* form was familiar to all. Listeners steeped in the social world of Roman Philippi could hardly have heard Paul's list of accomplishments without immediately reflecting upon the multitude of inscriptions that confronted them on a daily basis with the honors and achievements of their fellow-colonists. Paul thus appropriates Roman *cursus* ideology in order to present specifically Jewish reasons for boasting in a decidedly Roman framework. Philippians 3:5–6 constitutes Paul's pre-Christian *cursus honorum*.

Philippians 3:5–6 stands out as unique among Paul's autobiographical statements in several ways. Scholars have long noted what O'Brien refers to as the "tight form and terseness of these seven personal statements" (vv. 5–6).[42] Paul simply lists the various expressions one after another, without any connecting conjunctions. Verbal forms are strikingly absent as well, until the final phrase of the passage. The asyndetic structure brings to mind the economy of chisel and stone, rather than the more liberal material resources of pen and papyrus. The language contrasts markedly, in this regard, with the surrounding context, where Paul expresses his thoughts in complete sentences, generally employing appropriate connectives at every turn (vv. 2–3; vv. 7–11). O'Brien's diagram highlights the *cursus*-like structure of verses 5–6:

    περιτομῇ ὀκταήμερος
      ἐκ γένους Ἰσραήλ
        [ἐκ] φυλῆς Βενιαμίν
          Ἑβραῖος ἐξ Ἑβραίων
    κατὰ νόμον – Φαρισαῖος
      κατὰ ζῆλος – διώκων τὴν ἐκκλησίαν
        κατὰ δικαιοσύνην – τὴν ἐν νόμῳ – γενόμενος ἄμεμπτος.

The text should be compared grammatically and conceptually with the parallels in Galatians 1:13–14 and 2 Corinthians 11:22–29, where Paul also offers autobiographical statements concerning his Jewish past. The information given in Galatians 1, for example, directly parallels several phrases from Philippians 3.[43] The literary framework, however, is markedly different. In contrast to the *cursus* structure of Philippians 3, Paul presents his background in Galatians as a narrative framed in complete sentences, each of which is seamlessly integrated into the flow of the surrounding context. The parallel from 2 Corinthians is somewhat closer to our text structurally, but even there finite verbs are employed, and the grammar is much more varied, as Paul enumerates both his Jewish privileges and his sacrifices for the cause of Christ.

Note, as well, the twofold structure of the text, as diagrammed above. After listing circumcision (which may be regarded as the central point of dispute with the Judaizers), Paul presents his autobiography in two distinct sections, the first governed by the preposition ἐκ, the second by κατά. The honors enumerated in these two portions of the passage correspond, interestingly enough, to what social scientists call ascribed honor and acquired honor, respectively. Scholars define ascribed honor as a person's "basic honor level . . . inherited from the family at birth." Acquired (or achieved) honor represents honor conferred on the basis of deeds and accomplishments deemed virtuous by one's social peers.[44] It is important to note, in this regard, that the order in which Paul presents his Jewish status corresponds precisely to the typical structure of honor inscriptions found in the colony (see chapter four). In both Philippians 3:5–6 and the inscriptions from Philippi, ascribed honor precedes acquired honor. Thus, the elite class in Philippi present their birth status, followed by the honorific offices they have acquired:

> L(ucio) Decimio L(uci) f(ilio)
> Vol(tinia), q(uaestor), IIvir(o)[45]
>
> For Lucius Decimius, son of Lucius, of the tribe Voltinia, quaestor, duumvir

Similarly, Publius Marius Valens:

> P(ublius) Marius P(ubli) f(ilius) Vol(tinia) Valens or(namentis) dec(urionatus) hon(oratus), aed(ilis), id(em) Philipp(is), decurio,
> flamen divi Antonini Pii, IIvir, mun(erarius)[46]
>
> Publius Marius Valens, son of Publius, from the tribe Voltinia, honored with the decorations of a decurion, aedile, also decurion of Philippi, priest of the divine Antoninus Pius, duumvir, sponsor of games

The typical military *cursus* also began with ascribed honor (birth status) and proceeded to list the honoree's military achievements (acquired honor):

> C(aio) Mucio Q(uinti) f(ilio) Fab(ia)
> Scaevae, primopilo
> leg(ionis) VI Ferratae, praef(ecto)
> c(o)hort(is), ex testamento
> ipsius C(aius) Mucius C(ai) f(ilius) Fab(ia)
> Scaeva posuit[47]
>
> For Gaius Mucius Scaeva, son of Quintus, from the tribe Fabia, the first centurion of the Sixth Legion Ferrata, prefect of the cohort, on the basis of his own will, Gaius Mucius Scaeva, son of Gaius, has set up (this inscription)

It is helpful, in this regard, to compare Paul's presentation of his Jewish past in Galatians 1:13–14 with the structure of Philippians 3:4–6 and the *cursus* inscriptions from the colony, as outlined above. In Galatians Paul makes no attempt to order his honors in *cursus* form (ascribed honor followed by acquired honor). Rather, he focuses solely on his adult achievements (acquired honor) and makes no direct reference to his natal status (ascribed honor).[48] Although similar in content to 2 Corinthians 11 or Galatians 1, structurally Philippians 3 thus has more in common with Philippi's honor inscriptions than with the autobiographical statements found elsewhere in Paul's letters.[49]

There are other differences as well. Peter Pilhofer finds direct parallels for several of Paul's references among the symbols of social status that were important to persons in Roman Philippi:[50]

> *toga (virilis)* – περιτομῇ ὀκταήμερος
> *civis Romanus* – ἐκ γένους Ἰσραήλ
> *tribu Voltinia* – φυλῆς Βενιαμίν
> *Cai filius* – Ἑβραῖος ἐξ Ἑβραίων

It may very well be that Paul's expressions would have brought to mind the above parallels among those who first heard the letter. Pilhofer's arguments tend to persuade.[51] At any rate, given the preoccupation with citizen status in the colony of Philippi, the second parallel listed above – the one between Paul's tribe of Benjamin and *tribu Voltinia* – is certainly the most transparent. Supporting this assertion is the fact that φυλή is the Greek equivalent to the Latin *tribus*. Compare, for example, the Greek expressions φυλῆς Κορνηλίας (*tribu Cornelia*), φυλῆς Αἰμιλίας (*tribu Aemilia*), φυλῆς Πολλία (*tribu Pollia*).[52] It is also noteworthy that references to Paul's tribal origins are strikingly absent from the autobiographical parallels in Galatians and 2 Corinthians. In fact, the only other place where Paul refers to his membership in the tribe of Benjamin is Romans 11:1, also, interestingly enough, in a letter addressing persons living in a decidedly Roman context. As Pilhofer notes, the mention of Paul's tribe in Philippians can hardly be accidental. By drawing attention to his membership in the tribe of Benjamin (3:4), and then dismissing it as "rubbish" in the ensuing context (3:8), Paul pointedly challenges those who would privilege their Roman citizen status vis-à-vis their fellow-believers in the church in Philippi.[53]

Finally, Paul's *cursus* in Philippians 3 also stands out as exceptional in function and tone among Paul's various statements regarding his Jewish past. As a number of commentators have recognized, our text is unique among Paul's autobiographical statements in its paradigmatic nature. Galatians 1 and 2 Corinthians 11 are both transparently apologetic in tone. In each case Paul's primary aim is to defend himself and his ministry, not to offer himself as an example to his readers. Philippians 3, in contrast, presents Paul as a paradigm for his readers to follow (see vv. 15–17). Thus Peter Oakes specifically contrasts our text with the parallels in Galatians and 2 Corinthians, viewing Philippians 3:4–16 as one of several passages in the letter in which "Paul primarily writes about himself in order to give an example of the way he wants the Philippians to live."[54]

Not only, therefore, has Paul given his pedigree in Philippians 3 a distinct grammatical framework and vocabulary. He has also presented his Jewish honors (rather, his evaluation of them from his present perspective as a Christian) as a model for his readers to emulate. The reason in both cases, I maintain, relates to the social setting of Paul's intended audience. The recipients of the letter lived in a social context in which elite claims to ascribed honor (birth status) and acquired honor (virtuous deeds and civic and military posts) were proclaimed in the form of *cursus* inscriptions throughout the colony. As we have seen, moreover, these values and practices were replicated in miniature among the members of various cult groups and in other social settings. For Paul to dismiss his indisputably impressive Jewish *cursus* as "rubbish" (σκύβαλα, v. 8) would have profoundly challenged the social sensibilities of those steeped in the values of the dominant culture of Roman Philippi.[55]

Summary

Data gleaned from Acts and Philippians accords precisely with information found in the inscriptions from Roman Philippi. Concern with honor and social status deeply marked the social orientation of the colony, a reality of which both Luke and Paul were profoundly aware. Perhaps more than any of Paul's converts, Christians in the community at Philippi would have been under great pressure to conform, in their own social relations, to the marked verticality of the surrounding environment. As we have seen, voluntary associations attested from Philippi inevitably replicated the social stratification of the dominant culture. Philippian Christians would naturally tend to adopt similar values and, indeed, they did so, as later inscriptions indicate. In the second century, honors in the ἐκκλησία would be trumpeted in a fashion similar to the display of honors in the civic arena. A certain Αὐρήλιος Κυριακός, for example, publicly identifies himself as διδάσκαλος.[56] Ποσιδονία wants passers-by to esteem her as διακονίσση; Πανχαρία as ἐλαχίστη κανονική.[57]

Paul, however, will have no part of this, adopting, instead, a worldview diametrically opposed to the norms of the colony in which his converts reside. Paul's attitude toward the social values of the colony is evidenced both in his behavior, as portrayed in the Philippian narrative in Acts, and in the way in which he has crafted his salutation and his own autobiography in the letter to the Philippians. In his epistle Paul urges his readers to resist accommodation to the social verticality and pride of honors which so indelibly left their mark on public life in Philippi, by radically redefining, vis-à-vis the dominant culture, the kind of behavior to be honored among members of the Christian ἐκκλησία. And nowhere are Paul's convictions in this regard more apparent than in his presentation of the humility of Christ Jesus in 2:6–11. It is to that great Christological masterpiece that we now turn.

6

CARMEN CHRISTI AS CURSUS PUDORUM

> In humility regard others as better than yourselves.
> Philippians 2:3

Scholarly attention to Philippians 2:6–11 has generated an almost unmanageable bibliography.[1] Much of this work has been preoccupied with issues of ontological Christology, as commentators have sought to clarify the meaning of expressions such as μορφῇ θεοῦ, ἁρπαγμόν, τὸ εἶναι ἴσα θεῷ, and ἑαυτὸν ἐκένωσεν, and the implications of these phrases for our understanding of the nature of the incarnation. My concerns here relate not to ontology but, rather, to the manner in which Paul's picture of the self-humiliation of Jesus would have resonated in the readers' social context. I acknowledge that ontological questions can reasonably be asked of the text. Paul's purpose, however, is not to elucidate a static doctrine of the two natures of Christ but, rather, to engender behavior among his readers which he deems appropriate for those whose citizenship is in heaven.[2] To accomplish this end, Paul offers his readers a Jesus who embarks on what can only be viewed from the perspective of the dominant culture as a *cursus pudorum* – "a succession (or race) of ignominies." The imitation of Jesus, then, to which Paul calls his readers presupposes a wholesale inversion of the relational orientation of the dominant culture, particularly as we have seen it realized in the pronounced social verticality of the colony of Roman Philippi.

Philippians 2:6–8: a *cursus pudorum*

The broad framework of Ernst Lohmeyer's structural outline of Philippians 2:6–11 will be adopted here for the purpose of my analysis.[3] Lohmeyer divided the text into two strophes with three stanzas each. The first strophe is outlined as follows:

ὃς ἐν μορφῇ θεοῦ ὑπάρχων
οὐχ ἁρπαγμὸν ἡγήσατο
τὸ εἶναι ἴσα θεῷ

ἀλλὰ ἑαυτὸν ἐκένωσεν
μορφὴν δούλου λαβών
ἐν ὁμοιώματι ἀνθρώπων γενόμενος

καὶ σχήματι εὑρεθεὶς ὡς ἄνθρωπος
ἐταπείνωσεν ἑαυτὸν
γενόμενος ὑπήκοος μέχρι θανάτου
           [θανάτου δὲ σταυροῦ][4]

I am not concerned to defend the details of the above framework, for example, the subdivision of each stanza into three lines, and the manner in which these divisions are made. In the present connection, it is sufficient to note the clarity with which the author of our text, whom I tentatively assume to be Paul, has organized his picture of the humiliation of Jesus into three distinct and progressive stages, each marked by the presence of a finite aorist verb with various participial modifiers.[5]

What has not been sufficiently emphasized in the literature is that Paul's portrayal of Jesus consists of three progressively degrading positions of social status in the Roman world, corresponding to the structure outlined above, as Jesus descends a *cursus pudorum* from equality with God (Status Level One), through the taking on of humanity and the status of a slave (Status Level Two), to the public humiliation of death on a cross (Status Level Three).[6] I have diagrammed the text with movement both down and across the page, in an attempt to capture the social descent of Jesus' pilgrimage:

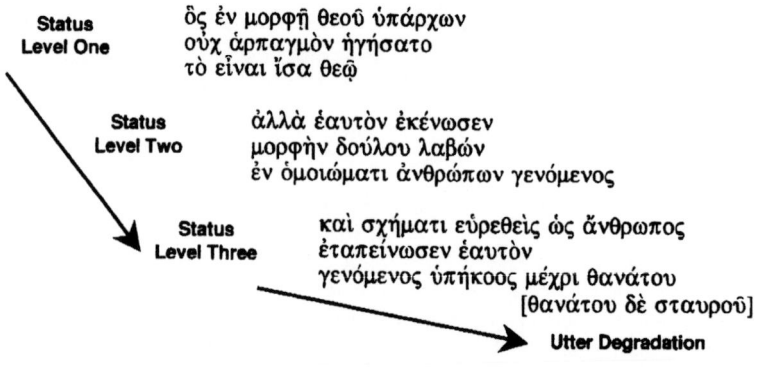

In the discussion that follows I will examine the text according to the three status levels outlined above. Special attention will be directed to those expressions in the passage which Paul utilized in order to challenge the Christians in Philippi to resist the temptation to accommodate themselves to surrounding social values. Most striking in this regard are the terms δούλου (v. 7) and σταυροῦ (v. 8), which represent, respectively, the most dishonorable public *status* and the most dishonorable public *humiliation* imaginable in the world of Roman antiquity. That a crucified δοῦλος is identified in the ensuing verses as one who is greatly honored by the deity – indeed, logically so (διὸ καί, v. 9) – utterly redefines social relations as understood among persons in the ancient world.

Status Level One: equality with God

Important ideas found in the first stage of Christ's *cursus* include ἐν μορφῇ θεοῦ, ἁρπαγμόν, and τὸ εἶναι ἴσα θεῷ. Interpretations of the first two expressions continue to resist scholarly consensus; ἐν μορφῇ θεοῦ, in particular, constitutes a notorious *crux* of Pauline Christology. I do not profess to offer any strikingly new alternatives for understanding these debated terms and phrases. I do suggest, however, that reading Philippians 2:6–8 against the social background of Roman Philippi tips the scales strongly in favor of specific interpretative options, some of which have played a part in scholarly dialogue for decades.

ὃς ἐν μορφῇ θεοῦ ὑπάρχων[7]

Earlier scholarship generally interpreted μορφῇ θεοῦ ("the form of God") in 2:6 as a reference to God's "glory" (δόξα): "that radiating brilliance of God by which the writers of the Old Testament and intertestamental literature often described him and his presence."[8] Others, following E. Schweizer, have seen in the phrase a reference to Christ's status, his original position vis-à-vis God.[9] More recently, Stephen Fowl has argued for taking μορφῇ in the traditional sense, as a reference to God's visible splendor or "glory," but with a "Schweizerian" twist. Paul draws upon the μορφή–δόξα connection in order to "[say] something about Christ's exalted status or position."[10] Fowl has accurately identified the meaning of Paul's expression, given the social situation of Paul's readers and his corresponding intentions in the hymn. The phrase ἐν μορφῇ θεοῦ directly refers to Christ's glory and does so in order to underline Christ's exalted social status, in preparation for the ensuing humiliation of his *cursus pudorum*.

The two primary objections to the μορφή–δόξα connection are easily dealt with in ways that further support my suggested interpretation of the passage. The first objection maintains that μορφή and δόξα are not, in fact, synonymous. The second challenge to the μορφή–δόξα connection relates to the broader context where, it is argued, the idea contained in δόξα cannot be applied to μορφή in the (clearly intended) parallel expression, μορφὴν δούλου (v. 7). Simply put, the first objection has missed the point, and clarification here renders the second objection a non-issue. The relationship argued for between μορφή and δόξα is not one of interchangeable synonymity. In our passage μορφή connotes, more generally, the visible form that is characteristic of the particular genitival modifier that happens to be in view. In verse 6, God (θεοῦ) is the modifier, and the μορφή, or visible manifestation, of God is his "glory." Paul thus has in mind here "Christ's eternal δόξα not because μορφή *equals* δόξα but because the μορφὴ θεοῦ is δόξα."[11] It is the entire expression, μορφὴ θεοῦ – not just μορφή, that is being read in terms of God's glory. This, in turn, paves the way for addressing the second objection, by preserving the (antithetical) parallelism between μορφῇ θεοῦ and μορφὴν δούλου. A change in genitival modifier – from θεοῦ to δούλου (v. 7) – demands a change in the connotation of μορφή: from δόξα to ἀδοξία, or something of the sort. The visible manifestation of God is "glory"; that of a slave is "dishonor" or "ill repute." All of this nicely accords with Paul's emphasis on social status throughout Philippians 2:6–11.

A final objection to interpreting μορφή in terms of visible form or appearance relates to the use of the preposition ἐν in the phrase ἐν μορφῇ θεοῦ. Some have found it unacceptably awkward to speak of a person "being in an appearance" (ἐν μορφῇ . . . ὑπάρχων). O'Brien responds: "The picture of the preexistent Christ clothed in the garments of divine majesty and splendour could be said to make adequate sense of the phrase."[12] This reference to glory as clothing, also taken up by Hawthorne, is of potential significance here, given the relationship between personal attire and social status in the Roman world (see chapter one).[13] O'Brien cites as parallel a phrase from Luke's gospel, where our participle and preposition appear in a similar connection: οἱ ἐν ἱματισμῷ ἐνδόξῳ καὶ τρυφῇ ὑπάρχοντες (7:25). In Luke, status and clothing are clearly in view. O'Brien suggests that the same is the case in Philippians 2: "The expression [ἐν μορφῇ θεοῦ] does not refer simply to external appearance but pictures the preexistent Christ as clothed in garments of divine majesty and splendour."[14]

We must proceed with caution here, since explicit references to clothing, as such, are not to be found in Philippians 2. Nevertheless, (a) the social setting of Paul's readers, (b) the emphasis in μορφή on outward appearance, (c) the Lukan parallel, and (d) the association of the ideas of "glory" and "clothing" elsewhere in biblical literature (Job 40:10; Matt. 6:29; Luke 12:27) all support the plausibility of a "glory"–"clothing" connection in the present context. In concert with Roman social values, then, the glory with which the preexistent Christ is clothed functions as a public expression of his social status.[15]

οὐχ ἁρπαγμὸν ἡγήσατο τὸ εἶναι ἴσα θεῷ

The political background of our passage will be treated in some detail below when I consider the significance of κύριος for Paul's argument (v. 11). Mikael Tellbe, however, correctly sees Jesus portrayed throughout the text as "an imperial figure with universal authority," and an allusion to the Roman emperor is already present in the first stanza of the hymn in the expression τὸ εἶναι ἴσα θεῷ.[16] Tellbe cites a variety of texts in which the idea of equality with God is specifically associated with a king or emperor. A second-century CE papyrus reads τὶ θεός; τὸ κρατοῦν. τὶ βασιλεύς; ἰσόθεος – "What is a God? Exercising power. What is a king? One who is equal with a God" (*Pap. Heid.* 1716.5). 2 Maccabees portrays a finally humbled Antiochus IV allegedly confessing, δίκαιον ὑποτάσσεσθαι τῷ θεῷ καὶ μὴ θνητὸν ὄντα ἰσόθεα φρονεῖν – "It is just to submit oneself to God and not to think that one who is mortal is equal to God" (9:12). Appian uses similar language when he discusses honors given to Julius Caesar by Augustus. Augustus' actions on behalf of Caesar provide the blueprint for later emperors to receive honors "equal to gods" (ἰσόθεοι) (*BCiv.* 2.148).

More problematic is determining the meaning of the much debated expression ἁρπαγμόν. A history of the interpretation could fill a chapter itself. Thankfully, R. W. Hoover's groundbreaking exploration of the linguistic background of the term has finally provided the basis for a clear understanding of the term in its literary and social context. Hoover insists on taking ἁρπαγμὸν ἡγήσατο as an idiom and concludes, "in every instance which I have examined, this idiomatic expression refers to something already present and at one's disposal. The question . . . is not whether one possesses something, but whether or not one chooses to exploit something."[17] The results of all this for the meaning of the expression can be seen in the translations of the RSV and the NRSV, respectively. The more recent NRSV translation reflects the influence of Hoover's analysis:

did not count equality with God *a thing to be grasped.* (RSV)

did not regard equality with God as *something to be exploited.* (NRSV)

Hoover's interpretation has not gone unchallenged, but it is fair to say that it now represents majority opinion in the scholarly community.[18] As the NRSV translation indicates, Hoover's understanding assumes that the preincarnate Christ already possessed what is expressed in the phrase "equality with God." That is, the "grasping" or "advantage-taking" expressed in ἁρπαγμόν "does not have τὸ εἶναι ἴσα θεῷ as its goal; rather, it begins from it."[19] It is thus the *manner* in which Christ utilizes his equality with God – not the attaining thereof – that is in view. This nicely accords with my identification of verse 6 as Status Level One in Christ's *cursus pudorum*. Given the location of verse 6 at the apex of the *cursus*, it makes good sense to view τὸ εἶναι ἴσα θεῷ as status *possessed* ("something to be exploited") rather than status *desired* ("something to be grasped"). The interpretation of Philippians 2:6–8 as a *cursus pudorum* thus further reinforces the viability of Hoover's interpretation of ἁρπαγμόν in the present context.

Understanding the various expressions of Philippians 2:6 as outlined above elucidates other debated issues. The relationship between μορφῇ θεοῦ and τὸ εἶναι ἴσα θεῷ, for example, has been an ongoing source of contention. An older interpretation of ἁρπαγμόν ("a thing to be grasped," RSV, above) encouraged some interpreters to see a significant distinction in meaning between τὸ εἶναι ἴσα θεῷ and μορφῇ θεοῦ earlier in the verse.[20] In view of the above discussion, however, which sees both τὸ εἶναι ἴσα θεῷ and μορφῇ θεοῦ as already in Christ's possession, it is preferable to understand the two phrases in close connection. As Hawthorne explains, "'the being equal with God' is precisely another way of saying 'in the form of God.'"[21] Reading the verse in this way also makes good sense of the grammar. Syntactically, the expression τὸ εἶναι ἴσα θεῷ is seen to refer back epexegetically to ὃς ἐν μορφῇ θεοῦ ὑπάρχων, so that we might translate the former "this divine equality."[22] In both cases the idea of status stands at the forefront.

We now return to the larger context of the stanza as Status Level One of Christ's *cursus pudorum*. The *cursus* reading and the above interpretation of the details of Philippians 2:6 are mutually informing. To summarize, Christ is first publicly presented, in his exalted status, as one whose outward appearance reveals him clothed in the garments of divine glory (ἐν μορφῇ θεοῦ ὑπάρχων). The clause that follows (οὐχ ἁρπαγμὸν ἡγήσατο τὸ εἶναι ἴσα θεῷ) then gives the reader "Christ's disposition or attitude toward that status."[23] This disposition, in turn, will be actualized in the behavior of Christ as he descends his *cursus pudorum* in the ensuing verses (vv. 7–8).

Finally, it is crucial to keep in mind that Christ's disposition and his behavior that follows are intentionally framed by the author to contrast with prevailing Roman convictions and practices relating to honor and social status. Paul, in his presentation of Christ at the apex of his *cursus* in Philippians 2:6, begins to radically reconstruct Roman social values for persons who desire to live life, according to the model of Jesus, as citizens of God's alternative community. In stark contrast to Roman rulers who claimed divine status and utilized their status to further enhance their own glory and honor – and in stark contrast to Philippi's local elite who replicated Rome's values in their own social world – Christ, who genuinely possessed divine status (ἐν μορφῇ θεοῦ ὑπάρχων), viewed his status as something to be willingly surrendered for the benefit of others. Those who wish to follow Jesus, Paul enjoins, must be similarly disposed (2:5).

Status Level Two: assuming the form of a slave

Jesus now begins the profound descent down his *cursus pudorum*. The phrase μορφὴν δούλου λαβών (2:7) will prove most informing in this regard, but I must first dispense with some preliminary issues relating to the interpretation of another important statement in the verse. The *crux interpretum* ἑαυτὸν ἐκένωσεν can be easily handled, for, as Gordon Fee has pointedly emphasized, the debate that has raged over this phrase has been quite unnecessary. Interpreters have been misled because they have assumed the presence of an unspecified genitive qualifier: Christ must have emptied himself "of something." This, in turn, has opened the door to ongoing speculation about the ontology of the incarnate Christ, a concern quite foreign (or, at any rate, secondary) to Paul's argument in Philippians 2. The idea that ἐκένωσεν needs a modifier of some sort – that Christ emptied himself "of something" – is a misleading assumption. In accordance with the progression of the text as an inverted *cursus*, and well within the semantic field of κενόω (as evidenced by specific usages of the term), ἑαυτὸν ἐκένωσεν in Philippians 2:7 should be understood metaphorically, to mean that Christ "emptied *himself*," he poured himself out.[24] The NIV paraphrase, "made himself nothing," nicely reflects the status concerns of the author as he penned the phrase.[25]

The manner in which Jesus "emptied himself" is revealed in two parallel participial clauses that are attached to the main verb. Both μορφὴν δούλου λαβών and ἐν ὁμοιώματι ἀνθρώπων γενόμενος are to be taken in a modal sense, describing the manner in which Christ "made himself nothing." The relationship between the two clauses is less easy to determine, but I suspect that the latter explains the former. That is, by "being born in human likeness" Christ was essentially taking on the form of a slave vis-à-vis his former exalted status as expressed in ἐν μορφῇ θεοῦ ὑπάρχων. For one who "existed in the form of God," becoming a man was tantamount to assuming servile status, humanly speaking.[26] It remains to consider the relationship between slavery and social status in the Roman world.

μορφὴν δούλου λαβών (2:7)

Some interpretations accord little consideration to the social world of Paul's readers as a possible background for elucidating the meaning of δοῦλος in Philippians 2:7. A particularly influential reading, which sees in δοῦλος an allusion to the servant figure in Isaiah 42–53, labors against a variety of objections, not the least of which are (a) the absence elsewhere of servant imagery for Jesus in Paul, and (b) the distinctly different Greek expression used for the idea in the LXX of Isaiah (παῖς μου, Isa. 42:1, *passim*). Other commentators, citing the universal lordship of Christ over all authorities, later enunciated in the passage (v. 10), surmise that δοῦλος (v. 7) refers to Christ's previous "thralldom to the powers of evil," willingly undertaken as part of his self-humiliation.[27] Although Pauline analogies to this second perspective are more easily identified (Gal. 4:3–5), the social location of Paul's Philippian readers opens the door to a much more contextually satisfying interpretation of the term. Neither Old Testament intertextuality nor bondage to cosmic powers is primarily in view. Rather, Paul uses δοῦλος in the present context specifically because of the negative connotations that slavery had for persons preoccupied with honor and social status in Roman Philippi.[28]

"The primary distinction in the law of persons is this, that all men are either free or slaves." So wrote Gaius in his second-century textbook on Roman law.[29] Things were hardly that simple, however, in everyday life, and determining the status of slaves has proven to be a vexing challenge to the social historian, since slavery in antiquity was not a monolithic institution. The majority of slaves can fairly be placed at the bottom of the social hierarchy, suffering to various degrees under the burdens of their tasks and the harshness of their taskmasters. Apuleius' graphic description of a group of rural slaves probably represents common fare in the Roman world:

Good, gods, what scrawny little slaves there were! Their skin was everywhere embroidered with purple welts from their many beatings. Their backs, scarred from floggings, were shaded, as it were, rather than actually covered by their torn patchwork garments. Some wore only flimsy loincloths. All of them, decked out in these rags, carried brands on their foreheads, had their heads half-shaved, and wore chains around their ankles. Their complexions were an ugly yellow; their eyes were so inflamed by the thick dark smoke and the steamy vapor that they could barely see. (*Met.* 9.12)[30]

Slaves in the mines were also notoriously brutalized:

But to continue with the mines, the slaves who are engaged in the working of them produce for their masters revenues in sums defying belief, but they themselves wear out their bodies both by day and by night in the diggings under the earth, dying in large numbers because of the exceptional hardships they endure. For no respite or pause is granted them in their labours, but compelled beneath blows of the overseers to endure the severity of their plight, they throw away their lives in this wretched manner, although certain of them who can endure it, by virtue of their bodily strength and their persevering souls, suffer such hardships over a long period; indeed death in their eyes is more to be desired than life, because of the magnitude of the hardships they must bear. (Diod. Sic. 5.38.1)

At the other end of the spectrum, however, were household slaves who were fortunate enough to serve in the homes of elite owners, some of whom treated their slaves with a modicum of dignity and respect.[31] Most exemplary in this regard was the special relationship Cicero shared with his slave Tiro, who became his master's confidant, secretary, and literary adviser, and whom Cicero later manumitted, in 51 BCE. Pliny, too, apparently acted toward his household slaves with some warmth and consideration:

I am always ready to grant my slaves their freedom, so I don't feel their death is so untimely when they die free men, and I allow even those who remain slaves to make a sort of will which I treat as legally binding. They set out their instructions and requests as they think fit, and I carry them out as if acting under orders. They can distribute their possessions and make any gifts and bequests they like, within the limits of the household.

(*Ep.* 8.16.1–2)

Tiro and the slaves whom Pliny has in view clearly had an easier life than those described in the excerpts from Apuleius and Diodorus.[32]

The differences in quality of life experienced by slaves serving as tutors in elite households versus slaves working on farms and in the mines have led Scott Bartchy to caution against viewing Roman slaves as members of a single social class. Nor should we situate slaves at the bottom of the social-economic pyramid. That position is more reasonably assigned to free day laborers, who generally fared much worse economically than slaves in the Roman world.[33] Others scholars maintain a more traditional view of ancient slavery. James Arlandson, for example, has recently asserted that slaves "had the lowest status of any class." For Arlandson, then, slaves possess a common status, and that status is to be situated, contra Bartchy, near the bottom of the social pyramid.[34]

Consideration of the complexity of social status provides a helpful pathway through this apparent scholarly impasse, while positively affirming the contributions of both Bartchy and Arlandson. A variety of factors – political power, wealth, natal origin, education, gender, occupation, and so forth – converged to determine social status in the ancient world. This was particularly the case for slaves. Bartchy's emphasis upon economic security and the relative honor of a slave's owner as the prime criteria for an individual slave's social location naturally generates a highly variegated picture of slavery, and Bartchy is correct to insist that the specificity of historical analysis produces example after example of slaves and freedmen at nearly every point along the social spectrum.

Social scientists, for their part, tend to operate at higher levels of abstraction than historians, and Arlandson's employment of Lenski's social-scientific model, which assigns slaves in agrarian societies to a single social stratum, has decidedly obscured the variegated reality of slavery in the Roman world. Yet the Lenskian approach is not without its insights, particularly in the present connection. Whether intentional or not, Arlandson's assignment of slaves to a single stratum in the social hierarchy strongly resonates with the thinking of the ancients themselves, at least at the level of elite ideology. Indeed, as we shall see below, focusing upon the common legal status of slaves, inherited at birth – as opposed to the specific social location of individual slaves – produces a rather uniform picture of slavery in the Roman world, and the referent "slave" takes on decidedly negative and socially shameful connotations in the symbolic universe of elite vocabulary. The Roman elite, utilizing as the fundamental evaluative criterion the natal status of the slave, generally relegated *all* slaves – rich or poor, powerful or powerless – to a single class which they situated decidedly below free persons of any stripe on the social pyramid.

As Dale Martin notes, "Slave terminology almost always carries negative connotations in Greco-Roman literature."[35] And it is slave terminology – not the social location of a particular Roman slave – that we are dealing with in the present interpretation of Paul's socially charged rhetoric in Philippians 2:7.

To summarize, although a slave attached to a wealthy οἶκος probably enjoyed a better standard of living than a free day laborer or a struggling peasant, the legal status of the slave in question – and the corresponding public dishonor associated with that status – persisted as the primary consideration of members of the elite who wrestled with the social anomaly of a wealthy or influential slave.[36] And this ideology was not only the province of the elite. Even poor free persons who engaged in servile occupations tenaciously and proudly asserted the honor of their freeborn status vis-à-vis the slave. The traveling companions in the *Satyricon* could not afford to purchase a slave, for example, so they hired a free man to carry their baggage. The narrator relates,

> the hired man, Corax, a shirker of work, kept putting down his bundle and cursing our hurry, and declaring that he would either throw the baggage away or run off with his load. "You seem to think I am a beast of burden or a ship for carrying stones," he cried. "You paid for the services of a man, not a horse. *I am just as free as you are*, although my father did leave me a poor man."
> (Petron. *Sat.* 117.11–12, Loeb, slightly adapted; my italics)

The Stegemanns accurately estimate the importance of legal status, inherited at birth, for determining social standing in the Roman world:

> some emancipated slaves held more political influence than many senators. Yet *the odium of unfree birth clung to them through their lives* and as such was, naturally, not only a problem of their own self-consciousness but also a social factor. For in the mind of the ancient elite, as we have seen, *it was origin, first and above all, that determined status.*[37]

The dishonor associated with slavery, viewed in generic terms by the elite, is widely attested. Dio begins his Stoic discourse on the true meaning of slavery and freedom with a telling description of the majority opinion he wishes to challenge: "Men desire above all things to be free and say that freedom is the greatest of blessings, while slavery is the most shameful and wretched of states (αἴσχιστον καὶ δυστυχέστατον ὑπάρχειν)" (*Or.* 14.1). The association of slavery and shame again occurs later in the same treatise (αἰσχρὸν εἶναι καὶ δουλοπρεπές; *Or.* 14.4), and in another discourse Dio categorically asserts, "No one of a servile background can develop any great pride" (*Or.* 52.8.5).[38]

The "odium of unfree birth," as the Stegemanns put it, above, was apparently difficult to shake, for freedom did little to erase the stigma of slavery for either the manumitted slave or his immediate descendants. Tacitus thus speaks for his elite contemporaries when he asserts that "the freedman is a slave at heart," as, we might add, were his offspring (*Ann.* 2.12). Dishonorable status, like honorable status, was closely connected to family origin, and even freeborn persons with servile ancestors were open to social censure by those of higher status.[39] The *topos* is a common one. Mark Antony, for example, taunted Octavian concerning his patriline, claiming that his great-grandfather was "a freedman and a rope-maker from the country about Thurii" (Suet. *Aug.* 2). Even an amorous affair with a freedperson could render a person of elevated rank vulnerable to the aspersions of others. Poppea Sabina, elite wife of Otho, seduced Nero and proceeded to insult the emperor, after she had gained his favor, by comparing Nero to her husband as follows:

> [Otho's] was true majesty of mind and garb; in him she contemplated the princely manner; while Nero, enchained by his menial paramour and the embraces of Acte [Nero's freedwoman lover], had derived from that servile cohabitation (*contubernio servili*) no tincture of anything but the mean and the shabby (*abiectum et sordidum*). (Tac. *Ann.* 13.46)

Given the social status of slaves, it was considered utterly anomalous for a slave to defend his honor in a public encounter. Cicero categorically asserts, "It belongs to slavery not to speak for or against anyone you wish" (*Sull.* 48).[40] "The slave," according to Phaedrus, "dared not say outright what he wished to say" (3, *prologus* 34–36). Someone should have informed Helvius Mancia. In a treatise entitled "Freely Spoken or Freely Done," Valerius Maximus narrates an entertaining confrontation between Helvius, the son of a manumitted slave, and the esteemed triumvir Pompey, which colorfully highlights the social anomaly of a person tainted with servile blood defending himself in a public setting. Helvius had publicly challenged Pompey before the censors. The challenge was inappropriate to begin with, given the differences in status between the two men, and the verbal sparring that ensued became quite scandalous. Pompey initiated the exchange of insults: "In the altercation Pompeius Magnus said that [Helvius] had been sent back from the underworld to make this charge, casting his lowly station (*humilitatem*) and his old age in his teeth" (6.2.8). Helvius responded in a manner totally out of character with his social status. Instead of cowering before his social superior, Helvius replied to Pompey that, yes, he had, indeed, just returned from the underworld where, as a matter of fact, he had seen a host of persons whom Pompey had unjustly sent there through the recent proscriptions! The narrator, Valerius, finds himself profoundly offended by Helvius' audacious assertions, as his editorial observations clearly show – but not because Helvius' prosopography of Hades is in any way inaccurate. No, our author's concerns relate instead to issues of social impropriety. This "son of a freedman" has, in Valerius' view, proven himself to be "[a] country townsman, smelling of his father's slavery (*servitutem paternam redolenti*), unbridled in his temerity, intolerable in his presumption" (6.2.8).

The poet Horace once claimed that he did not feel obligated, "as would a goodly number," to apologize for being the son of a freedman (*Sat.* 1.6.92). Here Horace stands out as quite exceptional among persons of his social status, and he was most certainly swimming upstream against a torrent of popular opinion in this regard. For when considered generically, by representatives of the dominant culture, the variegated picture of ancient slavery which characterized historical reality in the Roman world fades into the background, and the referent "slave" takes on uniformly negative social connotations, especially where public honor is concerned. Indeed, Ramsay MacMullen can go so far as to make the following incisive observation about the inverse relationship that obtained between slavery and honor in the Roman world: "That slavery even under a humane master negated pride and self-respect was its only essential evil, in the ancient mind."[41] Slaves, in the words of one Roman senator, are the "dregs of society" (Tac. *Ann.* 14.45).

An important issue informing our understanding of Paul's use of δοῦλος in Philippians 2:7 relates to the social stigma of slaves in the Roman army. Rome's citizen army served as a powerful public reminder of the difference in social status between slave and free in the Roman world, since slaves were generally prohibited from serving in the military. At several junctures in its history, however, necessity forced Rome to employ slaves as soldiers and, in each case, the practice was viewed as a highly regrettable compromise of tradition. Valerius Maximus opens his treatise "On Necessity" with the following introductory assertion: "The bitter laws and cruel commands of odious necessity have forced our city and foreign nations to suffer many things grievous not only to understand but even to hear" (7.6.1a). Valerius cites, as his very first example of things "grievous not only to understand but even to hear," the enrollment of slaves in the army:

> In the Second Punic War, when Rome's manpower was exhausted by several adverse battles, the senate on the motion of Consul Ti. Gracchus decreed that slaves be purchased publicly for use in war and to repel the onset of the enemy . . . How great is the violence of sour chance! The community that until then had scorned to have *capite censi* [non-propertied free men] even of free birth as soldiers added bodies drawn from servants' attics and slaves collected from shepherds' huts to its army as special strengthening. So sometimes a noble spirit yields to expediency and bows to the power of Fortune in cases where unless we choose counsels of safety those of handsome show lead to collapse. (7.6.1a)

It was probably easier for the residents of Philippi to recall the more recent employment of slaves in the army of the colony's founding emperor:

> Except as a fire-brigade at Rome, and when there was fear of riots in times of scarcity, [Augustus] employed freedmen as soldiers only twice: once as a guard for the colonies in the vicinity of Illyricum, and again to defend the bank of the river Rhine; even these he levied, when they were slaves, from men and women of means, and at once gave them freedom; and he kept them under their original standard, not mingling them with the soldiers of free birth or arming them in the same fashion.
> (Suet. *Aug.* 25)[42]

Given the disdain with which Romans viewed the anomalous presence of slaves in the army, those descendants of military veterans who formed a small but socially influential portion of the population of first-century Philippi would have been particularly sensitive to the stigma of servile status.

The relevance of all this for Philippians 2 should be patently clear. To ascribe to Jesus the status of δοῦλος (2:7) was to assign to him a position of greatest opprobrium in the social world of Paul's readers. It is hardly coincidental, moreover, that only in Philippians, among his letters, does Paul explicitly depict Jesus as δοῦλος. Paul's readers lived in what was arguably the most status-conscious city in the Roman East, a colony stamped, moreover, with a military mentality sharply attuned (a) to the social stigma of slavery and (b) to the contrasting honor associated with the patriline of an esteemed citizen soldier.

Status Level Three: the shame of the crucified

Jesus now reaches the utter nadir of his *cursus pudorum*, as I proceed to consider a portion of the text which is relatively transparent to the reader, at least with respect to lexicography and syntax. The derogatory connotations of humility (ἐταπείνωσεν ἑαυτόν) in the ancient world are well known, and O. Merk has even made specific application, in this regard, to the social setting of Philippi.[43] Most countercultural vis-à-vis ancient social values is the fact that Christ humbled *himself*. Being humbled was common fare in the ancient world, where males sought to augment their own honor and social status at the expense of the honor and status of their peers. Humbling *oneself*, on the other hand, was not within the purview of the values of the dominant culture. The content of Christ's self-humiliation, moreover, resulted in his utter degradation, as he underwent the most shameful public humiliation imaginable in the ancient world – death on a Roman cross.

ὑπήκοος μέχρι θανάτου

When Paul brings together the ideas of slavery (v. 7) and obedience (ὑπήκοος μέχρι θανάτου, v. 8) in Philippians 2, he draws upon yet another cultural script familiar to his Roman readers. In his study of the function of honor in Roman society, J. Lendon comments extensively on "the audible quiet of the ancient sources on the subject of an aristocrat's obedience."[44] Due to the stigma that slavery cast upon relationships that were based upon the obedience of one party to another, Roman aristocrats intentionally avoided obedience terminology in their interactions with one another. Where functional hierarchy did obtain, other metaphors were generally employed. A consul to a quaestor, for example, was like a father to a son.[45] Even Trajan, in his letters of appointment for equestrian officials, avoided all mention of obedience. Lendon explains the aristocratic aversion to the idea of obedience:

> These evasions are symptoms of more than the euphemistic concealment of an ugly reality; they were an attempt to ameliorate the acute discomfort that stark relations of obedience between one aristocrat and another inspired. This was a world where aristocrats, even privately, did not think of themselves primarily as servants of others.[46]

As Larry Hurtado has recently observed, moreover, "Jesus' crucifixion is explicitly mentioned as the extremity of his obedience."[47] The connection should not be missed. By referencing the idea of obedience (ὑπήκοος) specifically in terms of the shameful way that Jesus died (see below), Paul thus continues to portray Jesus as acting in a manner which sharply contrasts with the cultural values and social codes of the leading municipal figures of first-century Philippi.

θανάτου δὲ σταυροῦ

Martin Hengel has accurately identified θανάτου δὲ σταυροῦ as the most decisive statement in the humiliation of Christ in Philippians 2.[48] The grammatical emphasis that scholars have long noted in the expression perfectly accords, moreover, with my identification of θανάτου δὲ σταυροῦ as the point of final and utter degradation, the nadir of Jesus' social descent as portrayed in Philippians 2:6–8.[49] Two aspects of crucifixion deserve mention in connection with my reflections on the social environment of Philippi: (a) the social stigma attached to crucifixion, and (b) the association of crucifixion with slavery in the Roman mind. Before considering the social ramifications of crucifixion, however, some brief comments are in order concerning another interpretative issue surrounding σταυροῦ in Philippians 2:8.

Debate continues over whether the saving significance of Christ's death is in view in our passage, or whether Paul uses σταυρός simply to depict the historical event of Christ's death as an utterly shameful experience.[50] The dishonor associated with the cross is certainly present, as the discussion below will unequivocally demonstrate. I also find Christ's saving death in view in Paul's argument. Throughout the present chapter I refer to Jesus in Philippians 2 utilizing his status *for the benefit of others.* The idea highlighted in italics is nowhere explicitly specified in the text. It is, however, everywhere present "behind the text." Although I will argue below that the social stigma associated with crucifixion is at the forefront of Paul's σταυρός terminology in 2:8, I am convinced that Christians in the Philippian community who heard Paul's letter read for the first time would have readily understood Jesus' activities to have been accomplished on their behalf. This, after all, was a central aspect of Paul's gospel, and it also provides the ethical foundation for Paul's challenge to his readers to imitate Jesus by deferring to the needs of others in their own community relations (2:5). As Oakes observes of our passage, "Jesus abandons his privileges *for the sake of others.*"[51] We turn now to the social stigma of Roman crucifixion.

Among the ancients, death by crucifixion was universally deemed the most dishonorable experience imaginable. Christians were quite aware of the honor problem posed by a crucified Messiah. According to Justin Martyr, opponents of the Jesus movement "charge us with madness, saying that we give the second place after the unchanging and ever-existing God and begetter of all things to a crucified man" (*Apol.* 1.13.4).[52] As Hengel notes, Justin's ensuing response to this charge "make[s] it clear that the dishonour involved in the death of Jesus by crucifixion was one of the main objections against his being son of God."[53]

The association of the cross with public shame occurs in Christian and pagan literature alike. Celsus, for example, portrays Jesus as one who was "bound in the most ignominious fashion (ἀτιμότατα)" and "executed in a most shameful way (αἴσχιστα)" (Origen, *Contra Celsum*, 6.10).[54] Notice, as well, the explicit juxtaposition of "shame" and "cross" in Hebrews 12:2 (ὑπέμεινεν σταυρὸν αἰσχύνης καταφρονήσας). Centuries later Lactantius still wrestled with the question of why God did not choose for Jesus "an honorable kind of death" (*honestum . . . mortis genus*) but, instead, chose to use an "infamous kind of punishment" (*infami genere supplicii*) (*Institutiones* 4.26.29).[55] The musings of Melito of Sardis pointedly underline the social dissonance associated with the idea of a crucified God:

> He who hung the earth [in its place] is fixed there, he who made all things fast is made fast upon the tree, the Master has been insulted, God has been murdered, the King of Israel has been slain by an Israelitish hand. O strange murder, strange crime! The Master has been treated in unseemly fashion, his body naked, and not even deemed worthy of a covering, that [his nakedness] might not be seen. Therefore the lights [of heaven] turned away, and the day darkened, that it might hide him who was stripped upon the cross.   (*Homily on the Passion* 96)[56]

For Melito, it is the public humiliation of God, not his physical suffering, which he finds so troubling. So, also, for John Chrysostom: "Where can anything be found more paradoxical than this? This death was the most shameful of all, the most accursed . . . This was no ordinary death" (*Homily on Philippians* 8.2.5–11).[57] As Peter O'Brien remarks, "By first-century standards no experience was more loathsomely degrading than this."[58]

The shameful manner in which Jesus died, moreover, carried with it unavoidable implications for those who worshipped him, and Paul's status-sensitive readers at Philippi would surely have been uncomfortable with the fact that a logical line could be drawn, in this regard, from the cross of Christ to the social status of his followers. The shame of crucifixion was, in fact, to be widely utilized in precisely this fashion in later anti-Christian polemic. Caecilius, Minucius Felix's pagan interlocutor, reasons as follows:

> To say that their ceremonies center on a man put to death for his crime and on the fatal wood of the cross is to assign to these abandoned wretches sanctuaries which are appropriate to them and the kind of worship they deserve. (*Octavius* 9.4)[59]

Tacitus had already utilized the dishonor of the crucifixion of Jesus to cast aspersions upon the Christian movement. "Christus," Tacitus informs us, "the founder of the name, had undergone the death penalty in the reign of Tiberius, by sentence of the procurator Pontius Pilate." The resulting "disease" (*malum*) found its way to Rome, "where all things horrible or shameful (*pudenda*) in the world collect and find a vogue" (*Ann.* 15.44.3).[60] For Christians in Philippi, the sharp verticality of their social world would have served only to accentuate the foolishness and shamefulness of worshipping a crucified Christ.

A second aspect of crucifixion which informs our understanding of Philippians 2 is the explicit identification in the Roman world of crucifixion as a punishment particularly fitting for a slave.[61] The frequency with which slaves were crucified was so well known that the practice could serve as material for Plautus' comedies as early as the late third century BCE. A slave named Sceledrus, for example, proclaims, "I know the cross will be my tomb. There's where my ancestors rest – father, grandfather, great-grandfather, and great-great-grandfather" (*Mil.* 372). In another work, Plautus portrays a deceitful slave named Chrysalus expressing concern that his master will uncover his misbehavior. Should such occur, exclaims the slave, "[My master will] change my name for me the minute he gets back, and transform me from Chrysalus ['goldbearer'] to Crossalus ['cross-bearer'] on the spot" (*Bacch.* 362). Cicero will later identify the crucifixion of slaves suspected of rebellion as a tradition belonging to the *mos maiorum*, and the practice of crucifying slaves is attested throughout Roman literature.[62] The connection between slavery and crucifixion was embedded in the memory of Cicero's generation, which witnessed the crucifixion of some six thousand slaves along the Appian Way after the suppression of the revolt under Spartacus (Plut. *Crass.* 8; *Pomp.* 21; Appian, *BCiv.* 1.116). Little changed during the early imperial period. Slaves who avenged the cruelty of their owners, summarized a contemporary of Paul, "stood under the certain threat of crucifixion" (Seneca, *Clem.* 1.26.1).

The crucifixion of slaves was so widespread, in fact, that the expression *servile supplicium* ("slaves' punishment") came to be used as a technical phrase of sorts to refer to death by crucifixion – even where non-slaves were concerned. Scipio Africanus, for example, crucified a group of Roman deserters in Africa during the war with Carthage. Valerius Maximus, who relates the story, criticizes the general's decision: "Roman blood should not be insulted by paying the slaves' penalty (*servile supplicium*), however deservedly" (2.7.12).[63]

It is hardly an accident that crucifixion, the most dishonorable form of public humiliation which the socially conscious Roman elite could employ in their efforts to punish and discourage rebellion among the lower classes, finds itself so closely associated with slavery, the lowest class in the stratified social world of Roman antiquity. The juxtaposition of the two ideas – σταυρός and δοῦλος – served to compound the social stigma associated with both slavery and crucifixion in the ancient world and, thereby, to reinforce in the public arena the social hierarchy that served the interests of the dominant culture.

It would be wrong to conclude my discussion of the shame of the cross without citing the *locus classicus* for the relationship between crucifixion, slavery, and citizen status in the Roman world (each an important issue, as we have seen, for the interpretation of Paul's letter to the Philippians). I refer, of course, to Cicero's prosecution of Verres for crucifying Gavius of Consa, a Roman citizen. The text deserves extended citation. We pick up Cicero's speech just after his description of the flogging of Gavius:

> And so, gentlemen of the jury, in the middle of the forum in Messana, a Roman citizen was flogged. And the whole time, while he suffered, while the whip cracked, no groan, no cry of any kind was heard from the tortured man except "I am a Roman citizen." In reminding Verres of his citizenship, he thought that he would escape the flogging, but when he kept crying out and demanding the rights of citizenship, Verres ordered his staff to make for this poor tormented man a cross. That's right, a cross! . . . Gentlemen of the jury, this was the only cross ever set up in the part of Messana that overlooks the straits. Verres chose this spot, with its view of Italy, deliberately so that Gavius, as he died in pain and agony, might recognize that the narrow straits marked the boundary between slavery and freedom, and so that Italy might see her own son hanging there, suffering the most horrible punishment ever inflicted on slaves. To put a Roman citizen in chains is a wrong. To flog him is a crime. To execute him is almost parricide. And what shall I call crucifixion? So abominable a deed can find no word adequate enough to describe it.

Yet even a crucifixion did not satisfy Verres. "Let him gaze upon his native land. Let him die within sight of justice and liberty." Oh Verres, it was not Gavius, not some unknown man, whom you tortured and crucified in that place, but the universally acknowledged correlation between liberty and Roman citizenship.[64]

As Cicero's compelling rhetoric clearly demonstrates, the association of slavery with crucifixion ("the most horrible punishment ever inflicted on slaves"), on the one hand, and the "universally acknowledged correlation between liberty and Roman citizenship," on the other, occupied polar opposite positions in Rome's symbolic world of honor, shame, and social status.[65]

As a crucified slave, Jesus has arrived at the utter nadir of the *cursus pudorum* outlined in Philippians 2:6–8. If the δοῦλος/ὑπήκοος/σταυρός nexus constituted the sum total of the biography of Jesus known to Paul's readers in Roman Philippi, there would be no reason for them to follow Jesus and every reason to accommodate themselves instead to the colony's social values. Paul, however, assures his readers of a further reality which, he trusts, will compel those who hear his story fully to embrace his Jesus and to summarily reject prevailing cultural norms: God has assigned to Jesus the highest in honors specifically because of the manner in which Jesus chose to use the power at his disposal. And God's unique position at the apex of the social pyramid guarantees both the efficacy of his grant of honor and the public acknowledgment of Jesus' exalted status on the part of all created beings.

Philippians 2:9–11: reconstructing honor

As we discovered above, it is now commonly acknowledged that the expression οὐχ ἁρπαγμὸν ἡγήσατο τὸ εἶναι ἴσα θεῷ (v. 6) portrays Jesus as utilizing power and status in a manner diametrically opposed to the practices of the Roman rulers familiar to the readers. Roman emperors and, it will be recalled from the survey above, the elite in the colony of Philippi, were known for grasping at honors through self-assertion. Jesus' "equality with God" was, in contrast, not something he used for his own advantage. As the text proceeds to relate, Jesus instead willingly used his position for the good of others: he "made himself nothing by taking on the form of a slave... becoming obedient to the point of death – even death on a cross." Such a utilization of power – indeed, a voluntary relinquishing of power and prestige – would have struck members of the Roman elite as abject folly. As Pliny pointedly observed, "It is more uglifying to lose, than never to get, praise" (*Ep.* 8.24.9).[66] Jesus lost it willingly. Paul proceeds to assure his readers, however, that God's value system is utterly unlike that reflected in the social world of Roman Philippi. For it is precisely Jesus' willingness to relinquish his status in the interests of others that explains (διὸ καί, v. 9) his exaltation to the highest position of authority, and results in the ascription to him of the name (κύριος) that is above every name.

Grammatically, verse 9 marks the crucial transition in Paul's story of Jesus. The subject shifts sharply from Christ to ὁ θεός, and grammarians have consistently observed that the addition of καί in the expression διὸ καί denotes that "the inference (διό) is self-evident."[67] This would have only served to render Paul's rhetoric all the more arresting to the first hearers of the letter, since the honoring of a crucified δοῦλος would have been anything but a "self-evident" inference for persons steeped in the social realities of Roman Philippi.[68] No matter, for, as Paul proceeds to demonstrate, One with greater social status than any emperor has utterly redefined that which counts for honor in his alternative society.

Jesus' exaltation: the social background

Here we must appreciate the presence of a twofold cultural script which significantly informs Paul's portrayal of the exaltation of Jesus. First, as discussed in chapter two, individual aristocrats in the Roman world had the ability to confer honor upon one another. This common practice functioned, however, according to some very specific guidelines. In Lendon's words, "To be praised by any given aristocrat added to one's own prestige *in proportion to that aristocrat's prestige.*"[69] This is a crucial qualification. Lendon cites Symmachus, a highly distinguished fourth-century aristocrat, who, although over-modest, nevertheless reveals the above principle in action:

> My testimony can make no addition to your honour. For the old saying runs "to be praised by a praised man," and my humbleness cannot much help the brilliance of your reputation.
>
> (Sym. *Ep.* 9)

Epigraphic evidence clearly demonstrates that the cultural script described above was actively in play in the lives of the elite in Roman Philippi. Several inscriptions specifically cite the emperor as the individual bestowing an honor. Thus, Tiberius Claudius Maximus, veteran of the Dacian and Parthian campaigns, wishes all who read his *cursus* to appreciate the fact that he was decorated by Domitian and Trajan.[70]

The only local resident of Philippi, moreover, who was known to have been admitted to the senatorial order by the second century CE, Gaius Julius Maximus Mucianus, also owed his status to the direct intervention of the emperor. In accord with the social dynamic outlined above, Gaius' brother spares no expense to publicize, in the heart of the city (Philippi's forum), the emperor's role in honoring Gaius with the *latus clavus*:

> [C(aio)] Iul(io) C(ai) f(ilio) Vol(tinia)
> [M]aximo Muci-
> ano, viro cl(arissimo), la-
> toclavo hono-
> [r]ato a divo Pio
> ...[71]

> For Gaius Julius Maximus Mucianus, the son of Gaius of the tribe Voltinia, a *vir clarissimus*, honored with the latus clavus by the divine (Antoninus) Pius . . .

To be so honored by the emperor was to be honored by the most exalted person in the colony, indeed, by a divinity himself (*dio Pio*).

I suggest that Paul intentionally draws upon this cultural script in his portrayal of the exaltation of Jesus in Philippians 2. For Paul there remained One who far exceeded the emperor in rank and in his corresponding ability to bestow honor upon another. Paul's marked transition in subject from Christ to ὁ θεός (v. 9) draws attention to the exalted status of the One who honors Jesus. Given the status of the bestower, there can be no question of the efficacy of the grant of honor in the ensuing text. This is how the text would have been understood by the first hearers of the letter.

Secondly, as we learned above, honor, to be genuine, had to be publicly acknowledged: "To claim honor that the community does not recognize is to play the fool."[72] Here, as well, the relative prestige of the one granting the honor remains an important consideration. Lendon helpfully relates the ability of one aristocrat to confer honor upon another with the public nature of honor in Roman elite society:

> When one man honoured another in the Roman world, he granted him a quantum of honour, which, provided that the bestower was sufficiently distinguished himself, the aristocratic community at large then accepted that the recipient possessed; *a man's ability to mobilize aristocratic opinion in favour of another man was proportional to his own honour.*[73]

All of this insightfully informs our understanding of Christ's exaltation in Philippians 2:9–11. God intends for "every knee" to bend and "every tongue" to confess that "Jesus Christ is Lord, to the glory of God the Father" (vv. 10–11). Given the indisputable status of the bestower, Paul leaves his readers with the assurance that God's grant of honor to Christ is such that not only Lendon's "aristocratic community at large" (see the above quotation) but, indeed, "all sentient creatures" will acknowledge the exalted status of Jesus of Nazareth.[74] The utterly unexpected status reversal of Jesus finds its legitimization (διὸ καί), then, in the exalted position of the One who assigns to Jesus "the name above every name" (v. 9) – the social status of ὁ θεός guarantees the efficacy of his bestowal of great honor upon the crucified δοῦλος, Christ Jesus.

Jesus as lord: the name above every name

Central to the status bestowed upon Christ in Philippians 2:9–11 is the acclamation of Jesus Christ as κύριος. With most commentators, I understand "the name that is above every name" (v. 9) to be not Ἰησοῦς but κύριος (v. 11), taking the genitive in the phrase τῷ ὀνόματι Ἰησοῦ (v. 10) as possessive rather than explicative.[75] Before considering the background of κύριος, however, we should carefully note the threefold use of ὄνομα (vv. 9–10). It is commonly recognized that names were employed in antiquity in a manner quite distinct from their use in modern society, where we use a name simply as a means of distinguishing one person from another. Bauer speaks, for example, about the "efficacy" of a name in the ancient world, seeing in a name "something real, a piece of the very nature of the personality whom it designates, expressing the person's qualities and powers."[76] But even more than this is in view in the name ascribed to Jesus in Philippians 2:11 (κύριος). As the presence of the phrase ὑπὲρ πᾶν ὄνομα demonstrates, κύριος specifically highlights Christ's publicly acclaimed social status. The threefold use of ὄνομα confirms this observation. In an important discussion of the language of honor in Latin and Greek, Lendon squarely situates the ὄνομα word-group ("name," "fame"; including ὀνομαστός, "of name or note," "famous") in the semantic field of honor discourse.[77] In assigning to Jesus the "name that is above every name," then, God has given him "a title which outranked all other titles."[78] Status remains at the forefront of Paul's language in Philippians 2:9–11.

The acclamation of Jesus as κύριος in the present context again underscores Paul's intention to challenge the values of the dominant culture as reflected in the social practices of those wielding power in Roman Philippi. The origin of κύριος as a designation for Jesus on the part of

Aramaic-speaking Christians in the East has been generally acknowledged, and an intended connection in our text between Jesus as κύριος and the Old Testament name of God, "Yahweh," can hardly be disputed.[79] Philippian Christians who were familiar with the Old Testament would have appreciated Paul's reworking of this important text from the prophet Isaiah, as he now depicts Jesus as "the sharer of the unique lordship of Yahweh and the rightful recipient of such worship and praise as God alone may command."[80] One wonders, however, just how transparent this intertextuality would have been to a predominantly Gentile community. Much closer to the hearth, conceptually, was the association of κύριος with the Roman ruler and his status as lord of the empire. As N. T. Wright and others have increasingly recognized, "In the Mediterranean world where Paul exercised his vocation as the apostle to the Gentiles, the pagans, the fastest growing religion was the Imperial cult, the worship of Caesar."[81]

Tellbe has identified the designation of Jesus as κύριος as the most notable feature of Paul's Christology in the epistle.[82] Paul's concern to depict Jesus as κύριος in Philippians finds its explanation in the sociopolitical setting of Roman Philippi. It is likely that the term κύριος had become a common designation for the Roman emperor, particularly in the East, by the time Paul wrote Philippians. In fact, κύριος was already applied to the emperor by the time of Claudius. An Egyptian papyrus (49 CE), for example, reads as follows: Τιβερίου Κλαυδίου Καίσαρος τοῦ κυρίου (*P. Oxy.* 1.37.5–6). An ostracon from Thebes has the phrase Τιβερίου Κλαυδίου Καίσαρος Σεβαστοῦ Αὐτοκράτορος τοῦ κυρίου (Ostr. 1038). Under Nero, the description of Caesar as Lord became more widespread. In a 67 CE inscription from Corinth, for example, Nero is called ὁ τοῦ παντὸς κόσμου Νέρων, αὐτοκράτωρ μέγιστος and ὁ κύριος Σεβαστός (*SIG* 2.814.30–31, 55). The association of κύριος terminology with the ruler of the Roman world would probably, therefore, have played a vital part in the Philippians' political and social reality. Tellbe suggests that it would have been a part of the readers' religious reality as well. He maintains that the confession "the emperor is Lord" was religiously colored and thus quite similar to the confession "the emperor is God." Especially in the East, during the time of Nero, distinctions between the political and religious usages of κύριος terminology no longer obtained.[83] The manner in which Paul has reworked Isaiah 45 (above), moreover, along with the divine status assigned to the pre-incarnate Christ in verse 6, certainly suggests that Paul intends to contrast a divine Jesus with a divine emperor. The centrality of the imperial cult in first-century Philippi also points in this direction.

Here again, however, ontology (the divinity of Christ versus the divinity of the emperor) must not be allowed to overshadow function (the behavior of Jesus versus the behavior of the secular rulers), so that we do not lose sight of the practical implications of Paul's intended contrast for relations among the Philippian Christians. According to the logic of Paul's argument, it is specifically the unique *manner* in which he approached his power and status (vv. 6–8) which entitled Jesus to the status reversal that he ultimately experienced at the hands of God (vv. 9–11). The attitude and behavior of Jesus (vis-à-vis the earthly rulers) – not Christological ontology, as such – constitute the primary focus of the text.

There is little need to enumerate specific examples of the self-serving, honor-seeking ways of Roman rulers, for, as Tellbe notes, nearly every account of the emperors during the first century confirms that Roman rulers were known for "grasping their power through self-assertion, greed, rivalry, violence, and murder."[84] The contrast with Jesus could hardly have been more striking.[85] For Christ, the social status associated with equality with God (v. 6) was not something to be exploited for his own advantage but, rather, something to be willingly surrendered in the service of others, in a way that finally brought upon Jesus the utmost in public shame and social degradation. Jesus therefore utilized his authority in a manner that stood in diametric opposition to the way in which power and position were exploited by secular rulers, at both the imperial and local levels. Precisely for this reason, Jesus – not Caesar – receives the eminently honorable name κύριος at the hands of the only One whose status accords him the right to bestow such an honor upon another. Persons steeped in the social realities of first-century Philippi could hardly have missed Paul's point.

It will be helpful to offer here some reflections on the relationship of Philippians 2:9–11 to its immediately preceding context. Reading the hymn in light of the cultural values and social codes discussed in this chapter may contribute positively to the ongoing dialogue concerning the logic of the author and the literary unity of the passage. Christ's exaltation (vv. 9–11) has been viewed as particularly problematic for those of us (now the majority) who hold to an ethical interpretation of 2:6–11 in its present setting in the epistle. Larry Kreitzer frames the dilemma as follows:

> The difficulty is that there is no immediately obvious connection between the exaltation theme contained in these verses and the exhortation based upon the ethical example of Jesus that clearly underlies vv. 6–8. It is difficult to incorporate the final stanza of the christological hymn within an interpretation of the passage that focuses solely on the ethical example of Jesus.[86]

One could perhaps simply assume that Paul inserted into his letter a confessional hymn, the focus of which was decidedly Christological, but only part of which addressed the ethical needs of his argument. According to this reading, the ethical framework of this portion of the epistle cannot accommodate the whole hymn, and verses 9–11 are left "hanging awkwardly outside this new enclosure."[87] Such an assumption, however, remains unsatisfying, and commentators continue to search for more viable options. Rhetorical criticism has proven useful for properly situating Philippians 2:6–11 within the overall flow of the epistle but has yet to connect vv. 9–11 persuasively to the context of the hymn itself.[88]

Stephen Fowl's analysis of the place of Philippians 2:9–11 in the hymn has moved the discussion a step forward. Fowl reads both the humiliation and the exaltation of Christ under the rubric of suffering. Paul has challenged his readers to stand firm in the face of suffering (1:27–30). He now assures them that Jesus also suffered unjustly (2:6–8), but that Jesus was vindicated by God for his suffering and humiliation (2:9–11). The implication of Christ's example is that, if the Philippians remain faithful like Jesus, they, too, will find vindication at the hands of God the Father.[89] Fowl is correct to see a close relationship between Christ's humiliation and his vindication, one that nicely fits the epistolary context of the hymn. A problem persists, however, for those, like Fowl, who wish to see suffering as an ever-present *topos* in the epistle.

In the context immediately surrounding the hymn (2:1–4; 12–18) suffering is no longer in the foreground of the text, for Paul has shifted his attention from conflicts with outsiders (1:27–30) to relational issues within the Philippian congregation itself. This remains the case even if one insists that unity in the face of suffering is in view.[90] The shift in subject matter should not go unnoticed, for it reveals that Paul, in his portrayal of Jesus (2:6–11), is not (*pace* Fowl) offering promise of vindication for suffering at the hands of outsiders. Rather, Paul draws upon the attitude and activities of Jesus in order to construct a new *ethos* for interpersonal relations *among* community members.[91] It is not simply Jesus' suffering but, rather, the manner in which Jesus used his divine status which God vindicates in verses 9–11. The implication, then, is that God will fully and finally vindicate – that is, greatly honor – all who, like Jesus, use their status and power for the benefit of others in the community.

The exaltation of Christ (vv. 9–11) is, therefore, absolutely crucial to Paul's argument in the context of 2:5–11. Themes of *cursus*, honor, status, and power flow naturally throughout the text, from Jesus' humiliation to his exaltation, though in a decidedly countercultural way. As a reward for dishonoring himself for the benefit of others, Jesus is exalted to the highest place by One whose position at the very apex of the pecking order of social reality assures Paul's readers that the status reversal of this crucified δοῦλος will ultimately be acknowledged by all.

Finally, some observations are in order concerning the vexing issue of the origin of the Christ hymn. Was Philippians 2:6–11 originally a pre-Pauline liturgical confession appropriated and adapted by the apostle for its present setting in the epistle? I no longer find the arguments in favor of such a view to be particularly convincing. The manner in which verses 9–11 fit the "hymn," combined with the way in which the ethical interpretation of the whole of verses 6–11 – properly informed by Roman social values and practices – works in the surrounding context, leaves little need to postulate pre-Pauline composition for Philippians 2:6–11.

Arguments against Pauline authorship can be grouped into three general categories: structural, linguistic, and theological objections.[92] A persistent lack of consensus with regard to the poetic structure of the alleged hymn continues to compromise the structural argument against Pauline authorship. Scholars have utilized various criteria for sorting out the poetic structure, with the result that a number of words and phrases are omitted from the text in order to support a rather bewildering array of suggested reconstructions.[93] Until some degree of agreement is reached on the poetic layout of the passage, it will remain difficult to determine whether or not the grammatical structure of Philippians 2:6–11 is characteristically Pauline. Meanwhile, the progression of the text is quite clear when viewed from a broader thematic perspective. Nearly all commentators acknowledge a two-stage humiliation of Christ in verses 6–8, followed by his exaltation to a position of great honor verses 9–11. It is hardly accidental, I suggest, that this transparent thematic structure perfectly addresses the issues of power, prestige, and social status which characterized the relational universe of Paul's Philippian audience.

Linguistic objections to Pauline authorship are also increasingly less tenable. The uncharacteristic vocabulary often cited in favor of pre-Pauline composition stumbles over the fact that rare words occasionally occur in other texts that are indisputably Pauline. More to the point in the present connection, the linguistic argument falters completely when we consider that the presence of nearly every term generally cited as non-Pauline in our passage can be explained by the social scientific interpretation of Philippians 2:6–11 outlined in the previous pages. For example, each of the three key expressions not elsewhere used of Christ by Paul – μορφῇ θεοῦ, ἴσα θεῷ, δούλου (vv. 6–7) – is easily accounted for by the status concerns of Paul's argument. Other exceptional terms and expressions also make perfect sense in view of Paul's preoccupation with issues of honor, shame, and social status (ἁρπαγμὸν ἡγήσατο [v. 6], ὑπερύψωσεν [v. 9]), a preoccupation that finds adequate explanation in the social setting of the letter's recipients.

A final argument in favor of pre-Pauline authorship of Philippians 2:6–11 concerns the theology of the text. Proponents of this line of reasoning suggest that the soteriology of the passage differs markedly from Paul's own understanding expressed in other places, particularly because references to the saving significance of Christ's death and to the resurrection are strikingly absent from the text. To look for a fully nuanced Pauline soteriology is to beg the question, however, by presupposing that Paul's intentions in the passage are primarily soteriological. I maintain that Paul's central concerns in Philippians 2 are not soteriological but, rather, ecclesiological in nature. Paul specifically crafts his narrative of the humiliation and exaltation of Jesus in such a way as to subvert Roman social values and to encourage an alternative way of living together for members of the Christian community at Philippi. In such a context, the saving significance of Christ's death is assumed, and the position of honor gained by Christ as a result of his exaltation is much more to the point than the historical fact of his bodily resurrection. Given the respective backgrounds of the social and literary contexts, therefore, it is most reasonable to assume that Paul penned this Christological masterpiece solely to address the relational needs of the Philippian congregation.[94]

7

SUMMARY AND CONCLUSION

> All who exalt themselves will be humbled, and all who humble themselves will be exalted.
>
> Jesus of Nazareth (Matthew 23:12)

Gerd Theissen has recently identified renunciation of status as one of the two basic values of the primitive Christian ethic.[1] Paul's reconstruction of honor and shame in Philippians 2 constitutes an important expression of this value framed in distinctly Christological terms. I conclude my study with a brief overview of the materials covered in the previous chapters, followed by some reflections about the potential importance of my findings for properly situating the defining symbols and social values of early Christianity in their Greco-Roman setting.

Summary: reconstructing honor in Philippi

The summary that follows will proceed in the order in which I presented the materials in the first six chapters of the monograph. I will first provide an overview of the broader world of Roman social life, followed by a brief assessment of the ways in which these cultural values and social codes found expression in the colony at Roman Philippi. The survey concludes with a review of my treatment of the biblical materials relating to Philippi.

Roman social stratification and the *cursus honorum*

Viewing the population of the empire as broadly consisting of two social strata, the elite and the non-elite (the former representing less than 2 percent of the population), has proven to be a helpful heuristic device for macrosociological analysis of Roman life. As we have seen, moreover, the two-strata perspective corresponds precisely to the manner in which persons in Roman antiquity viewed their own social world. Lucian's division of the population into "the rich" and "the poor" (*Saturnalia* 19), for example, and Paul's familiar categories of "the strong" and "the weak" (1 Cor. 1:26–29; *passim*) typify the "broad binary division of society" which characterizes the viewpoint of nearly every ancient writer.[2]

Historical reality was significantly more complex. The elite class at Rome occupied two distinct *ordines*, senatorial and equestrian, each of which subdivided into a number of ranks and status groupings according to the honor rating of the various participants. Members of the local elite, in Italy and the provinces, constituted yet a third formal *ordo*, that of the decurions. Nor were non-elite persons a homogeneous social entity. Distinctions between slave and free, and, among the latter, between citizen and non-citizen, proved defining for day-to-day social relations. And then there were those who continue to resist facile classification due to their socially anomalous positions. Certain freedmen, for example, acquired wealth that would have qualified them for membership in an elite order, had they not remained indelibly stained by the servile status they had acquired at birth. Reflected in all of the above, and foundational to any analysis of Roman social life, is the ubiquitous tendency of the population of the empire to divide and subdivide into groups and subgroups, in order to clearly demarcate the social pecking order. Simply put, persons who lived in the Roman world participated in a highly stratified relational environment, and the privileged few who had the most to gain from the hierarchy intended it to remain that way.

Cicero's elite peers would have applauded his assertion that "rank must be preserved" (*Planc*. 15), and Rome's social verticality was creatively reinforced by various practices and legislation that ensured the preservation of the social status quo wherever Rome ruled. What people wore, where people sat at public events or private banquets, what people did (or, in the case of the elite, did *not* do) to earn a living, how people were treated by the judicial system, how much grain or olive oil persons received from the public dole – all of these common aspects of life were carefully regulated according to social status. Public processions at civic religious festivals and at the funerals of the aristocracy served further to remind both elite and non-elite of their appropriate positions in the hierarchy.

Social mobility across the profound chasm that separated the non-elite from the elite stratum of society was relatively uncommon. Advancement *within* the various social groups, however, was not only possible but even, in many cases, carefully scripted. I have in mind here Rome's *cursus honorum* and the replication of *cursus* ideology and praxis in local elite and non-elite settings across the empire. The senatorial *cursus* in Rome was a well-defined (if often compromised) sequence of honorific posts which included, in ascending order, the offices of quaestor, aedile, praetor, and consul. Personal and familial honor were central to one's advancement in the *cursus*. Life was lived – and honor won and lost – in the public eye, under the constant scrutiny of one's social peers, in a relational environment that Carlin Barton has appropriately identified as "a contest culture, a sometimes brutally competitive, hierarchical society in which one's status and being were perpetually tested."[3] Victors and their families publicly proclaimed the prizes won in these honor contests in *cursus* inscriptions that adorned public works and burial monuments in Rome and in the surrounding locale.

The populations of provincial towns in Italy and elsewhere replicated Rome's *cursus* ideology, along with the preoccupation with status and honor-seeking which characterized aristocratic life in the capital. Members of a local elite appropriated Roman titles such as quaestor and aedile, as they constructed their own sequence of honors to mark out advancement within the municipal decurion order. Provincial aediles and *duumviri*, in particular, engaged in urban benefaction, adorning the public works that they financed with inscriptions detailing their ascension through various honorific offices to their positions at the apex of the local *cursus*. As in Rome, attention was given in the towns and municipalities to the preservation of the hierarchy. Seating at public events was assigned, festival processions were organized, and justice was served according to social rank. The trickle-down effect of value replication guaranteed that persons in these local settings who did not qualify for decurion status nevertheless emulated the values and practices of their social betters. Non-elite voluntary associations thus boasted their own official posts, and, like their social superiors, *collegia* members publicly honored individuals (members or non-members) who served the associations as benefactors.

In the Roman world, as in most societies, hierarchy and rank were highly formalized in the military. A soldier's pay, the booty awarded after a victorious battle, land allotments upon retirement – even the square footage of a soldier's sleeping quarters – were all assigned in amounts directly proportionate to the soldier's rank. Competition was fierce for additional honors and decorations available to individuals who distinguished themselves on the battlefield. Retired veterans and their families publicly proclaimed the ranks achieved in the military *cursus*, and the honorific decorations won in battle, on sepulcher inscriptions erected across the empire.

At times, moreover, Rome's military hierarchy directly informed the non-military social hierarchy of a local municipality. In view here is the Roman practice of colonization, whereby retiring soldiers were rewarded by their superiors (the emperor during our period) with land allotments in conquered territories. The phenomenon generally involved the wholesale dispossession of local landholders by a large contingent of veteran settlers, who were assigned their respective plots of land according to military rank. In the case of Roman Philippi the process of colonization virtually guaranteed that the social organization of the newly established colony would replicate the military hierarchy reflected in the rank structure of the retired veterans.

Replication in Roman Philippi

Philippi was established as a Roman colony in 43 BCE and, again, by Octavian in 30 BCE. The refounding of the settlement as *Colonia Julia Philippensis*, after Augustus' victory at Actium, assured the colony of a special relationship with Rome and her first emperor. Aulus Gellius' observation – that Rome's "colonies seem to be miniatures, as it were, and in a way copies" of the mother city (*NA* 16.13.8–9) – is particularly on target in the case of Philippi, where Roman control of positions of power and influence (through membership in the decurion council), judicial practices (through the enforcement of *ius Italicum*), and social life at every stratum in the hierarchy (through value replication) mimicked life in Rome to a remarkable degree.

Most vital in linking the colony to Rome and its *princeps* was the ruler cult. The veneration of the Roman emperor and the Augustan family was apparently embraced with special enthusiasm in Philippi, a settlement initially populated with retired veterans who held their imperator in high esteem. And as we saw in a previous chapter, emperor worship served to reinforce the social hierarchy at Philippi in some rather significant ways. The assignment (by elite decurions) of prestigious honorific priesthoods to both their fellow-members of the elite (the flaminate) and to wealthy freedmen (the office of *Augustalis*) regularly reminded the populace of the social location of these respective groups in the hierarchy. Festival processions making their way to Philippi's forum in order of honor and rank further reinforced the social status quo. Even geography played a part, as the imperial cult's temple and the meeting house of the elite decurion council stood at opposite ends of the colony's geographical center of power, the Philippian forum.

Rome's *cursus* ideology and preoccupation with honor saw replication among both elite and non-elite in the colony. Decurions engaged in public benefaction and proclaimed their various offices and honors in inscriptions placed in Philippi's forum and the adjoining areas. Monuments unearthed in both of the colony's cemeteries similarly attest to efforts on the part of Philippi's elite class and their surviving family members to publicize in *cursus* form honors won by the deceased. Evidence for non-elite cultural values and social codes points in the same direction. The horizons were smaller, of course, since the non-elite vied for status and participated in a replicated honors race, not in the broader municipal sphere but, rather, in the more circumscribed confines of their voluntary associations and cult groups. Their values and behavior, however, prove remarkably similar to those of the colony's elite. Honorific offices and acts of public benefaction are attested for a number of non-elite cult groups, with the Silvanus cult boasting the greatest abundance of evidence along these lines. Silvanus worshipers in the colony subdivided into at least seven groups, which were identified, interestingly enough, as *decuriae*. A hierarchy of honors included priesthoods (*sacerdotes*) and the office of aedile (the same term is used in the colony's elite municipal *cursus* and in the senatorial *cursus honorum* at Rome). Members of the Silvanus group who possessed sufficient wealth made contributions toward the construction of the cult's temple edifice, and they were honored with public inscriptions detailing the specifics of their respective monetary gifts.

A careful survey of data from the colony, as evidenced in Peter Pilhofer's recent catalogue of extant inscriptions from the colony, can only lead us to conclude that persons in first-century Philippi were passionately preoccupied with honor, rank, and social status, and that the colonists felt strongly compelled to proclaim publicly the honors they had received, in order to lay claim to their social location in the pecking order of this highly stratified Roman settlement. The social orientation of Philippi, in turn, sheds much light upon Paul's rhetorical strategy in his letter to the young Jesus community at Philippi, as Paul seeks to persuade the recipients of his letter to resist the temptation to accommodate themselves to the relational values of their status-conscious culture.

Paul and the reconstruction of honor

An examination of the New Testament materials relating to the church in Philippi demonstrates the value of the above background materials for interpreting the biblical text. Luke's story of Paul's ministry in Philippi (Acts 16:11–40), for example, is unique among the journey narratives in its explicit identification of Philippi as a Roman colony, and in the charge it relates, namely, that Paul and his fellow missionaries were advocating anti-Roman practices. Only in the Philippian narrative, moreover, does Luke take pains to specify the precise titles of the local Roman magistrates and their assistants, though such officials would certainly have been present in other places where Paul ministered. The presence of these important bits of social realia, along with the special emphasis in the narrative upon the citizen status of the missionaries which concludes the account, assure us that the author of Acts was particularly sensitive to the issues of honor and social status so abundantly evidenced in the colony's inscriptional database.

The interpretation of Paul's letter to the Philippians similarly profits from a careful consideration of the settlement's social values. In his greeting in the letter Paul (a) refrains from calling attention to his apostolic office, (b) refers to himself and Timothy as "servants," and (c) specifically addresses community leaders with their formal titles ("bishops and deacons"). The combination of these elements is without parallel among the greetings in Paul's letters. The reason, as I suggested in a previous chapter, relates to the special temptation to privilege positions of honor and status, which would have faced higher-ranking members of a Jesus community situated in a social environment like Philippi. By refraining from calling attention to his own eminent status as God's chosen apostle and, instead, identifying church leaders by title, Paul thus models the reversal of Roman honor practices enjoined later in the epistle: "in humility regard others as better than yourselves" (2:3).

Also unique to Philippians is the structure and orientation of Paul's list of Jewish achievements in 3:4–6. The information concerning Paul's background is most profitably read as a catalogue of Jewish honors structured in Roman form. The syntactical economy of the text, along with the *cursus* arrangement, whereby ascribed honor (Paul's birth status) precedes acquired honor (Paul's accomplishments in Judaism), suggests that Paul has set the details of his Jewish past in a distinctly Roman framework. Paul's inclusion of his citizen tribe (Benjamin) points in the same direction, given the pervasive emphasis upon the Roman tribe *Voltinia* in the Philippian inscriptions. The text as it stands, therefore, constitutes Paul's pre-Christian *cursus honorum*, and would have been heard as such by persons constantly confronted with honor inscriptions in the public areas of Philippi. Paul's rejection of such honors as "rubbish" would have struck the recipients of the letter as markedly countercultural vis-à-vis the social values that characterized day-to-day life in the colony.

The great Christological passage in Philippians 2 is also best interpreted under the rubric of Roman *cursus* ideology. That Christ is presented in the passage in contrast to the Roman emperor and to imperial ideology can no longer be disputed. I have argued, in addition, that the structure of 2:6–8 is to be read against a Roman background. Paul has taken in hand Rome's *cursus* ideology and turned it on its head, so to speak, as he presents Christ descending a *cursus pudorum* from equality with God (Status Level One), to the status of a slave (Status Level Two), to the socially degrading experience of crucifixion (Status Level Three). Most astounding, from the perspective of Roman social values, Paul's Christ has descended his *cursus* willingly ("emptied himself," v. 7; "obedient to the point of death," v. 8), and he has received the highest of honors at the hands of God himself for his decidedly anti-Roman approach to power and status (vv. 9–11).

Conclusion: reconstructing honor in early Christianity

Homo hierarchichus. Thus begins the title of Louis Dumont's classic treatment of the caste system in mid-twentieth-century India.[4] Indeed, the expression is quite apropos for humanity in general, since social inequality seems to be a characteristic of life. As David Grusky has recently observed, "The human condition has so far been a fundamentally unequal one; indeed *all* known societies have been characterized by inequalities of some kind, with the most privileged individuals or families enjoying a disproportionate share of the total wealth, power, or prestige."[5]

While generally acknowledging the ubiquity of social inequality, social scientists continue to disagree about what has come to be identified in the literature as "the positive functionality of stratification." Functionalists tend to view social inequality as indispensable for properly motivating persons of different aptitudes and abilities to fulfill their respective roles satisfactorily in society. Conflict theorists rightly charge the functionalist perspective with ignoring internal power struggles within society and tacitly legitimizing existing social inequality. Consequently, conflict theorists have generally been more hopeful than functionalist sociologists about the potential for a non-stratified society some day in the future.[6]

I am not optimistic. It is important to distinguish here between the inevitability of social verticality, on the one hand, and the positive functionality of stratification, on the other. While I remain unconvinced that inequality always functions in ways advantageous to society, the inevitability of social stratification is increasingly difficult to deny. Recent treatments of social inequality, for example, have emphasized the emotional, and even biological, basis for status-seeking and social stratification.[7] History points in the same direction, as professedly radical egalitarians who have come to power, such as the Bolshevik and Chinese Communist revolutionaries, soon set up different, but no less hierarchical, social systems of their own in which, of course, party officials ended up at the top of the reconstructed pecking order of wealth, power, and prestige.[8] In the words of Joseph Schumpeter, the social structure of human society is like a multi-storied hotel which is "always occupied, but always by different persons."[9] Human beings seem to orient toward hierarchy by nature, and Francis Fukuyama is quite on target when he asserts,

> Imagining a flat, networked, nonhierarchical world of the future is tantamount to imagining a world without politics. This particular libertarian dream – shared, incidentally, by many human rights activists in Eastern Europe before the fall of the Berlin Wall – is no more realistic than the socialist dream in which politics becomes everything, or the radical feminist dream in which men somehow cease to be men.[10]

Even if it were possible, moreover, the realization of a non-stratified social utopia might prove highly disappointing. Western society has made significant strides in this direction and yet, as Carlin Barton so perceptively observes, our efforts to distance ourselves from the honor-oriented values of a contest culture like that of ancient Rome have created other problems, some of which may prove to be even more profound:

> Euro-Americans often attempt to minimize competition and discriminations (and thus hierarchy and envy, particularly when directed against themselves). But attempts to have differences without competition or comparisons have produced, as a paradoxical side-effect, a yearning for identity and a sense of honorlessness and nonbeing.[11]

The development in recent decades of a multi-million-dollar psychotherapeutic industry, along with a significant corpus of literature wrestling with the sense of social dislocation that has resulted from radical individualism and the corresponding reconstruction of the self in Euro-American society, suggests that Barton's observations are quite on the mark.[12] Barton concludes: "Fortunately or unfortunately, it is by comparisons and discriminations that we locate ourselves; it is by discriminations that we exist."[13]

And so it was for Mediterranean antiquity. The deep structure of the Roman social mentality was such that not even philosophers and slaves could escape honor's pale.[14] Nor, in the final analysis, could the early Christians. This is a key point. John Elliott has recently discussed a tendency in New Testament studies toward anachronism in the employment of social-scientific models in the study of ancient texts. Elliott thus labels

Summary and conclusion

as an "idealistic fallacy" the popular theory that Jesus was an egalitarian. As Elliott appropriately proceeds to observe, "The focus of Jesus' social teaching was not the *elimination* of status but rather the *inversion* of status."[15]

The same must be said about Paul's portrait of Jesus in Philippians 2. Early Christianity established itself in a markedly agonistic society in which the quest for public honor dominated the behavioral priorities of males of nearly every social rank. Persons like Paul who sought to challenge the values of their social world could hardly reject, in principle, notions of honor and shame without, at the same time, "shedding their skin," so to speak. Honor and status, as such, were simply non-negotiable. The *ingredients* of honor (what makes one honorable), however, were. In this regard, Paul's social agenda involved what Scott Bartchy has recently described as "the redefinition of the basis for attaining honor: serving rather than competing."[16] No longer would males who won victory over their peers in the incessant race for honors that characterized social life in the Roman world thereby earn the right publicly to proclaim their social status and to dominate increasing numbers of persons – male and female alike – in their circles of influence.[17] Paul's vision, rather, was for a community in which honor was to be granted to those who utilized their power and status sacrificially, for the benefit of others in the group.

Instead of rejecting in principle the social realities of honor and shame, therefore, Paul and those who shared his sentiments sought to reconstruct the cultural values and social codes of the Roman world by substituting, for those attitudes and kinds of behavior deemed honorable by the dominant culture, a radically alternative set of attitudes and kinds of behavior to be honored in the Christian *ekklesia*. That God himself had profoundly honored these very attitudes and behavior in the life of his servant Jesus assures Paul's readers that the alternative vision for social relations which he offers them is, in the final analysis, far superior to – and much more enduring than – the public pomp and status-conscious value system of the Roman world.[18]

I conclude with some brief observations about the manner in which Paul draws upon the symbol of the cross in Philippians 2, in view of current scholarly interest in the utilization of religious symbols for social engineering. It has become increasingly popular in recent decades to approach the use of religious symbols by the leaders of faith communities with a hermeneutic of suspicion – and with good reason, given the abuse perpetrated by those in power in a myriad local settings throughout the past and recent history of the Christian church. Among New Testament writers, Paul, especially, has become an object of postmodern deconstruction, the works of Elizabeth Castelli and Stephen Moore serving as but two representative examples.[19] The cross, in particular, is a powerful religious symbol fraught with potential for use and abuse. Moore, for example, reflects upon his own experience in the monastery during which the image of the tortured Jesus on the cross was used to enact what Foucault calls "the quiet game of the well behaved," that is, to reinforce the community's hierarchy.[20] And Moore, we can be assured, is hardly the only member of a faith community who has been challenged to submit to the authority of the F/father according to the analogy of Jesus on the cross.

One could hardly charge Paul, however, with similar rhetorical designs in Philippians 2. Paul, in his great Christological masterpiece, utilizes the image of crucifixion not to elicit the reluctant submission of the powerless to their social superiors but, instead, to encourage those with some status in the community to regard their social capital not as "something to be exploited" but, rather, as something to utilize – even renounce, if necessary – in the service of others. We know this to be the case because Paul portrays Christ submitting to the abhorrent physical and social death of crucifixion for the salvation of his people *willingly, from a position of absolute power and authority equal to that of God himself.* This is important because it clearly demonstrates that, by extension, Paul directs his challenge in the text not to those at the bottom of the community's status hierarchy but, rather, to the honorable in the community, to those in the Philippian church who could claim Roman citizen status, or, perhaps in a few cases, boast of membership in the elite stratum of the colony's population. Paul's message is quite transparent and, from the Roman perspective, decidedly subversive and anti-traditional: God honors persons of high status in the *ekklesia* who view their power as a resource to be used in the service of others in the community of faith – even if this means renouncing their social status, or, rather, exchanging their privileges in the colony for the superior position of honor and status which they, like Jesus, will receive at the hands of God.

NOTES

1   Roman social organization

1. Littlejohn (1972, 9).
2. Lenski (1966, x). Little has changed over the years with respect to basic definitions. Oxford's *Dictionary of the Social Sciences*, for example, has recently defined social stratification as the "systemic forms of inequality that divide societies and broadly impact occupational and social status" (Calhoun [2002, 466]). See also André Béteille, who similarly views stratification in terms of "the unequal positions occupied by individuals in society." Béteille appropriately cautions against being misled by the geological metaphor implied in "stratification": "The arrangement of persons in a society is enormously more complex than the arrangement of the layers of the earth; and social strata are not visible to the naked eye in the way that geological strata are" (1985, 831). For a judiciously chosen compendium of influential essays on social inequality, which constitutes a survey of the discipline as it developed during the second half of the twentieth century, see Grusky (1994). The editor's introductory overview is particularly helpful (Grusky [1994, 3–35]).
3. Others adopt a threefold typology: (1) *caste systems* (characterized by highly differentiated statuses with rigid borders and little opportunity for social mobility), (2) *estates* (societies like medieval Europe, which distinguish between clergy and nobility, on the one hand, and a broad category of peasants, merchants, and artisans, on the other), and (3) *class systems* (characteristic of industrial and post-industrial societies) (Calhoun [2002, 466]).
4. Lenski (1966, 210, author's italics. Chart from page 437, reproduced with permission).
5. Lenski identifies several classes as characteristic of agrarian society: governing, retainer, merchant, priestly, peasant, artisan, unclean, and expendable classes. In what follows, I have generally chosen to utilize Roman categories to describe the various strata of the social hierarchy, rather than to adapt the ancient source materials to Lenski's model. Saller has taken much the same approach in the recently updated *Cambridge Ancient History* (2000, 817–54). This is not to disparage a more formally sociological approach, however, since with certain refinements Lenski's model has proven its worth as a valuable heuristic device through which to view the social world of Mediterranean antiquity.

Two of the more sophisticated recent attempts to analyze the social structure of Roman antiquity are by Arlandson (1997, 1–119) and Stegemann and

Stegemann (1999, 53–95). Both treatments build on Lenski's groundbreaking work, alternately confirming and modifying Lenski's proposals based on evidence from ancient source material. For further study, see the substantial bibliographies in Arlandson and Stegemann, which reflect, respectively, American and continental European scholarship. Crossan should also be consulted, particularly for Roman Palestine (1998, 151–59). Crossan appropriates Kautsky's important refinement of Lenski's typology. Kautsky divides Lenski's agrarian society into two sub-categories: traditional and commercialized. The Roman empire exemplifies the latter category and this, in turn, elucidates such phenomena as the unequal distribution of landed resources and peasant revolts in the Roman world (Kautsky [1982, 25, n. 31]).

6. Hopkins (1978, 198).
7. Ibid.
8. Garnsey and Saller (1987, 109–10). Lenski comments on the uneven distribution of wealth in agrarian societies: "On the basis of available data, it appears that *the governing classes of agrarian societies probably received at least a quarter of the national income of most agrarian states, and that the governing class and the ruler together usually received not less than half.* In some instances their combined income may have approached two-thirds of the total" (1966, 228, author's italics).
9. Biblical citations are taken from the NRSV.
10. Greco-Roman sources are cited from the Loeb Classical Library, unless otherwise noted.
11. Loeb translation, slightly adapted.
12. As cited by Arlandson (1997, 27).
13. On Josephus see Hamel (1989).
14. Stegemann and Stegemann (1999, 57–58). The above discussion, while possessing the advantage of clarity, justly invites the charge of oversimplification in reducing ancient society to two social strata. The distinction between elite and non-elite blurs somewhat in real life. Garnsey and Saller draw attention, for example, to "a sizeable heterogeneous group of men of free birth [who] can be distinguished from both the elite orders and the humble masses" (1987, 116). Lictors, scribes, and other retainers of Roman magistrates are representative. Purcell's careful study of these retainer groups should be consulted (1983). Moreover, the assignment of a given individual to one or the other social stratum must answer to the multivalent criteria that social scientists have established for such classification. Stegemann and Stegemann, following Lenski, utilize power, privilege, and prestige as their defining categories (1999, 60–61). Arlandson (1997, 16–18) adopts Runcimann's guidelines instead (1968, 25–61): class, status, and power. Each author justifies the appeal to his threefold category based on confirming evidence from ancient sources. Complicating matters further is the fact that persons in the ancient world might find themselves meeting one or two of these criteria while lacking the other(s). A slave, for example, might be commissioned and empowered by his lord to manage landed estates, thus exercising a degree of power incongruent with his birth status (the technical expression is status inconsistency).

Nevertheless, for the purposes of macrosociological analysis of ancient society, it is fair to retain a twofold division, since this is precisely the way in which the ancients themselves viewed their social world (see above). In fact, as Garnsey and Saller note, the very existence of the retainer class of imperial aides, which they offer as a qualification to the assumption of a two-strata structure, actually serves "to confirm the essential dichotomy, insofar as their rank derived from their position as appendages to the ruling aristocrats" (1987, 116). Further confirmation comes in the form of the second-century distinction between the *honestiores* (more honored) and the *humiliores* (more humble). Although this legal bestowal of privilege on the elite did not come until the second century, it did not arise in a social vacuum but, rather, legitimized a position already occupied by a certain group of persons in Roman antiquity. See now Saller, who begins his examination of Roman social order with reference to "the broad binary division" of society and, after a lengthy discussion of the complexities of Roman social life, concludes by drawing attention, once again, to the contrast between "the élite few" and the "impoverished masses" (2000, 817, 827).

15. See Treggiari's helpful discussion of the history and origin of the Roman *ordines* (1996, 875–77).
16. At other times, an emperor might give an impoverished aristocrat the money necessary to retain his social status. Nero underwrote a fellow-consul, Valerius Messala, to the tune of 500,000 sesterces, and also assigned "an annual stipend" to Aurelius Cotta and Haterius, "though they had dissipated their family estates in profligacy" (Tac. *Ann.* 13.34).
17. The estimated figures for equestrians and decurions are from Stegemann and Stegemann (1999, 73–74). Oakes has recently estimated that some five hundred persons of decurial status lived in first-century Philippi (the figure includes extended family members). This would represent approximately 3 percent of the town's total population (2001, 47).
18. The translations are from Garnsey and Saller (1987, 114).
19. On the importance of public honor among Romans of every social stratum see Lendon (1997) and Barton (2001). For honor and shame as a foundational cultural script for understanding Mediterranean antiquity see Malina and Neyrey (1991, 25–66), and the works of deSilva (1999, 2000).
20. Thus, Saller identifies "distinctive clothing" as one of "the central symbolic expressions of the social hierarchy" (2000, 820).
21. The minimum age to don the *toga virilis* was fourteen years. It was a breach of convention, therefore, when "the manly toga was prematurely conferred on Nero" at thirteen (Tac. *Ann.* 12.41). Tacitus offers a characteristically biting commentary on Nero's social pilgrimage and, in doing so, underlines the importance of clothing as a public indicator of social status:

> The Caesar (Claudius) yielded with pleasure to the sycophancies of the senate, which desired Nero to assume the consulship in the twentieth year of his age, and in the interval, as consul designate, to hold proconsular authority outside the capital and to bear the title Prince of the Youth . . . at the games in the Circus, exhibited to gain him the partialities of the crowd, Britannicus rode past in the juvenile white and purple, Nero in the robes of triumph. "Let the people survey the one in the insignia of supreme command, the other in his puerile garb, and anticipate conformably the destinies of the pair!" (*Ann.* 12.41)

22. Everitt (2003, 71, my italics).
23. Zanker (1988, 15).
24. Julius Caesar had previously "denied . . . the wearing of scarlet robes or pearls to all except to those of a designated position and age" (Suet. *Iul.* 43). Caesar's own attire was later viewed as highly symbolic. Caesar, who ultimately ascended to the heights of sole power, also dressed in a way that stood out from his fellow-senators. As Suetonius relates, "They say, too, that he was remarkable in his dress; that he wore a senator's tunic with fringed sleeves reaching to the wrist, and always had a girdle over it, though a rather loose one; and this, they say, was the occasion of Sulla's *mot*, when he often warned the nobles to keep an eye on the ill-girt boy" (*Iul.* 45). Caesar also distinguished himself from his fellow-senators by occupying "a raised couch in the orchestra" at the theater (Suet. *Iul.* 76). Seating at public events was highly segregated according to social status (see below), the front of the orchestra being reserved for the senatorial order. Caesar's "raised couch," like the fringed sleeves of his senatorial tunic, places him both *among* and *above* his senatorial peers.
25. The same rule applied in the theater where, as we shall see below, the social hierarchy was reinforced in other publicly pronounced ways (Suet. *Aug.* 44). According to Wallace-Hadrill, Augustus' revival of the *mores maiorum* intentionally drew upon toga imagery: "Augustus, the citizen in his toga, stands as moral exemplar to his people" (1990, 158). See also Zanker on this: "It is astonishing how many portraits of Augustus made during his lifetime, both on coins and as honorific statues, show him veiled in a toga" (1988, 127; see 162–66).
26. Reinhold traces instances of usurpation of social status and status symbols from the mid-republican period down to the fourth century of the common era (Reinhold, 1971). Especially prevalent were attempts on the part of wealthy freedmen illegally to assume the privileges of the equestrian order. Slaves and freedmen procured gold-plated iron rings to pass themselves off as Roman knights (Pliny, *HN* 33.6, 23), and status-specific seating at public events was compromised on a number of occasions. By the time of Domitian, special attendants policed the fourteen rows reserved for equestrians in the theater in Rome, in order to insure that no one sat out of order (Mart. 5.8, 14, 23, 35; Suet. *Dom.* 8). Official attempts to prevent such behavior were never wholly effective.
27. Augustus' policy sought to redress recent compromises in the social hierarchy, which had resulted from (1) a leveling among elite status groups due to the social and political upheavals that characterized the last century of the republic, and (2) Julius Caesar's radical social policies (on Caesar's innovations see chapter two). Reinhold summarizes:

> Augustus not only halted the social leveling that was in process, but reorganized the social structure of the empire, moulding it more formally into an "estate" system of stratification with legal distinctions between statuses. Underlying the Augustan system was not only a Roman-Italian bias, but the decision to establish an imperial hierarchy of social classes with an increased range of social stratification everywhere in the empire.
> (1971, 279)

Decades ago Syme called Augustus "a small-town bourgeois devoted and insatiable in admiration of social distinction" (1939, 368).
28. The study of funeral practices has become something of a cottage industry among Roman social historians. On the issue of social status at Roman funerals, see Sumi's article about the use of mimes to portray the ancestral heroes of elite families (2002, 559–85). The excerpt from Diodorus, above, comes from a longer quotation by Photius, which is taken from his discussion of the funeral of L. Aemilius Paullus, the famous conqueror of Perseus who died in 160 BCE:

> Those Romans, who by reason of noble birth and the fame of their ancestors are pre-eminent, are, when they die, portrayed in figures that are not only lifelike as to features but show their whole bodily appearance. For they employ actors who through a man's whole life have carefully observed his carriage and the several peculiarities of his appearance. In like fashion each of the dead man's ancestors takes his place in the funeral procession, with such robes and insignia as enable the spectators to distinguish from the portrayal how far each had advanced in the *cursus honorum* and had had a part in the dignities of the state.
> (Diod. Sic. 31.25.2)

29. Flower (1996, 11). See the collection of the literary, epigraphic, and numismatic evidence for the *imagines* in an appendix to Flower's monograph (281–338).
30. Flower (1996, 127).
31. Flower (1996, 12). In the chapter that follows I will discuss in some detail the importance of honor in Roman social life.
32. Trans. Shelton (1988, 217).
33. The translations of Cicero are taken from Shelton (1988, 129–30), slightly adapted.
34. The translation of Plautus is Shelton's, as is the interpretation of *crux* as "one destined for crucifixion" (1988, 131).
35. The phrase "cluttering up your atrium," in the citation from Plautus, is revealing, since housing, too, was viewed in connection with social status. Thus, after describing in some detail the various rooms of a large Roman villa, Vitruvius observes (assuming a two-strata view of his social world), "Therefore magnificent vestibules (*vestibula*) and alcoves (*tabulina*) and halls (*atria*) are not necessary to persons of a common fortune, because they pay their respects by visiting among others [functioning as clients], and are not visited by others [as is the case with an elite patron]" (*De arch.* 6.5.1–2). See Joshel's careful examination of occupational inscriptions in the vicinity of Rome (Joshel, 1992). She notes that for Roman satirists "lying, cheating, vulgar tradesmen are stock figures along with rich, obnoxious freedmen, greasy foreigners, decadent nobles, needy clients, insensitive patrons and unchaste women" (63).
36. Apparently barbarians were not the only ones distracted by the social scene being played out in the audience at theatrical performances. As Horace had observed some years earlier, a critical observer could not help but "gaze more intently on the people than on the play itself, as giving him more by far worth looking at" (*Epist.* 2.1.197–98).

37. Up to this point the Frisians probably remained rather inconspicuous, since the theater has been conservatively estimated to hold some 17,500 persons (Beacham [1992, 160]).
38. Richard Saller has recently drawn upon the narrative to support his contention that seating at public events functioned both to portray and to legitimate the social hierarchy: "In this vignette the un-romanized Germans displayed their lack of understanding of the imperial order by their naivety about distinctions of seats at a public spectacle. The story (whether true in all details or not) shows the theatre as a teaching device, educating peripheral peoples about the Roman hierarchy of privilege" (2000, 821).
39. Augustus exempted the knights in question, allowing them to sit in the equestrian section, provided they could prove that "they themselves or their parents had ever possessed a knight's estate" (Suet. *Aug.* 40). Their refusal to exempt themselves, however, indicates the seriousness with which these regulations were viewed during the early principate.
40. Garnsey and Saller (1987, 117).
41. In Cicero's day, social segregation at the theater extended to the demarcation of a special section of seats for persons who were financially insolvent (*Phil.* 2.44). The practice of seating according to social status can, in fact, be traced back a good deal further. In 194 BCE Roman censors arranged for special seating at the games for the approximately three hundred members of the senate (Beacham [1999, 26], citing Livy 34.44.54).

    Initially, the *lex Roscia* (67 BCE) was not warmly embraced. Four years later, when the legislation's author, L. Roscius Otho, entered the theater, equestrians applauded, those behind them hissed, and "the two parties turned on each other, shouting out insults; the whole theater was in a state of turmoil" (Plut. *Cic.* 13, trans. Beacham [1999, 32]). Only a timely speech by Cicero prevented the situation from escalating into violence. It did not take long, however, for novelty to become normative. An inscription from Orange reserves places for equestrians in the first three rows of the theater. This suggests that the *lex Roscia* was respected, in principle, in the provinces during the imperial period. Fewer equestrians (in provincial towns) meant fewer rows (three versus fourteen in Rome). Kolendo estimates from the inscription that some 170 equestrians could find seating in the three rows reserved for the *ordo* in the theater in Orange (1981, 310).
42. By 80 CE further stratification *within* the orders surfaces in the epigraphic record. In the Colosseum, the *fratres Arvales*, a priestly college chosen from the most distinguished senatorial families, had special places reserved for them in the senatorial section of the audience. Among the two rows reserved for senators at the Colosseum, a further division also obtained: *viri clarissimi*, *spectabiles*, and *illustres*. The first row, nearest the arena, was reserved for the *illustres* and a portion of the *spectabiles*. The rest of the *spectabiles*, along with the *clarissimi*, sat in the second row. The seats of some two hundred individual senators are designated by name by the time of Odoacer (476–93 CE) (Kolendo [1981, 304]).
43. Information from Dio Cassius suggests that the provision for separate seating for equestrians at the circus was enacted in 5 BCE (55.22.4). The chronology of the various laws pertaining to seating at public events poses a variety of

challenges to the interpreter. It is often difficult to tell whether old practices are being renewed or new ones established. The identification of the various groups in the senatorial decree originating with Augustus (Suet. *Aug.* 44, above) remains an issue of scholarly debate. A detailed discussion is beyond the scope of this project. For the Augustan legislation, in particular, see Beacham's judicious treatment (1999, 123–25). See, too, Rawson (1987).

44. Caligula apparently utilized or, rather, violated the social demarcation of the theater *cavea* to satisfy his own perverted desire for amusement. Suetonius informs us that Caligula scattered "gift tickets" (probably vouchers of some sort entitling the bearer to a sum of money or grain) before the theater opened, "to induce the rabble to take the seats reserved for the equestrian order" and thus to start a fight (*Calig.* 26). According to Josephus, Caligula provided a private theater where "no seats had been set apart either for the senate or for the equites, so that the seating was a jumble, women mixed with men and free men with slaves" (*AJ* 19.86).

45. Although the responsibility to assign seating was at times delegated to lesser officials, ultimate authority rested with the emperor, as the decisions of Augustus and Claudius, above, clearly indicate (for prefects assigning seats in the Colosseum, see Kolendo [1981, 304, n. 26]).

46. A few examples: Hierapolis, Ephesus (Asia), Stobi (Macedonia), Lambaesis (North Africa), Tarraco (Spain) (Kolendo [1981, 310]).

47. *CIL* 1.594; 2.5439 = *ILS* 6087. The information is particularly valuable for the present study, since both Urso and Philippi were Roman colonies. The analysis that follows relies on Kolendo (1981, 305–7).

48. Kolendo (1981, 306).

49. *CIL* 1.593 = *ILS* 6085 (*lex Julia municipalis*); *CIL* 12.6039 = *ILS* 6964 (*lex Narbonensis de flaminio provinciae*).

50. Interestingly enough, this fourfold division (*coloni coloniae, incolae, hospites, adventores*) also figures in some inscriptions of a private character from Italy which regulated admission to the baths (*CIL* 9.5074 = *ILS* 5671; *CIL* 14.2979 = *ILS* 5672; *CIL* 11.6167 = *ILS* 5673). As Kolendo rightly observes, these divisions were "deeply rooted in the mindset of the inhabitants of the towns of the empire" (1981, 306, my translation).

51. Kolendo (1981, 315).

52. Beacham (1992, 166).

53. Saller (2000, 830).

54. Trans. Shelton (1988, 319).

55. Trans. Shelton (1988, 17). The whole of Juvenal's fifth satire treats the manner in which clients are entertained at table in the homes of their patrons and (with appropriate allowances made for exaggeration and fabrication) offers a colorful and insightful picture of Roman social values from a client's perspective.

56. Trans. Vermes (1995, 77–78).

57. Dio's own philosophical convictions, of course, accorded quite nicely with the peasant's relegation of the troubling inequities of daily life to the will of the "king of the gods."

58. Garnsey (1970, 279, my italics).

59. A standard treatment of the topic is Garnsey (1970).

60. A most important consideration here is the complex nature of modern society, with its extensive division of labor and activities, which, in turn, generates a multitude of overlapping social roles.
61. T. H. Marshall (1950, 30, my italics).
62. Isolating the legal system as a separate category proves a bit artificial here, since, as we have seen, seating at public events was, itself, codified in pieces of formal legislation. It is at this point that the fivefold grid, which I have designed as a heuristic device through which to view Roman social verticality (attire, occupation, seating at public events, seating at banquets, and the legal system), blurs somewhat, and the holistic nature of Roman social organization manifests itself.
63. Trans. Lendon (1997, 204).
64. Garnsey, from whom the citations in this paragraph have been taken, identifies discrimination between citizen and non-citizen in all legal spheres as "a permanent feature of the Roman judicial system" (1970, 262).
65. Trans. Shelton (1988, 12–13). See also *FIRA* 2 (407 [Paulus, *Opinions* 5.22.1–2]; trans. Shelton [1988, 13]):

> People who plot sedition and riot or who stir up the masses are, according to the nature of their social rank, either crucified, or thrown to wild animals, or exiled to an island. Those who dig up or plough up boundary markers, or who cut down boundary trees: (1) if they are slaves acting on their own, they are condemned to the mines; (2) if they are *humiliores*, they are sentenced to work on public construction projects; (3) if they are *honestiores*, they are fined one-third of their property and expelled to an island or driven into exile.

66. Littlejohn (1972, 10, my italics). A basic assumption of human inequality undergirds each of the public demarcations of the Roman social hierarchy surveyed in this chapter. Such a view of persons contrasts sharply with the pervasive ideological egalitarianism that characterizes American social values. This ideology, which persists despite the existence of marked status differences in American society, was pointedly symbolized early in America's history in Thomas Jefferson's order to have a round table replace the rectangular one at the White House, in order to relieve him of the necessity of stipulating the order of precedence at official receptions. The commentary by Lipset, Bendix, and Zetterberg is incisive: "This act was not a denial of the existing differences in rank and authority; it was rather a testimony to the belief that they were the accidental, not the essential, attributes of man. Among men of equal worth it is not in good taste to insist on the accidental distinctions which divide them" (1994, 316).
67. Trans. Garnsey and Saller (1987, 118).
68. Cited by Lenski (1966, 43).
69. Pascal, living in a world that had seen over a millennium of Christian influence, regrets these realities; Pliny affirms them.
70. See, for example, Saller's discussion of the Roman *salutatio*, the morning ritual in which the elite were formally greeted by their retinues of friends and clients. Saller calls the *salutatio* "a remarkable custom for its regular, precise visible display of status" (2000, 829; see 829–30). Note, also, Gardner (1986).

71. On food distribution see Saller (2000, 821) and the bibliography cited there. During the second century, for example, an imperial freedman gave a grant of money to the residents of Anagnia as follows: 20 sesterces to each decurion, 8 to each *sevir*, and 4 to each member of the *populus* (*ILS* 1909). Donahue's recent analysis of Roman public feasting particularly underscores the social function of these events (2003).
72. Garnsey and Saller (1987, 117).

2 Preoccupation with honor and the *cursus honorum*

1. Lendon (1997, 35). I am indebted to Lendon for much of what follows.
2. Lendon (1997); Barton (2001).
3. Barton's translation (2001, 37).
4. Malina and Neyrey (1991, 26). Honor and shame are "Core Values" according to John J. Pilch (1993, 95).
5. Moxnes (1996, 19). Moxnes's overview of honor and shame includes a balanced and insightful discussion of this important cultural value, as well as a helpful summary of the writings of cultural anthropologists who have addressed the issue in their studies of Mediterranean society. See also Moxnes (1993).
6. Lendon (1997, 73).
7. Lendon (1997, 35).
8. Downing has recently challenged the categorical assertions of Malina, Neyrey, and others who identify honor as *the* most important social value for persons in Mediterranean antiquity. Downing maintains instead that "'respect' ('honor and shame') is *an* issue of which we need to be aware, but that it is only dominant, 'pivotal,' central (the 'core') when, and where, it is clearly shown to be" (1999, 55, author's emphasis).

    It is certainly the case that much work remains to be done in refining our definitions of honor and shame, and it is reasonable to understand the value as one among several important aspects of Mediterranean social life. Downing is therefore on the mark to challenge the reductionistic tendency among certain exegetes to understand every interpersonal encounter in the New Testament primarily in terms of honor and shame. To support his contentions, Downing offers persuasive critiques of a number of recent, unconvincing attempts to read the gospel pericopes in this manner (58–70). To this degree, Downing's conclusion is a sound one: "The issue of honor, of respect in the community, is important, and it may even *on occasion* be of prime importance. It does not help to assume – irrespective of evidence – that it always must be dominant" (73, author's emphasis).

    What will continue to be debated, of course, is what counts for convincing evidence in any given text-segment. The one passage Downing cites as "a pericope whose overriding concerns are quite clearly 'honor' and 'shame'" is Luke 14:8–10, where honor issues are explicitly evidenced in the language (ἐντιμότερός σου; μετὰ αἰσχύνης; ἔσται σοι δόξα) (53). To be fair, Downing allows for the possibility that honor/shame might be important to a particular narrative even in the absence of explicit semantic indicators (60–61). He seems more comfortable, however, acknowledging the significance of the value for interpretation primarily in those passages that contain honor/shame terminology.

A strictly linguistic approach has the potential, however, to be unnecessarily limiting where the application of broad social values to biblical materials is concerned. Important social conventions are at times strongly reflected in a text even in the absence of specific semantic indicators. An illustration will prove helpful. The primary metaphor for the social organization of early Christian communities was the metaphor of family. Early Christian churches thought of themselves as surrogate Mediterranean kinship groups, and they exhibited behavior consonant with that social model. Often we find both family language and family-like behavior exhibited – or enjoined – in a single text-segment. 1 Corinthians 6:1–11 is illustrative. Paul challenges his readers to refrain from unfamily-like behavior (litigation), *and* he utilizes "brother" terminology in four instances to make his point. The family construct is clearly central here, as demonstrated by both Paul's language and the behavioral values that he promotes.

Note, in contrast, Acts 2:44–45 and 4:32–37. Neither passage contains kinship terminology in its near context. Nevertheless, as S. S. Bartchy has demonstrated, the behavior exhibited – the sharing of material possessions – is best understood as an expression of the Jerusalem Christians' conception of their community as a surrogate kinship group (1991, 309–18). That is, social values characteristic of the Mediterranean family best explain the behavior exhibited by the Jerusalem Christians despite the absence of family language in the surrounding context.

The same methodology should be applied to the value of honor and shame. The exegete will of course gravitate toward those texts containing explicit terminology as the most likely candidates for the application of the construct as a useful hermeneutical device. Certain other texts, however, which lack such semantic indicators, will also be better understood when viewed through the lens of this important social value. I hope to demonstrate in the present work that concerns for social status and honor serve as *the* primary social values energizing Paul's portrayal of Jesus in Philippians 2:6–11. To be sure, terms from the semantic field of honor and shame are present in the context of the passage (δοῦλος, 2:7; σταυρός, 2:8; ὄνομα, 2:9–10). But it is the structure of Paul's hymn to Christ, which reads like an inverted *cursus*, along with the social background of the colony of Roman Philippi, which provides the most compelling evidence for my thesis.

As Downing appropriately notes, the importance of honor and shame – or of any implicit cultural script, for that matter – in a given text must be demonstrated by the illumination it brings to the interpretation of the passage. Some of the recent attempts to apply the honor/shame construct to New Testament narratives are certainly forced and artificial; others, however, are quite convincing. The reader will decide whether the present treatment falls in the former or the latter category.

9. Lenski (1966, 37, author's emphasis).
10. MacMullen (1974, 118).
11. In a letter in which he informs a friend about a library he built and *alimenta* he financed for the children of his hometown, Pliny observes, "the cultivation of liberal inclinations . . . taught me to be free from the general bondage to avarice." Earlier in the letter, Pliny had specifically identified this "bondage"

with the "innate disposition to accumulate wealth" by which, Pliny regrets, "mankind is universally governed" (*Ep.* 1.8).
12. In view here is the practice of urban patronage, so prevalent in Greco-Roman antiquity. On the subject of Roman patronage in general, see Saller (1982) and Moxnes (1991). Nicols (1980) documents a change in the nature of the elite patron's traditional rewards, as Rome made the transition from republic to empire. During the republican era, the patron received from his clients votes at election time, soldiers for military campaigns, and the company of his clients as faithful retainers in public. The offices attained and battles won through the support of one's clients served, in turn, to enhance individual and familial honor. Centralization of power in the hands of the emperor put an effective end to these avenues of public honor. Instead, Rome now encouraged a new ideology in which patronage was defined more in terms of civic virtue. In Rome and in the provinces, the elite increasingly turned wealth into honor by spending their money on projects which benefited the public. Nicols refers to "the enormous (and virtually unparalleled) outpouring of private capital for public welfare in the second century" (1980, 385).
13. Moxnes (1991, 249–50).
14. Translated by MacMullen, who adds, "Note also the use of φιλοτιμία to mean not only the ambition for honor, but munificent giving (Plut., *Cic.* 8.1; *Phocion* 31.2; Dio Chrysos., *Or.* 46.3; LSJ s.v.), even forced contributions (Plut., *Eumenes* 4.3)" (1974, 168, n. 14).
15. MacMullen (1974, 62). A classic example in late republican history is Julius Caesar who, during his aedileship in 65 BCE, went into debt to the point of near bankruptcy in order to ingratiate himself with the masses by putting on extraordinary spectacles and gladiatorial exhibitions.
16. Barton (2001, 58).
17. Malina and Neyrey (1991, 25–26). See Pitt-Rivers (1966, 21).
18. Moxnes (1996, 20, author's italics).
19. Ibid.
20. Malina and Rohrbaugh (1992, 213). As Miriam Griffin has recently asserted in another connection, "The Romans could not accept that the conduct of the individual should not be governed in any way by the estimate of others" (1996, 196).
21. Lendon (1997, 36).
22. Barton (2001, 248–50).
23. Trans. Barton (2001, 19).
24. Trans. Lendon (1997, 97).
25. Trans. Lendon (1997, 91).
26. Valerius Maximus comments similarly: "Glory is not neglected even by such as attempt to inculcate contempt for it, since they are careful to add their names to those very volumes, in order to attain by use of remembrance what they belittle in their professions" (8.14, ext. 3).
27. Lendon (1997, 91).
28. In view of the above survey of the public nature of honor in the Roman world, I find Rohrbaugh's recent description of members of the elite class as "quasi-individualists" rather at odds with the evidence. Rohrbaugh opines, "Their survival was not at stake, and thus they could afford to act as a law unto themselves, beholden to no one. Their honor was displayed in their achievements

and possessions, not in their conformity or loyalty to a group" (2002, 35). I much appreciate Rohrbaugh's attempt to nuance the sweeping categorization of ancient Mediterranean persons as collectivist in orientation, a categorization which has characterized much of New Testament scholarship along these lines. The application of cultural anthropological models to Mediterranean antiquity, if not in its infancy, has barely reached adolescence, and increasing refinements will only enhance our understanding of the ancient world. I suspect, however, that Rohrbaugh has here swung the pendulum too far back in the opposite direction. Rohrbaugh's quasi-individualist elite classes whose honor was "displayed in their achievements and possessions" and who were "beholden to no one," sound more like the upper-middle-class Americans who live in my suburban Los Angeles neighborhood than the Roman elite we have encountered in the sources surveyed above.

29. Lendon (1997, 44).
30. Indeed, as Lendon notes, the "monolithic quality of ancient rhetorical education" served as a key factor in socializing many generations in many places to adopt common standards of honor (ibid.).
31. Ibid.
32. Thus, Helmut Halfmann: "The social status of a person's parents and distant ancestors was the most important criterion determining the position of an individual in Roman society" (1979, 28, my translation). Similarly, Anthony Barrett remarks in his recent biography of Livia, "The importance of family background as a virtual prerequisite to success in Roman society cannot be overstated" (2002, 4).
33. Not only were potential spouses evaluated on the basis of natal origin. Senators, too, were ideally to be chosen for their lineage. Thus Dio puts in the mouth of Maecenas a speech recommending as senators, first and foremost, "those of noblest birth" (Dio Cass. 52.19.1).
34. Saller (1994, 110).
35. Others attempted to acquire undeserved social status in different ways and were severely punished for their deceptions. Suetonius tells us that Claudius "confiscated the property of those freedmen who passed as Roman knights and ... forbade men of foreign birth to use the Roman names ... Those who usurped the privileges of Roman citizenship he executed in the Esquiline field" (*Claud.* 25).
36. The right educational training and rhetorical skill could prove decisive. According to Valerius Maximus by "campaigning in the courts M. Cicero won the highest offices and a most eminent status" (*summos honores amplissimumque dignitatis locum*) (8.5.5).
37. Bourdieu (1977, 15).
38. Lendon (1997, 36–37).
39. Lendon (1997, 37).
40. The discussion that follows leans heavily on Lendon (1997, 40–41). Lendon (41, n. 51) cites Val. Max. bks. 3–6; Cic. *Planc.* 60; Sall. *Iug.* 1.3; Plut. *Cat. Min.* 1.1, 16.4.
41. Malina (1996, 48).
42. The topic has received increasingly nuanced treatments in recent years. See, for example, Creighton (1990, 279–307).
43. I owe this citation to deSilva (2000, 24).

44. Lendon (1997, 41, citing Tac. *Ann.* 4.38). The efficacy of honor as a moral constraint was particularly idealized by Roman imperial writers who wrote about the past. Livy, for example, describes a time (*c.* 300 BCE) when the only punishment backing up an important piece of legislation (*lex Valeria de provocatione*) was the formal declaration that the offender had committed a dishonorable act (*improbe factum*). He remarks, "I believe that this seemed a sufficiently strong sanctioning of the law – such was the shame (*pudor*) of men in those days" (Livy 10.9.6; trans. Barton [2001, 20]).
45. Scholars have become increasingly sensitive to the lack of personal privacy that characterized Roman social life, and Barton has recently underscored the close relationship that existed between this lack of privacy and what she calls "the critical social function of shame," a relationship that finds its most colorful expression, during the republican era, in the office of the Roman censor. According to Plutarch, the censor – in Barton's words "a sort of chief shamer" – possessed the power "of examining into the lives and manners of the citizens ... to watch, admonish, and chastise, that no one should turn aside to wantonness and forsake his native and customary mode of life." Plutarch explains:

> Its creators [of the office of censor] thought that no one should be left to his own devices and desires, without inspection and review, either in his marrying, or in the begetting of his children, or in the ordering of his daily life, or in the entertainment of his friends.
> (*Cat. Mai.* 16.1–2)

Excessive personal privacy was correspondingly viewed as a perilous commodity. Thus, Suetonius writes of Tiberius on Capri, "Moreover, having gained the licence of privacy, and being as it were out of sight of the citizens, he at last gave free rein at once to all the vices which he had for a long time ill concealed" (*Tib.* 42). Among the Romans, then, life was to be lived in the public eye, for the public good. Barton's summary is only slightly overstated: "The Roman way demanded a degree of mutual surveillance and inhibition that modern Americans might find only in an Orwellian nightmare or a maximum-security prison" (2001, 23).
46. Lendon (1997, 176).
47. The translation "Honors Race" (with the capitalization) is taken from Anthony Everitt's engaging biography of Cicero (2003, 12).
48. Primary sources outlining the origins and duties of the Roman magistrates include Cicero (*Leg.* 3.3.6–9; *Off. passim*), Varro (*Ling.* 5.14.80–82), *Digest* 1.2.16–28 (Pomponius), and Polybius (6.12.1–9).
49. When an esteemed senator received his callers in the morning a cry went out, "first the praetor, second the tribune" (Juv. 1.01). It was a noteworthy inversion of traditional priorities when Nero's grandfather, Lucius Domitius, "only an aedile, forced the censor Lucius Plancus to make way for him on the street" (Suet. *Nero* 4).
50. The *lex Villia Annalis* (180 BCE) set minimum ages for holding the praetorship and the consulship, and required a minimum interval of two years between the end of one office and the beginning of another.
51. Early emperors did not, however, simply appoint persons to the magistracies; influence was much less overt. Augustus, for example, restored popular

elections in 27 BCE, but continued to arrange for the election of his chosen candidates by an informal exercise of *auctoritas* known as *commendatio* or *suffragatio*. The actual choice of candidates was transferred to the senate upon the accession of Tiberius, from which time the people were presented with a single list of candidates chosen by the senate (with the emperor's approval) (Brunt [1984, 429]). The senate also continued to be involved in dispensing the honors associated with the various promagistracies, at least until the end of the first century (1984, 431).

Emperors, however, still managed to have their way. Tiberius, for example, carefully guarded his control over the dispensing of honors in the *cursus*. In 16 CE, a senator named Asinius Gallus introduced a motion that would have brought significant innovation to the *cursus*. According to Tacitus, Gallus moved "that the elections should determine the magistrates for the next five years, and that legionary commanders, serving in that capacity before holding the praetorship, should become praetors designate at once, the emperor nominating twelve candidates for each year." As Tacitus aptly proceeds to observe, "There was no doubt that the proposal went deeper than this, and trespassed on the arcana of sovereignty." Senators whose magistracies were assured five years in advance would not be nearly as pliable to the emperor. Tiberius responded by rebuffing the motion with a persuasive speech to the contrary (*Ann.* 2.36).

52. http://www.livius.org/ct-cz/cursus/cursus_honorum.html.
   [The publisher has endeavoured to ensure that the URL is correct and active at the time of going to press. However, the publisher has no responsibility for websites and can make no guarantee that a site will remain live or that the content is or will remain appropriate.]
53. Nero will later deal with a vacant consulate in a more traditionally appropriate manner: "When one of them died just before the Kalends of January, he appointed no one in his place, expressing his disapproval of the old-time case of Caninius Rebilus, the twenty-four hour consul [the name of Julius Caesar's appointee]" (Suet. *Nero* 15). Caesar's indiscretions with respect to the *cursus* tradition were not easily forgotten.
54. Lendon (1997, 21). The bestowal of these insignia on non-office-holding senators was one thing. It was downright scandalous when they were given to non-members of the elite. Pliny, more than a half-century after the event, simply could not seem to get over the fact that Pallas, a freedman of Claudius, was once honored by the senate with the insignia of a praetor. Pliny, who apparently stumbled across a monument to Pallas in Rome, felt compelled to assert in a letter written shortly thereafter that it was a "ridiculous farce" for such honors to be "thrown away on such dirt and filth" (*Ep.* 7.29.3; see also *Ep.* 8.6; Suet. *Claud.* 28; Tac. *Ann.* 12.53).
55. The reverse could obtain. Instead of a person being viewed as inferior and undeserving of an honor, a distinguished man might gain no honor – or even be dishonored – by being assigned a lowly post. Lendon adds, "At such a junction he is described as being 'above his office,' a revealing phrase, in that it implies the precision with which the honour of men and of offices could be totaled up and compared" (Lendon [1997, 181]; see Plut. *Prae. ger. reip.* 811b; SHA *Comm.* 3.3).

56. Suetonius relates another significant violation of traditional practice on the part of Claudius:

> Though he had declared at the beginning of his reign that he would choose no one as a senator who did not have a Roman citizen for a great-great-grandfather, he gave the broad stripe even to a freedman's son, but only on condition that he should first be adopted by a Roman knight. Even then, fearful of criticism, he declared that the censor Appius Caecus, the ancient founder of his family, had chosen the sons of freedmen into the senate; but he did not know that in the days of Appius and for some time afterwards the term *libertini* designated, not those who were themselves manumitted, but their freeborn sons. (*Claud.* 24)

57. Lendon (1997, 40).
58. Lendon (1997, 185).
59. Beck (1996, 181). Each grade in the cult was also under the protection of one of the planets (ibid.).
60. Kloppenborg (1996, 26).
61. Kloppenborg (1996, 23).
62. Translation from Lewis and Reinhold (1966, 322).
63. Lendon notes,

> Aristocrats fastidiously excluded freedmen from positions of honour in their realm, from the town senate, from being mayor or aedile. Very grand persons even sneered at freedmen's free-born sons. But freedmen (although not slaves) are extremely common as honoured officials in Italian trade guilds under the empire, guilds with many free-born members. The dishonouring taint of servile origin was felt less in communities of honour lower down in society; in a burial society even a freedman benefactor might have attributed to him the supreme prestige embodied in *maiestas*. (1997, 98).

For a recent survey of voluntary associations, with special emphasis on Macedonian groups, see Ascough (2003).

64. Kloppenborg (1996, 21).
65. Trans. Shelton (1988, 116).
66. Trans. Lendon (1997, 246).
67. Lendon (1997, 97). Joshel's collection of inscriptions reveals numerous examples of slaves and freedmen (of both genders) preoccupied with claims and grants of honor (1992).
68. Thus Barton insists that "emotionally the slave was every bit as sensitive to insult as his or her master. The plebeian was as preoccupied with honor as the patrician, the client as the patron, the woman as the man, the child as the adult" (2001, 11).
69. Garnsey and Saller (1987, 123). Early discussions of Roman social mobility include Hopkins (1965) and Weaver (1967).
70. MacMullen (1974, 88).
71. Garnsey and Saller (1987, 124).
72. Trans. Arlandson (1997, 23).

73. On advancement through the army see Halfmann (1979) and Saller (2000, 835–38). For the social opportunities available to freedmen and others of non-senatorial, non-equestrian status, Purcell's important study of the *apparitores* is quite insightful (1983). I suspect, however, that he is overly optimistic about the availability of these retainer posts to the masses of *ingenui* and *liberti* across the empire. Purcell's assertion that "almost no boundary between social groups was impervious to the power of personal patronage or the effects of economic success" (1983, 126), while technically accurate, must be qualified with the observation that the great majority of the empire's residents were undoubtedly neither well connected nor economically successful. Saller's summary is a sound one:

> Most of the empire's population worked in the countryside, where the nature of economic production offered few opportunities for significant social advancement. The condition of free rural labouring families should not be imagined to have been entirely static: hard work, good or bad luck with harvests and herds, and the division or accumulation of land through inheritance must have produced improvements and declines in family fortunes over the generations. Yet it is difficult to see how the meagre and uneven surpluses of peasant farming could have generated dramatic promotion into the leisured élite for very many.
> (2000, 834)

74. The quotations are from MacMullen (1974, 89, 91). The parenthetical comment in the second quotation is mine.
75. Saller describes the pathway to upward mobility through the military as "extremely narrow," noting that "only a few tens of thousands out of the empire's many millions were recruited into the legions each year, and only one or two out of the thousands of veterans retiring each year rose to the ranks of procurator" (2000, 836).
76. For the Delos Poseidonists see McLean (1996, 197).
77. Walker-Ramisch (1996, 134; she is citing MacMullen [1974, 76]).
78. Recent excavations of a mithraeum at Caesarea provide tangible evidence of this truth. The mithraeum lay beneath and enjoyed a connection (through a light tunnel) with a structure labeled by excavators as the "Honorific Portico." The Portico contained a garden decorated with monuments and plaques honoring various of the city's (and the province's) past elites. As Beck observes, "The two integrated structures nicely encapsulate Mithra's relationship to its secular context," a relationship of conformity and the reinforcement of the social status quo (1996, 178).
79. Lendon (1997, 33).
80. Lendon (1997, 73).
81. Reinhold (1970, 38).

3 The Roman colony at Philippi

1. Inscriptions from Philippi are generally cited according to the numbering system used by Pilhofer (2000; e.g. 348/G356). Dates are given where Pilhofer provides them; most dates remain somewhat conjectural. Philippi's forum was rebuilt during the second century, with the result that much evidence

dates to the period after that time. The conservative nature of Roman social values assures us, however, that the concerns for honor and hierarchy reflected in later inscriptions are likely to have characterized first-century Philippi, as well.

I generally follow Pilhofer's reconstruction of the often fragmentary inscriptions. Discussion of debated portions will be limited to those terms and phrases that specifically inform my study of the social orientation of the colony. Round parentheses – "( )" – expand abbreviations into full terms; square brackets – "[ ]" – enclose portions of an inscription which were broken off or otherwise unreadable but which have been restored with a significant degree of confidence. For other notations see Pilhofer (1995, 13).

2. For an overview of the history of Philippi, see Pilhofer (1995, 86–87) and Koukouli-Chrysantaki (1998, 5–35).
3. Krenides means a site "with many springs." Appian notes, "Philippi is a city that was formerly called Datos, and before that Krenides, because there are many springs bubbling around a hill there" (*BCiv.* 4.105). Appian probably has the Krenides-Datos chronology backwards. It appears that the Thracian settlement Datos was renamed Krenides by the Greeks (Koukouli-Chrysantaki [1998, 5, n. 2]).

Technically the pre-360 BCE inhabitants were not Thracians, since they had migrated from the west, rather than from Thrace in the east. Affinities with the Thracians, however, are such that those *in situ* when the Macedonians first arrived continue to be referred to as Thracians in the scholarly literature (Oakes [2001, 11–12]).
4. For the request to Philip for help we rely on information from Stephanus Byzantius: "The Krenidians were warring with the Thracians. Because of Philip's helping, they renamed it for Philip" (Koukouli-Chrysantaki [1998, 6, n. 4]).
5. The mines were apparently exhausted by Roman times (Oakes [2001, 21]).
6. The Greek period has left some remains. An inscription dated to the second century BCE portrays Philippi organized and administrated as a typical Greek city (348/G356). Oakes cites other evidence for pre-Roman Philippi (2001, 20–21).
7. Literary sources for the Battle of Philippi include Appian (*BCiv.* 4.105–38), Dio Cassius (47.35–49), and Plutarch (*Brut.* 38–53; *Ant.* 22). Strabo claims that the settlement at Philippi was "enlarged after the defeat of Brutus and Cassius" (*Geographia* 7, fr. 41).
8. A Roman colony was not viewed as an independent *polis* but, rather, as a daughter congregation of Rome. Citizens of Philippi identified themselves according to their membership in the tribes of Rome itself. Thus, one of the first veterans settled in Philippi, Sextus Volcasius, claims membership in *Vol(tnia tribu)* (418/L266 in Pilhofer's collection [2000], discussed by Bormann [1995, 21]), and a formal ceremony proclaiming the establishment of Philippi as a colony recalls the founding of Rome under Romulus (1995, 30–32, citing numismatic evidence).
9. Hendrix (1992, 315). Some inscriptions demonstrate the use of Greek on the part of masons and other trade workers, but the proliferation of Latin during the first two centuries of the common era remains quite striking. Although Latin will again recede into the background as early as the third century, the language

dominates in inscriptions from the first and second centuries, and there can be little doubt that the Romans were the most influential group of people in the colony when Paul first arrived in Macedonia. Every person listed as a *duumvir* or decurion during the first century is a Roman. As Pilhofer concludes, "Power in the colony lay in the hands of the Roman residents and *only* in theirs" (1995, 91, my translation and italics). The uniqueness of Philippi in this regard is most apparent when the colony is compared with other settlements in Macedonia and Achaia. Cassandra, Dion, Pella, and Corinth contained many Greek inscriptions alongside those in Latin. In Philippi, particularly the city itself, one must look long and hard for a single one (1995, 119).

10. The theater was Roman through and through. The *archimimus* (chief mime) Titus Uttiedius Venerianus occupied his position for thirty-seven years (476/L092). We also find evidence of a *choragiarius* named Marcus Numisius Valens (287/L378). On the theater, see Collart (1928, 74–124).

11. For a comparison with Roman colonies in the East, see Levick (1967, 161) and Millar (1990).

12. "A person like Paul who came from the East to Philippi entered another world. Roman colonies could be found also in Asia Minor, but none was so markedly 'Roman' as Philippi" (Pilhofer [1995, 92]). Corinth, as well, differed from Philippi in ways that directly inform my study. Though decidedly Roman in nature, the colony at Corinth, in contrast to Philippi, exhibits little evidence of any significant veteran population (Spawforth [1996, 170–71]). Even more pronounced were the differences between Philippi and Greek cities which were not Roman colonies, and these differences were not without significant implications for the construction of a city's socio-religious value system. D. R. Edwards, for example, in an informing study of power and religion in the Greek East, has generated a model of accommodation to Roman hegemony among Greek elites which appears quite distinct from that which we find in Roman Philippi (1996). Edwards shows how Greek elites integrated the worship of local civic deities into Roman power structures, thereby accommodating Roman hegemony while, at the same time, preserving their indigenous heritage. He offers the city of Aphrodisias, whose local deity was Aphrodite, as a representative example of such a phenomenon:

> Here local elites long understood the power of the emperors within the rubric of their deity, Aphrodite. As we shall see, they maintained identity and pride by defining Roman power within their view of cosmic power, an action essential for their political and social identity . . . Like many from the elite classes in the Greek East, elites in Aphrodisias promoted a dialectic in which local or Roman power confirmed the power of their civic deity and its proponents; in turn, the power of the deity affirmed local or Roman power. (1996, 19)

The salient point here is that early Philippi (42 BCE to late first century CE), in contrast to cities like Aphrodisias, had no local Greek elite with a corresponding civic deity, so that the construction of Edwards's "dialectic" between Greek and Roman religious power and symbols proved unnecessary. It is not surprising, in this regard, that both "Philippi" and "Philippians"

are conspicuously absent from the indices at the end of Edwards's monograph.
13. It is important to remember that Octavian was still in the process of establishing the parameters of his position as sole ruler of the empire at this time (Bormann [1995, 15]). A number of Antony's supporters were settled in the colony, including the disbanded Legion XXVIII, a legion of Antony's (418/L266; see also Collart [1937, 235]).
14. For the numismatic data see Collart (1937, 232, and Table 30, No. 8–11) and Gaebler (1929, 260–69, Table 1).
15. Two altars with the words *VIC(toria) AUG(usta)* appear on one side; *COL(onia) PHIL(ippensis)*, along with a plow (an image closely associated with the foundation of a Roman colony), appear on the other side.
16. On the importance of the goddess Victoria for Roman imperial propaganda and, specifically, the use of the goddess in *Res gestae* to justify Augustus' civil and religious reforms, see Fears (1981b). The association of Augustus with Victoria represents the fruition of developments that had begun earlier during the civil wars when, one by one, "the elements of the ideological framework of the Roman state were being detached from associations with the concept of collective authority in the *res publica* and were being transformed into extensions of the personality of individual charismatic dynasts" (Fears [1981a, 882]). The goddess Victory, for example, traditionally associated with guardian deities Jupiter and the Discouri, began to appear in consort with a victorious general as early as the time of Sulla. Fears observes, "When men came to believe that the charisma of victory no longer resided in the collective entity of the *res publica* but rather in the figure of an individual leader, communal authority and republican government were doomed and monarchy the only reality" (1981b, 824). See also Gagé (1933).
17. 201/L305.
18. 208/L461.
19. 254/L442.
20. 203/L314.
21. 281/L371.
22. 282/L370 (Tiberius, 36 or 37 CE).
23. 452/L164.
24. The quotation ("a distinctly Augustan character") is from Bormann (1995, 34, author's emphasis). The connection between Augustus and Philippi was an enduring one. Augustus' name formed part of the name of the colony until at least the middle of the third century, as indicated by coins and inscriptions (Collart [1937, 238]).
25. Velleius Paterculus claims to be unable to provide the name of a single non-military colony founded after *c*. 95 BCE (Vell. Pat. 1.15.5). For Roman colonization see Keppie (1983, 1984); for Philippi in particular, see now Bormann (1995, 11–29).
26. Bormann (1995, 22); Portefaix (1988, 60).
27. Oakes (2001, 25, 49); de Vos (1999, 236–37).
28. Tellbe (2001, 213). See, too, Brunt (1971, 236, 261); Appian, *BCiv*. 4.115.
29. The size of the colony can only be conjectured. Pilhofer, utilizing as his point of departure the refurbished theater (second century CE), which seated some

8,000 persons, offers 5,000 to 10,000 persons as a reasonable estimate of the population during the second century (1995, 75–76). Oakes suggests about 15,000 residents, given the geographical size of the colony and the density of analogous settings like Pompeii (2001, 45).
30. Nor were the troops always happy with their allotments. Percennius, leader of the 14 CE mutiny in Pannonia, lamented the fact that soldiers were rewarded for their service by being "settled in some waterlogged swamp or untilled mountain" (Tac. *Ann.* 1.17).
31. Salmon (1969, 137–38).
32. Bormann (1995, 20). On the population of Philippi at the time of the founding of the colony, see Collart (1937, 175–77) and, now, Oakes (2001, 19–24). Strabo speaks of a "little settlement" (κατοικία μικρά) before the defeat of Cassius and Brutus (*Geographia* 7, fr. 41), but his information is quite confused (Oakes [2001, 22–23]).
33. Oakes (2001, 19–20, 29–30).
34. Bormann (1995, 20, my italics).
35. Alcock (1993, 106–15).
36. Oakes is using "Greeks" at this point in his discussion for "non-citizens who were largely Greek-speakers" (2001, 50).
37. "To be sure, Romans were not in the majority numerically, as might be (wrongly) assumed from the Roman character of the city, but *the cultural atmosphere was Roman through and through*" (Pilhofer [1995, 92, my italics]).
38. This principle of value replication should be kept in mind as we evaluate our literary sources. As some are now recognizing, the works of elite authors do not necessarily obscure social life as experienced by other status groups in the empire. D. R. Edwards, for example, opens his discussion of religion and power in the Greek East by acknowledging the "distinct bias" that characterizes our source materials: "they primarily represent an elite perspective." He does not, however, find this bias irretrievably problematic for ascertaining the social values of non-elite groups, since "the perspective of elites in the Roman world dominated most of the political, religious, and social landscape" (1996, 12).

    The phenomenon of value replication, moreover, is apparently not limited to pre-industrial, agrarian societies such as those of the ancient Mediterranean world. André Béteille, in a discussion of Max Weber's classic distinction between social classes and status groups, observes that "the relations between status groups are relations of emulation. Emulation by inferiors of the styles of life of their superiors provides stability to the prevailing system of stratification" (Béteille [1985, 832]).
39. As demonstrated by Krentz, who finds an unusual number of military terms and metaphors in the letter (1993). See also Geoffrion (1993). One could, of course, argue that Paul's own situation (i.e. Roman custody) has generated the military imagery in the epistle. It is not unreasonable, however, to assume that Paul here has in view the social setting of the Philippian congregation.
40. For the rank structure during the principate and social relations in the army see Breeze (1974) and MacMullen (1988), respectively.

41. The figures are from Speidel who is quite optimistic about their accuracy, due to some recent archaeological findings (1992, 106). See also Breeze (1971), Dobson (1972), and Jahn (1984).
42. Speidel (1992, 105).
43. Webster (1969, 191–94).
44. Macmullen (1974, 94).
45. Burnett, Amandry, and Ripollès (1992, 308, nn. 1646–49).
46. The description of the ritual comes from Gaebler's interpretation of the various images on coins minted at Philippi's founding (1929, 255–70, see 260–69). For a helpful summary see Collart (1937, 226–27) and Salmon (1969, 29–30).
47. Evidence from Dio suggests that Augustus also installed as colonists in Philippi some of Antony's party in Italy whose land he appropriated and gave to his own veterans (Dio Cass. 51.4.6). See the discussion in Collart (1937, 228–29).
48. 418/L266 (reign of Augustus; for dating see Bormann [1995, 20]).
49. For the praetorian cohort, see Collart (1937, 232), and Burnett, Amandry, and Ripollès (1992, 308, n. 1651). Oakes estimates the number of praetorians at one thousand (2001, 25).
50. According to J. B. Campbell, a legionary received a *praemium* of 12,000 sesterces, and a praetorian received 20,000 (1984, 162).
51. "After the conclusion of service, the military hierarchy is converted into a social hierarchy" (Bormann [1995, 23]). With time, however, the military orientation of Philippi probably receded somewhat, so that Oakes appropriately cautions us not to overestimate the number of veterans in the colony, and assumes there was a "negligible proportion of veterans" among the hearers of Paul's letter. He agrees with Bormann, however, that "there was probably a high proportion of veterans among the colony's authorities." Oakes suggests that about a quarter of those boasting decurion status were veterans (2001, 53). I suspect the percentage was higher, at least during the first half of the first century. The military presence in Philippi, moreover, was not limited to the colony's resident veterans and their descendants. Philippi's location along the Via Egnatia meant that the empire's armies would pass by on a regular basis in their east–west journeys. According to Suetonius, Tiberius marched through Philippi on his way to Syria in 20 BCE (*Tib.* 14). Ongoing challenges from indigenous tribes also guaranteed that Roman troops would never be far from Macedonia.
52. Lendon (1997, 243).
53. Cited by Lendon (1997, 246).
54. The translations of Caesar's *Gallic War* are Lendon's (1997, 244, 239).
55. Maxfield (1981, 113, 116–17).
56. Lendon (1997, 246).
57. Lendon (1997, 261, citing Dio Cass. 56.42.2; see also 265). Tellbe claims that veteran soldiers "were well known for being the most traditional and loyal ritualistic supporters of the civic cults" (2001, 217).
58. 202/L313. It is beyond the scope of this project to discuss the various technical terms (titles left untranslated above) representing various military posts. On this see Pilhofer and the bibliography cited there (2000, 219).

59. 058/L047. Although dating must remain conjectural, Pilhofer suggests a possible date at the time of Claudius or Nero, in which case Paul could hardly have missed the large monument alongside the Egnatian Way (2000, 65).
60. 522/L210. I count some seven ranks or titles in the inscription, as well as the imperial decorations referred to above. The inscription represents one of the most detailed descriptions we possess of a career in the Roman army. See the extensive commentary in Speidel (1970). The inscription is also discussed by Breeze (1971), who uses it as evidence for reconstructing pay grades and rank structure in the Roman army.
61. 219/L353. Several inscriptions detailing a combination of military and civic posts will be cited in the following chapter. The same phenomenon can be observed in several inscriptions from the colony at Scupi (Birley [1986, 212–14]).
62. This consensus (Beare [1959, 7–9]); White [1995, 250–51]) has recently been challenged by Bormann (1995, 60–70). Bormann, however, underestimates the persistence of local cults during the Roman period, as Pilhofer has rightly observed (1995, 47–48).
63. Bormann (1995, 32–67).
64. L. R. Taylor (1931, 12–14).
65. It is difficult to know whether or not living emperors received divine honors in Philippi, but it is patently clear that the veneration of deceased, divinized emperors and their families constituted a central component of the colony's religious and social life. A tradition obtained whereby the divinity of Julius Caesar was directly associated with Philippi. Thus Valerius Maximus relates the appearance of *divus Iulius* to Cassius before the battle of Philippi, saying that Cassius had failed in his attempt to kill Caesar, since his divinity guaranteed his immortality (1.6.13; 1.8.8). Augustus' association with the goddess *Victoria* also encouraged the development of the cult.

    I suspect that the more overt honors given to living emperors as gods, which characterized the cult in certain Greek cities in the East, would have been tempered by the decidedly Roman nature of the colony. The establishment of the *ius Italicum* at Philippi, for example, suggests an imperial cult more in line with Italian practices, where the honoring of the *genius* of the emperor, rather than his outright divinization, was the norm (important treatments include L. R. Taylor [1931], Price [1984], Fishwick [1987], and now Gradel [2002]). Given the identification of the region as the homeland of Alexander the Great, however, a more pronounced worship of the currently reigning emperor (particularly Caligula and Nero) at Philippi cannot be entirely ruled out. During his mid-twenties, Alexander had portrayed himself as a son of Zeus and, encouraged by Persian and Egyptian practices, had begun to seek worship in Greece and Macedonia. Though initially unenthusiastic, his local subjects established a vibrant cult to Alexander after his death. The Alexander cult lasted well into the Roman era and "provided both a model and an inspiration for the Roman imperial cult four centuries later" (Wright [2003, 56]); for the influence of Alexander on Roman practices, see now Erich S. Gruen (1998).
66. Analyses of the archaeological digs around the forum are found in Bormann (1995, 41), Sève (1989–90), Sève and Weber (1988, 477–79), and Koukouli-Chrysantaki (1998, 14–16). See, too, the summary in Tellbe (2001, 214–17).

67. Koukouli-Chrysantaki (1998, 16).
68. Hopkins (1978, 220, n. 33).
69. This applies to civic religion in general in the ancient world. Although one could fairly argue for some distinction between the sacred and the secular where newer cults and mystery religions are concerned, the sacred/secular dichotomy can only be anachronistic and misleading when applied to public, civic religion. Thus, Beard and North observe that pagan priests in the official cults "never (or only in exceptional circumstances) stood apart from the political order." Religious power, in this regard, was "embedded within the social and political order" (1990, 1–2). Note Cicero's conviction that "the worship of the gods and the vital interests of the state should be entrusted to the direction of the same individuals, to the end that citizens of the highest distinction and the brightest fame might achieve the welfare of religion by a wise administration of the state, and of the state by a sage interpretation of religion" (*Dom.* 1).

The modern, Euro-American perspective, which assumes that politics and religion are two distinct spheres of life (public and private, respectively), has in no small way distorted our understanding of ancient paganism and, I might add, of early Christianity as well. Until recently, for example, interpreters of Paul have tended to depoliticize his writings, focusing, instead, almost exclusively on Paul's theological insights. The rediscovery of the close connection between politics and religion in the ancient world affords us the opportunity not only to understand Roman religion better but also to gain a "fresh perspective" on Paul, for whom, we may confidently assume, politics and religion also constituted mutually informing categories (Wright, 2001).
70. Price (1984, 7).
71. Garnsey and Saller (1987, 167).
72. Hopkins (1978, 198).
73. Bormann lists some fourteen inscriptions describing priests and priestesses of the imperial cult (1995, 42–44).
74. 700/L738 (first century CE).
75. 001/L027 (first century CE).
76. Evidence from elsewhere in the empire extends our understanding of the formal aspects of the flaminate. The *Lex de flaminio provinciae Narbonensis*, from Vespasian's reign, institutionalized the imperial cult in the province of Gallia Narbonensis, addressing extensively the office of *flamen* (*CIL* 12.6038). Much of the legislation is "devoted to specification of the symbols placing this new official in the ranks of the élite of the city of Narbo" (Saller [2000, 820]), the symbols including: (a) being accompanied by lictors, (b) having the right to sit in the front row at public games (between senators and decurions), and (c) special clothing for the *flamen* and his wife. We may assume that similar privileges accompanied the flaminate in Philippi.
77. 002/L028 (first century CE).
78. 226/L344. See Pilhofer for a proposed restoration of this fragmentary inscription (2000, 240–43). Julia's identity as *sacerdos* in the imperial cult is not disputed on any reading.
79. On the *Augustales* see now the article by John Scheid in the new Pauly (1997). Scheid maintains that even if the *Augustales* did not constitute a proper *corpus* and *ordo* until the second century, they were formally organized according

to the analogy of the *ordo decurionum* from the outset (1997, col. 292). See also Ostrow, who also identifies the group as a functional (if not official) *ordo* and offers a helpful summary of the social function of the *Augustales*:

> To understand the role of *Augustales* as well-to-do freedmen at the municipal level, we must recall that the freed slave, though a citizen, was barred from an active role in the political life of his town. He could hold neither any magistracy nor a seat on the town council. For the wealthy freedman in particular, recognition of this fact must often have been a troubling realization indeed. But inscriptions make clear, from their frequent mention of the various public honors accorded to individual *Augustales*, that the institution aimed in part to provide successful municipal freedmen with a path to civic esteem that all but equaled the prestige of the local ruling classes themselves. The newly selected *Augustalis* will have paid for his privilege with expensive public benefactions (food, temples, public entertainments), but he will at last have achieved the satisfaction of a surrogate public career. (1990, 365)

Finally, the presence of *Augustales* in the colony reinforces the view (argued above) that Philippi was more Roman in orientation than other colonies in the East, since although *Augustales* are attested "in hundreds of towns across Italy and the western Roman world," they are found "only very rarely in the East" (1990, 364).

80. Collart (1937, 269). Bormann discusses two stone blocks which served as seats for the theater and which show the marks *AUG PO*, indicating that the seats were reserved for the Augustan priesthood (1995, 98). *Lex Coloniae Genetivae* 66 offers a striking parallel: *eisque pontificib(us) augurib(us)q(ue) ludos gladiatoresq(ue) inter decuriones spectare ius potestasque esto* ("These priests and augurs shall have the right and the authority to view the games and gladiatorial spectacles [seated] among the decurions") (Bormann [1995, 46, n. 89]).
81. 037/L037.
82. 455/L083.
83. Clarke (2000, 29), drawing upon the work of Beard, North, and Price (1998, 215).
84. Compare the description of a public procession honoring the goddess Isis in Apuleius (*Met.* 11.8–17).
85. Bormann (1995, 67).
86. Pilhofer (1995, 47–48).
87. Pilhofer, who charges Mikael Tellbe (1994) with greatly overemphasizing the role of the imperial cult during the first century, could fairly be charged with underestimating its importance. It is surely unreasonable, for example, to compare ("Ähnlich") first-century evidence for the ruler cult at Philippi with evidence for Isis, and to summarily dismiss both as unimportant in reconstructing first-century religious life in the colony (Pilhofer [1995, 93, see n. 6]). Sharply distinguishing Caesar worship from the Isis cult are (a) the refounding of the colony by Augustus, (b) the emperor's special relationship with his veterans, and (c) the late-first-century (and overwhelming second-century) evidence for the veneration of the imperial family – all of which point to a thriving ruler cult during the mid-first century CE.

Koukouli-Chrysantaki fairly surmises, then, that "Paul must have strolled in the forum, where statues of Augustus and his family stood, together with monuments of the Julio-Claudian emperors, eminent citizens of the Colonia Augusta Iulia Philippensis, and the local Thracian kings" (1998, 16).

88. In the Thracian population, Philippi's veteran colonists apparently encountered a people as preoccupied with public marks of social status as the Roman settlers themselves: (Dio to his interlocutor:) "Well, now have you ever been in Thrace?" "Yes." "Then you have seen the women there, the free women, covered with branded marks, and having the more such marks and the more elaborate in proportion to their social standing and that of the families to which they belong?" (Dio Chrys. Or. 14.19).
89. Pilhofer (1995, 89).
90. The same might be said of Greek influence. The milestones that were erected between Neapolis and Philippi on the Via Egnatia are initially bilingual (first Latin, then Greek) – Latin, however, clearly dominates along the last kilometer before the city (Pilhofer [1995, 119]).
91. Sack (1986, 19). See also R. B. Taylor (1988).
92. Neyrey (2002, 61).
93. Everitt (2003, 49).
94. See Bormann for a discussion of the archaeological evidence relating to the temples (1995, 41–42), and Koukouli-Chrysantaki for the *curia* (1998, 15).
95. Dorcey (1992, 3).
96. The Isis sanctuary, as well, established itself a century later across the Via Egnatia, some 300 meters from the forum of the city (Pilhofer [1995, 75]).
97. Witherington (1998, 490). Non-elite cults that did gain a foothold in the city were generally aligned with the cult of the emperor. In a recent article examining the status of rural cult sites in Greece, Susan Alcock discusses "the abandonment of these small country cults" during the early Roman period, as the population of southern Greece increasingly migrated from the countryside to local towns and cities (Alcock [1994, 253]). Inscriptional data suggests that the same dynamic played itself out in the north. The resulting amalgamation of rural and urban religion in any given setting would depend on elite structures of religion and power in the local town or city. The decidedly Roman orientation of Philippi meant that, as adherents to local cults (and to local expressions of foreign cults, like Isis and Cybele) moved from the country to the city, "many of the local gods were subordinate to Roman politics of religion and gradually became integrated into the civic cults" (Tellbe [2001, 216]). Second- and third-century inscriptions thus portray the cults of Cybele and Isis, for example, devoted at the same time to the cult of the emperors. The local cult of the Thracian Horseman also found itself associated with emperor worship.
98. Whittaker (1997, 148).

4 Honor and status in Philippi

1. 213/L347 (second century CE).
2. 217/L348 (second century CE).
3. 214/L349 (second century CE).
4. 215/L350 (second century CE).

5. 218/L352 (second half of second century CE).
6. 219/L353 (second half of second century CE).
7. I am not alone in finding a particular "pride of honors" in Philippi. See the quote from Pilhofer in the summary at the end of this chapter.
8. 198/L307. On the identification of the building as a records house see Sève (1996, 177).
9. 233/L332. The inscription is composed of several fragments of which I have only reproduced four. The identification of the *Iunior* of the library with Gaius Oppius derives from a third inscription found in the forum, set up by a person named Gaius Oppius Montanus Junior (231/L341). The same individual is honored in yet a fourth inscription, also found in Philippi's forum (235a/L804).
10. 228/L331 (161 or 175 CE).
11. Sève (1996, 173).
12. 229/L342 (second half of second century CE). The only other senators attested in Philippi before the fourth century are Gaius Julius Maximus Mucianus (240/L465, below) and Lucius Salvius Secundinus (386a/L839).
13. 232/L336.
14. 240/L465.
15. 061/L050 (second century CE).
16. 249/L373.
17. 252/L467 (second–third century CE).
18. Forbis (1996, 5, 9).
19. Forbis (1996, 4).
20. 257/L445.
21. 87/L265. See Pilhofer for above interpretation (2000, 85).
22. 386a/L839. The word *adlectio* is a technical term for a practice first attested under Claudius and Vespasian, which later became permanent under Domitian. The *adlectio* was a special mark of distinction whereby a young senator, before attainment of the legal minimum age, or an equestrian (often advanced in years), could be placed in a specific rank of the senatorial class (Halfmann [1979, 82]). Houston focuses particularly upon adlection under Vespasian, which Houston regards as "one of the most significant events of his principate" (1977, 35).
23. 395/L780 (after 161 CE).
24. See the following inscription, as well as 438/L077, where the *cursus* ascends from quaestor through aedile to *duumvir*. For a helpful overview of the function of the decurion council and the various magistrates in a Roman colony or municipality, see Clarke (2000, 41–58). The standardization that characterizes our surviving fragmentary evidence allows us to apply data derived from cities in Spain, for example, to Roman settlements elsewhere in the empire. In this regard, Curchin's study of Roman Spain becomes important for understanding the governmental structure and the responsibilities of elite office-holders in a colony like Philippi (1990).
25. 396/L781.
26. Patron (031/L121, first century CE); *irenarch* (120/L618); quaestor, aedile, and *duumvir* (438/L077).
27. 004/L030 (first century CE).
28. 001/L027 (first century CE).
29. 492/L110.

Notes to pages 99–105   193

30. 493/L113.
31. 026/L123. The inscription was found in Kavala.
32. 249/L373.
33. A grave inscription for Titus Flavius Alexander, erected by his son, Titus Flavius Macedonicus similarly attests to the holding of important municipal magistracies by more than one family member. The father served as "decurion of Philippi." The son boasts that he himself has been "honored with the decorations of a decurion," the likely prelude to the honor of the office itself (502/L247; see also 493/L113, above).
34. 350/L448.
35. 340/L589. See Pilhofer for interpretation (2000, 347).
36. Cybele: 321/L377. Isis and Serapis: 252/L467; 307/G410.
37. 524/L103 (second century CE); 525/L104; 597/G221. See Pilhofer's discussion of Dionysus (1995, 105).
38. 133/G441.
39. 148/L682, 163/L002, 164/L001, 165/L003, and 166/L004. The Silvanus association is the best-attested cult group in Philippi, one which has generated a substantial bibliography (see Pilhofer [1995, 108–13] and [2000, 170–83]). Dorcey's volume on Silvanus should also be consulted (1992).
40. See the maps of the cult sites in Dorcey (1992).
41. Dorcey (1992, 3).
42. A remarkably complete catalogue of members is found in 163/L002. See Pilhofer for a list of slaves and freedmen cult members (Pilhofer [1995, 109–10]).
43. Readers will be familiar with the household conversion of the Philippian jailer in Acts 16. Among Silvanus worshipers in Philippi, Pilhofer identifies a *pater familias* named Gaius Paccius Mercuriales whose whole family (including his sons, a freedman, and a slave) belonged to the cult (Pilhofer [1995, 110]).
44. Marcus Alfensus Aspasius (164/L001; 163/L002), Lucius Volattius Urbanus (163/L002), and Macius Bictor (166/L004). 163/L002 appears to list two different priests, but the two names were engraved by different hands at different periods in the inscription's history. See Pilhofer (1995, 110–11).
45. 164/L001, line 2.
46. 213/L347. See the discussion earlier in the chapter.
47. 163/L002, lines 1–2; 164/001, lines 1–2, 24–25.
48. 166/L004; see Pilhofer's comments (2000, 183).
49. 164/L001. The interpretation of certain terms and phrases remains in doubt, so the translation must remain somewhat provisional. The salient point – the replication in non-elite settings of public honors awarded for benefaction – remains clear, at any rate.
50. MacMullen (1974, 76).
51. 588/L236, 177/L014.
52. 451/L158, 519/L245.
53. 529/L106.
54. 321/L377.
55. Pilhofer (1995, 145–46).
56. 057/L046.
57. 535/G207.
58. 142/G2562; also 143/G563, 144/G298.

59. 451/L158.
60. 132/L303 (second–third century CE). Another physician attested in the Philippian inscriptions had a father who is specifically designated as a decurion (*decurio*) in the inscription (322/L379). The lack of such a designation here implies that Quintus Mofius Euhemerus was not a member of the decurion class.
61. 175/L012 (second–third century CE).
62. 581/L239 (second–third century CE).
63. 022/G220.
64. 333/L268, 344/L449, 350/L448, 432/L163, 525/L104.
65. Oakes (2001, 33).
66. Pilhofer cites Léon Heuey, who had noted this connection more than a century ago (Pilhofer [2000, 461]).
67. 476/L092 (first century CE).
68. A number of scholars have commented on the inscription. See the discussion and bibliography in Pilhofer (2000, 459–63). Another person involved in the theater identifies himself as *choragiarius*, loosely translated as "a supplier of stage properties" (287/L378; translation from Glare [1985, 311]).
69. 270/L387.
70. 321/L377.
71. 392/L624 and 394/L779.
72. 416/L166.
73. D. B. Martin (1990, 47).
74. Gamicus, who identifies himself as "freedman of Pontius Novus" (*libertus Ponti Novi*) is an exception (558/L408, first–second century CE).
75. D. B. Martin (1990, 48).
76. "I take this as an indication that persons in Philippi were *especially proud* to display their ranks and offices" (Pilhofer [1995, 142, his italics]). Pilhofer sees Philippi as exceptional in the degree to which honor and status were emphasized in the settlement, and he sees this reflected in Philippi's epigraphic database. See Pilhofer's discussion, subtitled "Posten und Pöstchen in Philippi" (1995, 142–44).
77. 476/L092 (Pilhofer [1995, 142]).
78. 040/G040; "Was it necessary for Ἐνκόλπιος, who had a sarcophagus with an inscription made for his patron, to designate himself an ἀπελεύθερος in this inscription, and thereby hand down to posterity his own social status?" (Pilhofer [1995, 143]).

5 Acts and Philippians

1. The Philippian narrative in Acts stands out in a number of ways, and scholars consistently comment on the rich attention to detail which characterizes the story. The topographical and historical references, along with the detailed knowledge of technical terms relating to civic administration, are without parallel in Acts. Pilhofer concludes that the author was a Greek-speaking, non-citizen resident of the city of Philippi (1995, 157). For present purposes it is important to note that the author introduces Macedonia as "the *most explicitly Roman* territory that Paul has entered" (Staley [1999, 125, his italics]).

2. Witherington (1998, 489).
3. See now Pilhofer's extensive argument for the reading ἥτις ἐστὶν πρώτης μερίδος τῆς Μακεδονίας πόλις. He argues from epigraphic evidence that μερίς is a technical term relating to the partitioning of Macedonia into four districts in 167 BCE. The districts were numbered 1 through 4, from east to west, and Philippi was located in the first district. Luke possessed this local knowledge and, for this reason, used μερίς instead of his more common, non-technical, expression, μέρος (2:10; 19:1; 20:2) (Pilhofer [1995, 160–65]). On the textual problem see also Ascough (1998).
4. Pilhofer cites Pisidian Antioch (13:14; 14:19–20), Iconium (13:51; 14:1, 19, 21; 16:2), Lystra (14:6, 8, 21; 16:1–2), Alexandria Troas (16:8, 11; 20:5–6), Corinth (18:1; 19:1), Ptolemais (21:7), Syracuse (28:12), and Puteoli (28:13) (1995, 159–60). See on this, in addition to Pilhofer, Levick (1967) and Zahrnt (1988).
5. This represents the standard view of the passage, argued anew by Pilhofer (1995, 189–93). For various treatments of the charge against the missionaries see Sherwin-White (1992, 79), Haenchen (1971, 496), I. H. Marshall (1980, 270), Conzelmann (1987, 131–32), Johnson (1992, 295), and Rapske (1994, 117–18). Schwartz's creative alternative (1984) – that Paul's accusers are fellow-Jews – has been decidedly refuted by Pilhofer (1995, 189–91) and, again, by de Vos (1999b, 55–56).

As de Vos rightly observes, however, the majority view is not without problems in its own right. Not only were Romans rather accommodating to foreign cults; the Jews, in particular, were granted special privileges. The charge against the missionaries, that Jews were violating Roman customs, then, is not, in de Vos's view, "a charge that fits" (the quotation is taken from the title of his essay). De Vos therefore identifies the accusation as it stands in Acts 16:21 as a piece of Lucan redaction which the author substitutes for the more historically plausible charge of magical practices, in order to distance the missionaries from any association with magic.

I am more optimistic than de Vos about the historical veracity of the charge, and I believe that de Vos's commendable application of social-scientific models (deviance labeling; status degradation ritual) would work quite well with the text as it stands. In either case, however, the accusation that the missionaries are promulgating anti-Roman customs remains the primary thrust of the charge, and this is my point in the present connection.
6. Witherington (1998, 496). See, too, Pilhofer's arguments for the identification of the στρατηγοί as the *duumviri iure dicundo* (1995, 195–97).
7. Pilhofer (1995, 193).
8. The Philippian narrative should also be compared with events in Iconium (14:1–7), where the local rulers are also introduced with the non-technical ἄρχοντες (14:5) which, unlike the Philippian account, receives no further specificity in the ensuing context.
9. Peter Garnsey (1970, 268).
10. I am among those who understand Paul to be a Roman citizen. Peter van Minnen has persuasively argued that Paul was probably a descendant of a Jewish freedman who had received Roman citizenship upon manumission (1994). Others favorable to the idea that Paul was a Roman citizen include Hemer (1989, 127) and Hengel (1991, 6–15). W. Stegemann (1987) and Lentz

(1993, 131–33) argue to the contrary. For further bibliography see Hengel (1991, 101, n. 58).
11. Bruce (1990, 366).
12. Rapske (1994, 134).
13. Oakes (2001, 61).
14. Pilhofer (1995, 121–22).
15. 600/L229.
16. Tellbe (2001, 214). On the *ius Italicum* see Watkins (1979, 1983). In Watkins's view, the history of *ius Italicum* is inseparable from that of Rome's citizen colonies. He concludes, "A Roman citizen colony was a part of the Roman state, was located on *ager Romanus*, and its settlers had the same rights and privileges in Roman law as did all other *cives*" (1983, 319–20).
17. 232/L336 (second half of second century CE).
18. "the term *colonia* refers to the community of citizens with full rights, to the *Philippenses*, that is, to the colonists, to their descendants, and to those previous residents of the region who had been naturalized and enrolled among the number of the colonists, while *res publica* designates the common realm of the colony, whose population consisted of elements that differed with respect to their legal status and which were organized into communities enjoying various prerogatives" (Papazoglou [1982, 106]).
19. Recent attention to the issue of citizenship on the part of Claudius may have fueled preoccupation with the franchise in a Roman colony like Philippi. Although liberal in his policy to extend citizenship in the provinces, Claudius was adamant about preserving social and legal distinctions between citizen and non-citizen. He executed persons *civitatem Romanam usurpantes* (Suet. *Claud.* 25).
20. See Johnson (1992, 303) for the interpretation of 16:37–39 as an honor contest.
21. The parallel with Jesus' honor reversal in Philippians 2 may be even more pronounced than indicated in the above discussion. Jennifer Glancy has recently provided a nuanced interpretation of the social function of public flogging in the Roman world (2004). In her view, scholars who focus solely upon the legal status of persons who are whipped by Roman magistrates (Acts 16:22–23) "overlook the *meaning* of such treatment for those shaped by Roman *habitus*" (124, author's italics). She proceeds to observe, "Citizen or not, free or slave, a beaten body was a dishonored body; any free person who was publicly stripped and battered with rods suffered an effective reduction in social status" (124). Even more to the point in the present connection is the semiotic relationship Glancy proceeds to uncover between flogging and slavery: "whipping, which brings dishonor to the one who is whipped, is suitable only for slaves, so one who is whipped, even if legally free, warrants description as servile" (125). Both Jesus (Phil. 2:7) and the missionaries, then, willingly assume slave status for the benefit of others, only to be vindicated in the striking honor reversals that conclude their respective narratives (Phil. 2:9–11; Acts 16:37–39).
22. The bibliography on Paul's πολιτεύομαι/πολίτευμα terminology in Philippians is ever-expanding. Clarke's discussion is a good place to begin (2000, 192–97); see, too, Pilhofer (1995, 127–34), as well as Tellbe (1994), Cotter

(1993), and Ascough (2003, 146–49). With most commentators, I understand πολιτεύομαι and πολίτευμα to be loaded with political connotations, referring to an alternative citizenship among the people of God, in pointed contrast to the emphasis on membership in the Roman citizen tribe *Voltinia*, which was so prevalent in the colony. A secondary contrast, with a replicated πολίτευμα experienced by members of voluntary associations, is also possible (Ascough [2003, 148–49]).

Peter Oakes's analysis has been particularly helpful in this regard. It is likely that those in the church who did possess Roman citizen status were almost exclusively non-elite Romans. Their citizenship thus had the potential to become the primary status marker distinguishing them socially from their fellow-Christians, particularly when confronted by official persecution. Paul's insistence on an alternative, superior πολίτευμα, to which all God's people belong, would have challenged any tendencies on the part of Roman church members to privilege their colonial citizen status (Oakes [2001, 55–76]).

23. Timothy, of course, is also included under the rubric "servants of Christ Jesus." This, too, is unique in the Pauline corpus. As Hawthorne has observed, in all his other letters Paul "puts a distance between himself and his colleagues by describing only himself as 'slave,' or 'apostle,' or 'prisoner' of Christ Jesus – never anyone else" (1983, 3). This departure from Paul's standard practice has been explained in a variety of ways (see Hawthorne [1983, 4], for the views and their respective adherents). In a letter full of examples, it is likely that Paul includes Timothy under the heading "servants of Christ Jesus" in preparation for his presentation of Timothy in 2:19–24 (note the use of ἐδούλευσεν to describe Timothy's sacrificial behavior in 2:22). That Paul, however, remains the sole author of the letter is indicated by the first-person singular Εὐχαριστῶ τῷ θεῷ μου ("I thank my God," 1:3), which follows the opening greeting.
24. O'Brien (1991, 45).
25. Fee (1995, 62). Fee labels Philippians a "hortatory letter of friendship," building on the works of Stowers (1991) and White (1990).
26. Some scholars, moreover, are now expressing reservations about the facile identification of Philippians as a letter of friendship. Reumann, for example, acknowledges influence from the friendship *topos* in the epistle but doubts that there is enough evidence to classify Philippians formally as a friendship letter (1996).
27. Sass (1941), Ollrog (1979, 184, n. 108), and Schenk (1984, 77) read the term in this way. The view can be found as early as John Chrysostom, who says, "This is a great honor, to be *a slave of Christ*" (*Homily on Philippians*, 2.1.1–2; trans. M. J. Edwards [1999, 217], translator's italics).
28. Fee (1995, 63).
29. Fee, for example, argues for a double connotation (1995, 63).
30. O'Brien (1991, 45). Others who interpret the term in this way include Silva (1992, 40–41), Hawthorne (1983, 5), and Best (1968, 375).
31. Bormann rightly relates Paul's description of himself and Timothy as δοῦλοι Χριστοῦ Ἰησοῦ in 1:1 to the "niedrige soziale Stellung" ("humble social position") of Christ, portrayed as δοῦλος, in 2:7 (1995, 219). This is also

the conclusion of Ascough (2003, 123, n. 59) and Garnsey (1996, 186–87). See the following chapter for a detailed discussion of the dishonor associated with slavery in the Roman world.

32. Winter reads ἐριθείαν and κενοδοξίαν (2:3) in terms of behavior commonly adopted in the competitive realm of municipal office-seeking (1994, 98–100). Ascough has recently suggested that Paul's language here should instead be read against the backdrop of the "interpersonal rivalry and competition, with particular attention to φιλοτιμία" that characterized non-elite voluntary associations. Ascough concludes, "Such 'love of honour' was the motivating factor for many benefactors of the associations. In contrast to this striving for honour in the associations, Paul's injunction that the Philippians 'do nothing from selfishness or conceit' indicates that they are not to compete with one another but 'in humility count others better' than themselves (2:3)" (2003, 144). The above citation is particularly illuminating, since Ascough is wholly preoccupied with arguing for analogies – not contrasts – between Paul's Macedonian congregations and the Greco-Roman associations, thus the title of his monograph, *Paul's Macedonian Associations*. Indeed, the quotation cited above is one of the few places in the book where Ascough acknowledges a distinct difference in relational orientation between the associations and Paul's Christian communities, and here, I might add, Ascough and I are quite in agreement.

33. For bibliography on ἐπισκόποις καὶ διακόνοις see the commentaries of Fee, O'Brien, and Silva, along with the classic monographs of Schweizer (1961), von Campenhausen (1969), and now R. A. Campbell (1994). For a contextually sensitive study of the qualifications for leadership in the early Christian movement, Clarke's monograph (2000) is now a standard work. The traditional view, that Pauline egalitarianism and charism ultimately degenerated into hierarchical institutionalism, with a corresponding increase in formal positions of authority in the church, has now been challenged by Campbell, who offers an alternative theory based on the household settings of early Christian communities (1994). Accompanying the focus on the household matrix of the early church is an increasing tendency to view the whole idea of formal office in the New Testament period as "sociologically inaccurate and historically anachronistic" (Elliott [2003, 81]). Offices, as generally understood, involve "clearly delineated positions and accompanying responsibilities in a hierarchically organized administrative system, positions and responsibilities for which one qualifies by prescribed training and qualifications" (2003, 81). Early Christian groups, in contrast, were led by persons whose status in the community arose from their roles as senior members of households and who exercised their authority in traditional, informal ways.

With Elliott, I am optimistic that increasingly rigorous analysis along social-scientific lines will bring much needed clarification to the long-standing debate over early church leadership. Yet Elliott fails to consider another possible analogy, namely the use of the terms in question to designate formal positions of oversight in certain Greco-Roman voluntary associations (Ascough [2003, 129–33]). For the purposes of my argument, however, it is sufficient to note that the leaders of the Philippian church – whether formal "officers" or heads of households – were individuals of honor and repute in the community (note Elliott's title:

"Elders as Honored Household Heads" [2003, 77]). Even more to the point, they could apparently boast recognized titles that were associated with their positions ("bishops and deacons"). It is Paul's exceptional use of these titles in Philippians 1:1 that I am addressing in the present connection.

With a degree of reluctance I retain the NRSV's translation "bishops" at various points in the above discussion. The rendering is highly anachronistic, given the manner in which "bishop" was used in later church history. I was tempted consistently to substitute "overseers" (with the NIV), since the expression is relatively unencumbered with ecclesiastical baggage and highlights the function, rather than the status, of the position. I have chosen to retain "bishops" in places, however, precisely because I believe that honor, not function, is at the forefront of Paul's usage of the term in Philippians 1:1. This, of course, fails to address the problem of anachronism – let the reader beware. Perhaps translating the terms as capitalized titles, "Overseers and Deacons," would both avoid anachronism and preserve the honorific emphasis of Paul's language, but this strikes me as a bit distracting.

34. "the Roman atmosphere of the colony" (Pilhofer [1995, 147]).
35. Thus, I disagree particularly with one of the options offered by Silva, who suggests that Paul may be attempting to buttress the authority of the congregational leaders in the face of "grumbling" (2:14–15), after the analogy of Moses and the Israelites in the Old Testament (1992, 143–44; see 144, n. 80). Others suggest that Paul singles out the leaders because of their special involvement in sending the gift with Epaphroditus (Beare [1959, 48–49]). Best was on the right track in linking the mention of the officers together with the omission of "apostle" as a self-designation, and then seeing here a mild rebuke to leaders who took pride in their superior position (1968, 373–74). For other views see the discussion in O'Brien and the works cited there (1991, 49). O'Brien's preference (after J.-F. Collange) is much too general: "The titles show [Paul's] regard for them but at the same time prepare for the criticisms that follow. As leaders of the congregation they have a special responsibility for oversight and service, and this will involve them in tackling the issues the letter raises" (49–50). These statements, however, could apply to any of Paul's congregations. The sole occurrence of "bishops and deacons" demands a more situation-specific explanation. The colony's preoccupation with social status, particularly evidenced in the public pride associated with the attainment of honorific office, readily provides that explanation.
36. I also assume the integrity of the letter in its present form. The identity of the subjects of Paul's invective in 3:2–3 and the integrity of the letter are not unrelated, as deSilva reminds us (1994). Rhetorical studies have proved favorable for those who assume the integrity of Philippians (see Dalton [1979], Garland [1985], Watson [1988], and Alexander [1989]). The direction that scholarly opinion has taken in recent years can readily be grasped by comparing the assessments of two important dictionary articles authored a generation apart. Koester began his 1976 article on Philippians in the *IDB Supplement* with a categorical reference to Philippians as a "composition of three letters" (1976, 665). More recently, Fitzgerald, after discussing the various positions in some detail, cautiously concluded that "the presumption

of the letter's literary integrity is probably correct" (1992, 321). So, also, Ascough (2003, 116). Even more optimistic is Pretorius, whose interaction with Wick's recent monograph compels him to assert that "the design and composition of the letter renders it nothing less than a literary masterpiece" (1998, 558).

Viewing the letter as a unity, in turn, opens up the whole epistle as a source of evidence to determine the identity of those to whom Paul refers in 3:2–3. The perspective I have adopted, that Christian Judaizers are in view, clearly represents majority opinion, although some have opted for non-Christian Jews (for example, Hawthorne [1983, 125–26] and Beare [1959, 101]). See the commentaries of Fee (1995, 294) and O'Brien (1991, 357) for bibliography and a discussion of the issue, as well as the fine overview of the various options presented by Williams (2002, 54–60). Sanders's essay should also be consulted. He affirms the view that Jewish Christians are in view in Paul's polemic in Philippians 3:2–3 (1986, 83–84).

A final issue concerns the degree of immediacy of the dangers Paul warns against. Were a distinct set of opponents threatening the Philippian Christians as Paul wrote? Or is Paul speaking in more general terms? The latter appears to be the case. DeSilva, for example, cites sociological studies showing how invectives like Paul's are utilized by beleaguered sectarian groups in order to encourage in-group cohesion and strengthen boundaries vis-à-vis outsiders (see also Wick [1994, 89–96]). Others have noted the paradigmatic tone of Philippians (Paul as an example for his readers to follow), as compared with the significantly more defensive posture Paul adopts in Galatians and 2 Corinthians, where distinct groups of opponents are clearly in view. DeSilva's summary is a sound one:

> We may conclude that Paul is not particularly concerned with any one or any number of groups of opponents. He is not facing a polemical situation as in Galatia or Corinth. Rather, he is using a common strategy for building up unity and cooperation within a group: warning about the presence of hostile and dangerous groups on the outside, against whom the Philippians need to present a united front. He chooses as examples of these hostile groups those factious believers and opponents that he encountered in Galatia and Corinth. (1994, 31–32)

37. O'Brien sees only a "passing allusion to circumcision" even in the first use of the phrase, in 3:3, and suggests that Paul is using the "in the flesh" throughout in its fuller theological sense (1991, 364). Udoh, at the opposite end of the spectrum, equates "in the flesh" with "in circumcision" each time the phrase occurs in verses 3–4. Not until verse 5 does Udoh see Paul expanding his focus to Jewish privileges in general (2000, 223–24).
38. Most recently, Oakes has emphasized the Jewish focus of verses 2–9, though he remains somewhat open to a broader understanding (2001, 117; see also Gnilka [1976, 187]).
39. The quote is from O'Brien (1991, 364). Those who interpret "in the flesh" comprehensively include BDAG (916) and Caird (1976, 134).
40. Fee (1995, 303).
41. O'Brien (1991, 364).
42. For the quotation, and the diagram that follows, see O'Brien (1991, 368–69).

43. As deSilva has observed, the first half of our text resembles 2 Corinthians 11:21b–23, the second echoes the contents of Galatians 1:13 (1994, 37). But the parallels begin earlier than verse 5. Sanders, for example, finds parallels to each of the phrases in Philippians 3:2–3 in either Galatians or 2 Corinthians, and he uses these parallels to argue that the agenda of the opponents – the circumcision of Gentile converts – was the same in all three situations (1986, 82–83).
44. Moxnes (1996, 20). Charlotte Wolf has identified this twofold typology of ascribed and achieved honor as the most important and useful one in a sociological literature "replete with typologies of status" (1985, 826).
45. 214/L349 (second century CE).
46. 395/L780 (after 161 CE).
47. 218/L352 (second half of second century CE).
48. But see 2 Corinthians 11, where Paul does, indeed, begin his list of honors with the status ascribed to him at birth.
49. Betz has maintained that Philippians 3:5–6 is thoroughly Pharisaic, with respect to both content and structure (1977). I prefer to understand the structure of the text in Roman terms, the content as Jewish, as argued above.
50. Pilhofer (1995, 123–27).
51. The first parallel on Pilhofer's list seems somewhat farfetched until one considers the relationship between the assumption of the toga and formal enrollment in one's citizen tribe, which occurred together in a public ceremony marking a significant rite of passage in Roman social life (see chapter one). Correspondingly, for Jews circumcision was the rite of passage inextricably linked to membership in the nation of Israel (see Pilhofer [1995, 126]).
52. Pilhofer cites epigraphic, papyrological, and literary evidence. The Vulgate translates our phrase *de tribu Beniamin* (Pilhofer [1995, 125, n. 20]).
53. The above background makes it completely unnecessary to elaborate, as most commentators have done, on the importance of Benjamin among Israel's tribes (Fee [1995, 307]; O'Brien [1991, 370–71]; Lohmeyer [1953, 129]; and Hawthorne [1983, 132–33]; but see F. W. Beare [1959, 106]). Pilhofer rightly questions whether Paul's audience would have possessed the Jewish background necessary to understand the reference in the subtle ways suggested by scholars who highlight the uniqueness of the tribe of Benjamin (1995, 125–26). The phrase φυλῆς Βενιαμίν is no more intended to highlight Benjamin's superiority among the tribes of Israel than *Voltinia* in the Philippian inscriptions is intended to imply comparison with other Roman citizen tribes. In both cases, the point is simply to proclaim one's membership in a recognized citizen tribe. Residents of the colony of Philippi who could make such claims took pride in their tribal membership because it marked them out as Roman citizens. Paul in Philippians 3:4 uses φυλῆς Βενιαμίν in similar fashion.
54. Oakes (2001, 103). The debate whether Philippians 3 is paradigmatic or apologetic is closely connected to other interpretative issues surrounding the letter, not the least of which are the identification of Paul's alleged "opponents" in Philippi and their presence (or lack thereof) in the colony at the time when Paul writes. See the note at the beginning of this section.

55. Wright, for very different reasons, has similarly concluded that Paul intended Philippians 3:2–11 to function as "a coded challenge to Caesar's empire" (2000, 182).
56. 071/G437.
57. 077/G067.

6   *Carmen Christi* as *cursus pudorum*

1. Those wishing to amass a bibliography on the passage should begin with R. P. Martin (1983) and with O'Brien's commentary, which is relatively thorough to 1991 (186–88). For more recent studies, consult the bibliography found in the collection of essays edited by Martin and Dodds (1998, 163–69), and various references cited in the works of Holloway (2001) and Oakes (2001).
2. I am not convinced that it is Paul's intention simply to present the "drama of salvation," apart from any ethical emphasis. Käsemann's influential attempt to refute an ethical reading of Philippians 2:6–11 and interpret the passage, instead, in solely kerygmatic terms, as a portrayal of the drama of salvation, has not won the day (1950). Such attempts to markedly separate the Pauline "indicative" from the "imperative" run the risk of minimizing the non-negotiable connection for Paul between doctrine and ethics. Philippians 2 is clearly a case in point, since in the present context the hymn both (a) describes Christ's act of salvation on our behalf (vv. 6–11) and (b) serves as an ethical challenge to the readers (v. 5). Thus, Pretorius pointedly refers to the "seemingly self-evident notion of the exemplary use of Christ's self-sacrifice" in the text (1998, 549). The ethical trajectory of the text was certainly "self-evident" to ancient commentators (for example, Ambrosiaster, who finds in our passage a challenge to "imitate" and "follow the example" of Jesus [*Epistle to the Philippians*, 2.8.1–2]). See Hurtado's refutation of Käsemann's position (1984), and O'Brien's extended discussion (1991, 253–62). Morgan's fine overview of Käsemann's programmatic essay should be consulted on this as well (1998). Those who read the text as an ethical example now include Peterman (1997, 114), Holloway (2001,121–22), and Oakes (2001, 188–90).

The kerygmatic interpretation has traditionally been associated with a view that interprets verses 6–11 as a pre-Pauline composition, adapted for use in Philippians. This interpretation, too, must be argued anew. To be sure, many scholars continue to insist that the passage could not have been composed to fit its present context, and they suggest that Pauline authorship is unlikely on other grounds as well (Brown [1998, 9–10]; R. P. Martin [1983, 215]). Dissenting voices, however, are growing more numerous. Fowl maintains that the hymn remarkably supports the argument of Philippians as a whole (1990, 31–45; 1998, 146–48). Others who question pre-Pauline origin include Hooker (1978), Fee (1992), and Tellbe (2001, 254). Fee challenges the various poetic reconstructions of the text, including Ernst Lohmeyer's (see the diagram and discussion in the pages that follow). Most recently, Wright has argued from both structure and content that Paul is likely to have penned the passage (2003, 228).

The social scientific reading of the text which I outline in the following pages may inform the discussion in several ways. First of all, when interpreted as I suggest, the passage perfectly resonates in (or, rather, against) the recipients' social context, thus reducing the need to postulate earlier composition. Secondly, the reading advocated here undermines lexical objections to Pauline authorship, since a number of the expressions typically cited in this regard (οὐχ ἁρπαγμὸν ἡγήσατο; ἐκένωσεν; μορφῇ; ὑπερύψωσεν) can be easily accounted for in view of Paul's emphasis upon honor, shame, and social status. Thirdly, my argument that Philippians 2:6–11 constitutes Paul's countercultural response to Roman *cursus* ideology – that verses 6–8 represent an inverted *cursus honorum* – also accords quite nicely with the ethical interpretation of the passage discussed above. As mentioned in chapter four, recent studies of Roman honor inscriptions have underscored their social function in the broader municipality. The bestowal of praise upon a civic benefactor in the form of a public inscription was intended not only to honor the individual in question; it also functioned as a source of public encouragement to motivate *others* to serve the city in similar fashion. Elizabeth Forbis thus refers to "The ability of Roman honorary inscriptions... to encourage virtuous behavior with the promise of public recognition," and claims that "the primary function of the inscriptions' honorary language was to present the honorand as an *exemplum* of virtue, rather than to express appreciation for his or her achievements" (1996, 5, 9). A number of the Philippian inscriptions appear to function in precisely the manner Forbis has described, including certain inscriptions that publicly honor the members of non-elite voluntary associations for contributions to building projects undertaken by their respective groups (the Silvanus cult, for example). In our passage, Jesus is greatly honored for his saving act of benefaction on behalf of his people (vv. 9–11). A loose analogy would suggest that Paul presents Jesus – the "honorand" in Philippians 2 – as the *exemplum, par excellence*, of Christian virtue, in order to encourage others in the Christian community to adopt the same attitudes toward power and social status in their mutual relations.

Finally, with respect to the various suggestions for poetic structure, while I remain unconvinced by all the details of Lohmeyer's proposal, his basic three-part structure for verses 6–8 corresponds nicely to the three distinct levels of social status reflected in "equality with God," "the form of a slave," and "death on a cross," respectively (see below on Christ's *cursus pudorum*). A threefold structure of some kind seems to be present by design, therefore, at least in verses 6–8.

3. Lohmeyer (1961, 5–6). See the recent appreciative review of Lohmeyer's work by Brown (1998). The diagram is given as presented by Brown (1998, 8).
4. The brackets reflect Lohmeyer's identification of θανάτου δὲ σταυροῦ as a Pauline gloss. Fitzmyer, who argues for an Aramaic original, follows Lohmeyer in viewing θανάτου δὲ σταυροῦ as the only phrase that is certainly Pauline (1988). Hofius has argued, in contrast, that θανάτου δὲ σταυροῦ was part of the original hymn (1976, 3–17). As mentioned above, I am inclined to assume that Paul penned the hymn, including the phrase in question. Whether Pauline or not, grammarians consistently identify θανάτου δὲ σταυροῦ as intentionally emphatic, and this will be an important point in the discussion to follow (O'Brien [1991, 230]; Fee [1995, 215]; BDF, para. 447(8)).
5. Those who challenge Lohmeyer's threefold arrangement tend to identify in verses 6–8 two logical and syntactical sections, corresponding to Christ's

incarnation (vv. 6–7c) and death (vv. 7d–8), respectively (Hooker [1978, 158–59]). My *cursus* reading works best with a three-part outline, since I focus not only upon the two "movements" of Christ in his humiliation (issuing in incarnation and death, respectively) but, more specifically, upon the three levels of social status portrayed in the passage (see below). The presence of three – not two – finite verbs in verses 6–8 suggests to me that Paul designed the text to be read in this way. The result is much the same, at any rate, since the contents of verses 6–8 reveal three levels of social status apart from structural considerations.

6. Oakes discusses the lowering of status in 6:6–8 but does not make a connection between the text and Roman *cursus* ideology (2001, 199–200). As he observes, a two-stage presentation of Christ's humiliation is distinctive among Paul's writings. Elsewhere the downward movement occurs in a single act (197, citing Rom. 8:3 and 2 Cor. 8:9).

7. For the various interpretations of the many debated expressions in our passage see the fine commentaries of O'Brien and Fee. For ἐν μορφῇ θεοῦ see Hawthorne's recent survey of the options and the references he cites (1998). Least persuasive, in my view, are interpretations that see in μορφῇ θεοῦ a reference to the account of Adam's creation in Genesis 1:26. Associated with such a perspective is the view that ἐν μορφῇ θεοῦ refers solely to Christ's humanity. The idea has a long pedigree, having experienced a renaissance of sorts in recent decades in the works of Murphy-O'Connor (1976), Howard (1978), and Dunn (1980, 114–21; 1988, 74–83), to name a few. Cogent refutations of these views are to be found in Feinberg (1980, 21–46), Fee (1995, 203, n. 41), Hurtado (2003, 122), and in O'Brien's extended discussion (1991, 263–71).

The sociological interpretation advocated here favors a view which understands Paul to be presenting Christ as preexistent in the opening strophe of verse 6, since the effect of Paul's rhetoric depends upon the social distance between the phrase ἐν μορφῇ θεοῦ ὑπάρχων and the expression θανάτου δὲ σταυροῦ, as Jesus descends his *cursus pudorum*. On Christ's preexistence see now Hurtado (2003, 121–23) and Habermann (1990, 91–157).

8. The quotation is from Hawthorne who continues to read the expression in this way (1998, 101). Older commentators taking the view include Meyer (1875, 80) and Weiss (1959, 2.478). More recently, O'Brien has ably defended the view (1991, 208). See now also Bockmuehl, who arrives at similar conclusions (μορφῇ θεοῦ = God's visible appearance) by drawing upon imagery found in Jewish mystical texts (1997; 1998, 128–29).

9. Schweizer (1955, 96). R. P. Martin also takes the phrase in this sense (1976, 96).

10. Fowl (1998, 142).

11. Strimple (1979, 261, author's italics).

12. O'Brien (1991, 209).

13. Hawthorne (1998, 101).

14. O'Brien (1991, 211).

15. A conceptual parallel is found in Philo, who refers to Caligula, dressed up as a god or goddess, as θεοῦ μορφή (*Leg.* 110).

16. Tellbe (2001, 256).

17. Hoover (1971, 118).
18. O'Neill has challenged the view (1988), as has Vollenweider (1999). Supporting Hoover's general thesis are O'Brien (1991, 215–16), Hawthorne (1998, 102–3), Wright (1986), and, somewhat more tentatively, Fee (1995, 207). Fowl calls Hoover's interpretation, as defended by Wright, "the definitive word on the clause" (1998, 142).
19. O'Brien, summarizing the views of Hoover and C. D. F. Moule (O'Brien [1991, 216]).
20. R. P. Martin's interpretation (1983, 143–53) has been challenged on these very grounds. See Wright (1986, 324–28; 332–33).
21. Hawthorne (1998, 104).
22. O'Brien (1991, 216); also Hawthorne (1998, 104); cf. BDF, para. 399(1).
23. Fowl (1998, 142).
24. Fee (1995, 210).
25. Oakes's assessment of the way in which the first listeners would have heard the text is quite on target: "The hearer will undoubtedly compare [μορφὴν δούλου] with ἐν μορφῇ θεοῦ and conclude that the content of ἐκένωσεν is some sort of lowering of position – in fact, a lowering of position which is about the most extreme that the Universe could offer" (2001, 194).

    Understandably, given the importance of the Christological controversies at the time, most ancient commentators who discussed ἐκένωσεν found themselves preoccupied with issues of ontology. Some church fathers, however, squarely situated the expression in the context of honor and status, as outlined above (translations from Edwards [1999, 242–45]):

    > By *emptying* the holy Scripture signifies becoming of no account . . .
    > Assuming the form of a slave, he concealed the dignity which was his.
    > (Theodore of Mopsuestia, *Epistle to the Philippians*, 2.2)

    > We must understand this *emptying himself* to consist not in any loss or privation of his power but in the fact that he lowered himself to the basest level and condescended to the meanest tasks.
    > (Marius Victorinus, *Epistle to the Philippians*, 2.67)

    > He *emptied himself* when he bowed to injuries and slanders, when he heard unspeakable insults and suffered indignities.
    > (Novation, *De Trinitate*, 22.8–9)

26. I was encouraged to discover that Oakes reads the clauses in this way and argues persuasively against alternative interpretations of ἐν ὁμοιώματι ἀνθρώπων γενόμενος (2001, 194–95). Those, for example, who counter that a Jew like Paul would never equate slavery with human nature miss the point, for social status, not an evaluation of human nature, is in view in the text. Oakes aptly summarizes:

    > The crux is that it is not δουλεία which is synonymous with humanity, even in Christ's case. It is the distance between δουλεία and being like God that is synonymous, in Christ's case, with his becoming human. Between being like God and being like a slave, there is the widest status gap imaginable by Paul's hearers. Paul is saying that for Christ to become human meant that deep a drop in status. (2001, 196)

27. For arguments in favor of the Isaianic servant background see Cerfaux (1959, 374–97), Robinson (1955, 103–4), and Talbert (1967, 150). Those arguing for the more cosmic interpretation (enslavement to the powers) include Fuller, from whom the quotation is taken (1965, 209). See Hurst (1998, 87, 94 n. 40) for arguments against both views.

   In view of Paul's use of Isaiah later in the text (verse 9–11) it may be premature summarily to dismiss an Isaiah connection surrounding δοῦλος in verse 7. Jeremias and, more recently, Bauckham find allusions to Isaiah 52–53 through Philippians 2:6–11 (Jeremias [1963, 182–88]; Bauckham [1998, 135]). Perhaps the connotation of δούλου is twofold. As scholars have noted, however, both δούλου and σταυροῦ represent marked departures from LXX terminology in Isaiah. Appeals to an alternative Greek Vorlage (Aquila used δοῦλος instead of παῖς for Isaiah's servant) serve somewhat to ameliorate these difficulties (Strimple [1979, 266]), but an explanation of the presence of δούλου in the same context as σταυροῦ is closer at hand. As we shall see below, a close association obtained, in the Roman mind, between slavery and crucifixion, a connection surfacing often in our source material. This suggests that, whatever Isaianic allusions might be present in the passage, the semantic resonance of δοῦλος in the social context of Paul's readers remains at the forefront of Paul's rhetoric.

   The above discussion of the meaning of δοῦλος raises, in turn, the thorny hermeneutical issue of the general lack of congruence between the intentions of an author and the interpretative abilities of his or her hearers/readers. Even if one acknowledges, for the sake of argument, that Paul consciously intended the numerous references to Isaiah which Bauckham and Jeremias claim to have found in Philippians 2:6–11, it cannot be easily assumed that the Philippians who first heard Paul's letter would have been able to appreciate the author's subtle intertextual allusions. What is clear, given the Philippians' social context, as outlined in chapters three and four, is that the negative connotations of δοῦλος with respect to honor and social status would have most impressed the first hearers of the letter. For a nuanced and insightful discussion of the limited ability of Paul's readers to understand his Old Testament allusions, see now Stanley (1999).

28. O'Brien, following Moule, also understands the expression μορφὴν δούλου λαβών "against the background of slavery in contemporary society," without, however, special reference to the social situation in Philippi (O'Brien [1991, 223]; Moule [1970, 268]). Oakes's demographic study again proves informative. Oakes estimates the slave population in the Christian community at Philippi at about 16 percent (2001, 61). Paul's utilization of δοῦλος terminology to refer both to himself (and Timothy) and to Jesus would not have been missed by the recipients of the epistle.

29. *Inst.* 1.3.9, cited by Treggiari (1996, 873).

30. Trans. Shelton (1988, 176).

31. Certain slaves were not without some resources. One collegium, for example, which required "an initiation fee of 100 sesterces and an amphora of good wine," had slaves among its members (*CIL* 14.2112).

32. Shelton rightly qualifies Pliny's assertions, however, suggesting that "the slaves working on the farms he owned may have received less sympathy from him than did his household slaves" (1988, 184). Household slaves,

themselves, were hardly insulated from maltreatment. Juvenal writes about a slave hairdresser abused by her matron:

> Poor Psecas, whose own hair has been torn out by her mistress, and whose clothing has been ripped from her shoulders and breasts by her mistress, combs and styles her mistress's hair. "Why is this curl so high?" the mistress screams, and at once a whipping punishes Psecas for this crime of the curling iron and sin of a hairstyle.
> (6.490–93, trans. Shelton [1988, 177])

The kitchen staff might experience similar injustice: "You say, Rufus, that your rabbit has not been cooked well, and you call for a whip. You prefer to cut up your cook, rather than your rabbit" (Mart. 3.94, trans. Shelton [1988, 177]). Even some of the more apparently humane treatment was, in the final analysis, rather utilitarian in its motivation:

> Slaves become more eager to work when treated generously with respect to food or more clothing or time off or permission to graze some animal of their own on the farm, and other things of this kind. The result is that, when some rather difficult task is asked of them or some rather harsh punishment is meted out, their loyalty and good will toward their master is restored by the consolation of these former generosities. (Varro, *Rust.* 1.17.7)

Maltreatment at times reached such heights that emperors felt compelled to intercede on behalf of slaves. Claudius, for example, manumitted a number of ill slaves, who had been abandoned on the isle of Aesculapius in the Tiber simply because their masters had been "loathe to provide them with medical care" (Suet. *Claud.* 25). Hadrian forbade the murder of slaves at the hands of their owners and the sale of slaves to pimps or gladiatorial entrepreneurs "without first showing good cause" (SHA, *Hadr.* 18.7–11).

33. Bartchy (1992, 66).
34. Arlandson (1997, 98). So, also, Ascough (2003, 47). Arlandson, following Lenski, situates "unclean," "degraded," and "expendables" below slaves in the social hierarchy, but he clearly places slaves below urban day laborers and rural landless peasants (see chart on [1997], 22).
35. D. B. Martin (1990, 46).
36. Petronius' *Satyricon* characteristically reflects the two perspectives outlined above. The author's portrayal of Trimalchio constitutes the classic expression of the elite stereotype of the boorish freedman who can never rise above his natal servile status. For Petronius, birth is determinative, and Trimalchio's wealth will never afford him true nobility. The tirade of Hermeros, an ex-slave in the *Satyricon*, assures us, however, that "successful freedmen were sensitive to the insults implicit in this elitist ideology and responded by emphasizing their personal accomplishments in buying their freedom and accumulating wealth" (Garnsey and Saller [1987, 121]; see also Juvenal 4.1; 6.84).
37. Stegemann and Stegemann (1999, 60, my italics).
38. Trans. MacMullen (1974, 116).
39. Dio, whose Stoic persuasions lead him to hold views contrary to cultural norms, attempts in a lengthy treatise to disassociate the concepts of freedom

and slavery from natal status. Dio argues that if a man is virtuous in character, "it is right to call him 'noble,' even if no one knows his parents or his ancestors either." Dio acknowledges, however, that majority opinion will continue to insist, to the contrary, that "it is impossible for anyone to be 'noble' without being 'well-born' at the same time, or for one who is 'well-born' not to be free; hence we are absolutely obliged to conclude that it is the man of ignoble birth who is a slave" (*Or.* 15.31–32).
40. Trans. MacMullen (1974, 116). Thus, Epictetus, who experienced at firsthand the stigma of slavery, wrote, "When you see someone cringing before another or fawning on him against his real opinion, you can with confidence say this fellow is no free man" (4.1.55; trans. MacMullen [1974, 116]).
41. MacMullen (1974, 199, n.89).
42. Death was the punishment assigned to slaves who attempted to enter the army by misrepresenting themselves as free men (Pliny, *Ep.* 10.29–30).
43. Merk (1968, 177–78).
44. Lendon (1997, 20).
45. Pliny, *Ep.* 4.15.9; Cic. *Fam.* 13.10.1.
46. Lendon (1997, 21).
47. Hurtado (2003, 237).
48. Hengel (1977, 62), to whom I am indebted for much of what follows.
49. O'Brien (1991, 230); Fee (1995, 215); BDF, para. 447(8). See now Williams's treatment of Paul's cross terminology as "a rhetorical or argumentative metaphor" (2002, 40). Williams sees Paul drawing upon the image of the cross in Philippians 2:8 "to encourage unity amid suffering and internal strife" (39–40).
50. Those who see the saving significance of Christ's work in the expression include Schneider (1971, 575), Gnilka (1976, 124), and Hengel (1977, 89–90).
51. Oakes (2001, 116, my italics).
52. Trans. Richardson (1970).
53. Hengel (1977, 1, n. 1).
54. Trans. Hengel (1977, 7).
55. Trans. Hengel (1977, 7, n. 10).
56. Cited by Hengel (1977, 21).
57. Trans. M. J. Edwards (1999, 250). For Augustine, too, it is not only the physical suffering Jesus endured but, particularly, the social stigma of crucifixion which his followers must be prepared to embrace: "He humbled himself, being made obedient even unto death, even death on a cross, so that none of us, though being able to face death without fear, might shrink from any kind of death that human beings regard as a great disgrace" (*On Faith and the Creed*, 11; trans. Edwards [1999, 250]).
58. O'Brien (1991, 231).
59. Trans. Hengel (1977, 3).
60. Hengel's translation. Hengel finds in the Tacitean phrase "death penalty" (*supplicio adfectus*) an echo of the "slaves' punishment" – *servum supplicium* (see below), based on Valerius Maximus 8.4.1 (1977, 3, n. 3).
61. Hengel utilizes the connection to argue persuasively for the unity of the passage (1977, 62). I am more interested here in Paul's juxtaposition of crucifixion and slavery to emphasize the utter shamefulness of the humiliation of Christ.

Notes to pages 146–51

62. *Verr.* 2.5.12. Other sources relating the crucifixion of slaves include Dionysius of Halicarnassus *(Ant. Rom.* 5.51.2; 7.69.1); Livy (22.33.2; 33.36.3); Orosius (5.9.4); Appian *(BCiv.* 1.120); Dio Cassius (49.12.4; 54.3.7); Petronius *(Sat.* 53.3).
63. Trans. Hengel (1977, 51, n. 1). Others who use *servile supplicium* to refer to death by crucifixion include Tacitus *(Hist.* 4.11, 2.72); Horace *(Sat.* 1.8.32); and Livy (29.18.14).
64. *Verr.* 2 (5) 162, 168–170 (trans. Shelton [1988, 287]).
65. Roman colonists at Philippi would have been particularly sensitive to this "correlation between liberty and Roman citizenship," since Augustus, Philippi's founder, had enacted specific measures to reinforce the boundaries between slave- and citizen-status as part of the reforms initiated during his principate:

    > Considering it also of great importance to keep the people pure and unsullied by any taint of foreign or servile blood, [Augustus] was most chary of conferring Roman citizenship and set a limit to manumission... Not content with making it difficult for slaves to acquire freedom, and still more so for them to attain full rights, by making careful provision as to the number, condition, and status of those who were manumitted, he added the proviso that no one who had ever been put in irons or tortured should acquire citizenship by any grade of freedom.
    > (Suet. *Aug.* 40)

66. The translation is Lendon's (1997, 193).
67. BDAG (198); O'Brien (1991, 233); Fee (1995, 220, n. 10).
68. I go in a markedly different direction here than Oakes, who attempts to explain Paul's "therefore" on the basis of contemporary expectations that a worthy candidate for ruler would naturally (διὸ καί) be raised to power (2001, 151–60). In the words of Oakes, "The logic of this was heard as natural because self-sacrificing, morally good acts were a common legitimization of imperial power" (2001, 208). Quite the contrary, in my view, for I maintain that Jesus is exalted precisely because his attitude and behavior, as illustrated in verses 6–8, fly in the face of Roman social conventions. Willing submission (ὑπήκοος) to the double shame of servile status (δούλου) and crucifixion (θανάτου δὲ σταυροῦ) goes far beyond the allegedly analogous "self-sacrificing, morally good acts" reflected in Oakes's parallels. Only the status of the One who is portrayed as bestowing honor upon Jesus in the ensuing verses can legitimate the wholly unexpected "therefore" of Philippians 2:9 (see "Jesus' exaltation: the social background," immediately below) – thus the sudden change of subject from Christ to ὁ θεός in verse 9.
69. Lendon (1997, 48, my italics). The dynamic surfaces often in the context of patron–client relationships. According to Saller, when a patron attempted to broker an honor of some sort for a younger client by canvassing with a superior, "The success of the young man depended on, and was a reflection of, the *auctoritas* of his supporter" (Saller [2000, 849]).
70. 522/L210.
71. 240/L465.
72. Malina and Rohrbaugh (1992, 213).
73. Lendon (1997, 48, my italics).
74. The latter phrase is taken from R. P. Martin (1998, 3).

75. Moule takes the name to be "Jesus," maintaining that verses 9–11 focus upon "Jesus," and not "Lord": "Because of the incarnation, the human name, 'Jesus,' is acclaimed as the highest name; and the Man Jesus thus comes to be acclaimed as Lord, to the glory of God the Father" (1970, 270). This reading, however, misses the status reversal reflected in the text, whereby, as O'Brien observes, "θεός (2:6) becomes δοῦλος (v. 7) and is exalted to be κύριος (v. 11)" (1991, 238). For the various arguments in favor of viewing κύριος as the intended referent for τὸ ὄνομα τὸ ὑπὲρ πᾶν ὄνομα, see, in addition to O'Brien, Fee's discussion (1995, 221–22).
76. BDAG, 712.
77. Lendon (1997, 278).
78. The quotation is from Hawthorne, who proceeds to add that God also bestowed on Jesus "a nature which coincided with that title" (1983, 91). Hawthorne thus sees designation, rank, and substance (Bauer's "qualities and powers") present in the name κύριος. While this may be the case, I understand rank (status) to be at the forefront of Paul's intentions here, due to the progression of the passage and the Roman imperial background (see below on κύριος).
79. The discussion that follows relies on Tellbe (2001, 250–52). On the Palestinian origin of the confession of Jesus as Lord, see Hurtado (1993, 560–69; 2003, 108–12). The κύριος–Yahweh connection finds its roots in (a) the use of κύριος for Yahweh in the LXX and (b) the corresponding substitution of κύριος for Yahweh in the Jewish synagogue (Fee [1995, 225]).
80. R. P. Martin (1983, 257). See also Kreitzer on this (1998, 119).
81. Wright (2001, 22).
82. Tellbe summarizes,

> The title is used altogether fifteen times, and permeates the letter; it is used *personally* of Paul's relationship to Christ (3:8; cf. 2:19, 24; 4:10), *corporately* of the "Lord" of the Philippian church (1:2; cf. 3:1; 4:1, 23), and *universally* as the "Lord" of the cosmos (2:10–11; 3:20–21) ... the letter to the Philippians also exhibits the highest frequency in the *corpus Paulinum* of the phrase ἐν κυρίῳ, stressing the new existence in and relationship to Christ as the "Lord." (2001, 251, his italics)

83. Tellbe (2001, 252).
84. Tellbe (2001, 256). Tellbe cites, for example, Suet. *Calig.* 22; *Claud.* 26, 29, 34–37; *Nero* 26–29, 33–39, 53; Tac. *Ann.* 14.59, 64–65; 15.60. The list could go on and on. Interesting in this regard is Dio Chrysostom's use of the verb ἁρπάζω to express improper ways of exercising a ruler's authority, in contrast to his presentation of the ideal ruler (*Or.* 4.95).
85. We need not assume that Paul is contrasting the attitude and behavior of Jesus with that of a specific emperor. Tellbe rightly rejects as unconvincing various attempts to read the behavior of a specific emperor as the foil against which Paul places the activities of Christ (Bornhäuser [1933, 453–55], Caligula and Nero; Seeley [1994, 69], Caligula). Tellbe rightly counters that "the text should rather be viewed as positing a general contrast between Christ's exaltation and the pursuit of power among earthly rulers" (2001, 256).
86. Kreitzer (1998, 113), who has nicely summarized the present state of affairs on the issue. R. P. Martin, who joins Käsemann in arguing for a kerygmatic

interpretation, views the problem of verses 9–11 as the strongest argument against an ethical interpretation of the text (1983, 85).
87. Kreitzer (1998, 114), who rejects such a reading.
88. See Kreitzer (1998, 114–16). He discusses the contributions of Robbins (1980), Watson (1988), Bloomquist (1993), and Basevi and Chapa (1993).
89. Fowl (1990, 95). Others who attempt to account adequately for the cogency of verses 9–11 within an ethical interpretation of the passage include Stanton (1974, 102–3) and O'Brien (1991, 262).
90. I have no problem with viewing suffering as a secondary theme in 2:1–11. Unity is not unrelated to suffering in the letter, as Geoffrion has demonstrated, particularly for 1:27–30 (1993, 35). See also Oakes's nuanced treatment of the themes of unity and suffering in the epistle. I find myself attracted to his assertion that "The practical outcome of standing firm under suffering is a call to unity" (Oakes [2001, 176]). It is unity, however, that is clearly at the forefront of Philippians 2:1–11. Suffering has receded into the background, and verses 6–11, in particular, must be viewed primarily as an effort on Paul's part to influence the *ethos* of interpersonal relations *among* church members, rather than as a paradigm for enduring suffering at the hands of outsiders. See, most recently, Ascough's extended discussion of what he deems "a concern with internal community relationships" that he sees reflected "throughout the letter" (2003, 139; cf. 139–44).
91. 2:1–5 points decidedly in this direction, whether we translate the prepositional phrase ἐν ὑμῖν (2:5) "among you" (my preference) or "in you" (referring to an inner disposition). As Ascough appropriately observes, "The introductory verse (2:5) suggests that the hymn is setting up the basis upon which the community is to relate to one another" (2003, 143). Moule's translation of verse 5 nicely captures Paul's intention in this regard: "adopt towards one another, in your mutual relations, the same attitude that was found in Christ Jesus" (1970, 265).
92. The categories are O'Brien's (1991, 198), picked up and modified by Williams (2002, 66–68).
93. On the lack of scholarly consensus, see Hooker (1978, 157).
94. See note 2 above. Oakes, with whom I am in general agreement, appropriately qualifies his affirmation of the Pauline origin of 2:6–11 by reminding us that even here Paul is drawing upon and reworking previous Christological convictions in order to meet the needs of the Philippian congregation (2001, 208–10). This incisive observation is of no little importance for reconstructing the developmental trajectory of Christology in early Christianity, and it renders the title of the important collection of essays edited by Martin and Dodds – *When Christology Began* (1998) – quite misleading.

7   Summary and conclusion

1. Theissen's other basic value is love of neighbor. Renunciation of status, in Theissen's view, ameliorates vertical inequality. Love of neighbor relativizes the ethnic and social boundaries that so indelibly marked life in the ancient world (1999, 64–80).
2. Saller (2000, 817).
3. Barton (2001, 237).

4. Dumont (1967).
5. Grusky (1994, 3, his italics).
6. The exchange between functionalists and conflict theorists, known in the literature as the Davis–Moore debate, has waned somewhat in recent decades with the introduction of poststructuralism. See the discussions in Béteille (1985) and Calhoun (2002). Seminal essays in the debate include Davis and Moore (1945) and Tumin (1953).
7. On the possible biological basis for status and hierarchy see the fascinating studies by Frank (1985, 21–25) and Raleigh *et al.* (1996). A connection has been established in studies of chimpanzees between success in achieving dominance in the simian hierarchy and a corresponding rise of serotonin level in the simian brain. Researchers have also been able to decrease the dominance of different monkeys in the hierarchy by manipulating serotonin levels.
8. On the failure of the socialist experiment in Eastern Europe, and other communist countries such as China, North Korea, and North Vietnam, see Lenski's important article and the references cited there (1994). Lenski identifies "internal, systemic factors" as a major source of the economic and social dysfunction that characterized these allegedly egalitarian societies. Particularly problematic was a misled Marxist optimism concerning human nature. The egalitarian orientation of Marxist ideology generated a substantial limitation on wage differentials for various occupations. The expectation was that "once socialism was established and the means of production were owned by all, moral incentives could replace material incentives and workers would find work intrinsically rewarding" (Lenski [1994, 58]). The result, of course, was quite the opposite. In Czechoslovakia in the early 1960s, for example, wage differences were reduced to the point that highly skilled professionals such as engineers earned but 5 percent more than unskilled laborers. Instead of working "for the sheer joy of working and for the satisfaction of contributing to society's needs," talented young people simply dropped out of school, recognizing that the negligible financial rewards of professional life simply did not justify the sacrifice and commitment demanded by a college education (58). The results of the communist experiment, Lenski suggests, demonstrate the viability, at least in part, of functionalist social theory. He concludes that all of this evidence seems to confirm Davis's (1953) assertion that successful incentive systems involve (1) motivating the best qualified people to seek the most important positions and (2) motivating them to perform to the best of their ability once they are in them (59).
9. Schumpeter (1953, 171).
10. Fukuyama (1999, 230). Fukuyama's whole chapter on economics and social hierarchy should be consulted (212–30).
11. Barton (2001, 95, n. 38).
12. See, especially, the works of Cushmann (1990, 1995).
13. Barton (2001, 95, n. 38).
14. Andrew Clarke claims that "social status was the ubiquitous measure of all personal relationships and interactions" in the Roman world (2000, 7).
15. Elliott (2002, 87).
16. Bartchy (2003, 146).

17. For the idea that the domination both of other males and of females constituted a key aspect of ancient patriarchy, see Bartchy (2003, 136). Scholars remain intrigued by the ways in which Paul appears to subvert various aspects of ancient patriarchy. Larson has recently maintained, for example, that Paul's enemies in Corinth appealed to gender norms in order to discredit the apostle. Paul's response – redefining weakness, humility, and suffering as "badges of honor in God's eyes" – constitutes "a rejection of certain traditional standards of masculinity" (2004, 94). Larson bases her argument upon ancient conceptions of gender:

> The essence of the Greco-Roman concept of masculinity was that a "real" man does not cede power or control to another, as slaves and women do. As traditionally constructed, masculinity was closely tied to the concepts of personal freedom and power over others and was incompatible with Paul's concept of "willing slavery" in Christ. (91)

The exercise of "power over others" was, of course, at the heart of what it meant to be an honorable elite male in the ancient Mediterranean world, and the indissoluble connection, in this regard, between honor and masculinity has important implications for our interpretation of Jesus' inverted *cursus* in Philippians 2:6–8. The profound reconstruction of honor undertaken by Paul in his portrayal of Jesus apparently constitutes a significant redefinition of traditional views of gender as well.
18. It is preferable, therefore, to refer to early Christianity's reconstruction of honor as an *inversion* of status (with Elliott), rather than as a *renunciation* of status (Theissen), since the former expression more readily suggests a redefinition of what counts for status and honor among the followers of Jesus, rather than the renunciation of status in principle (suggested, but perhaps not intended, by Theissen's phrase). Those who emulated the attitude and activities of Jesus might, indeed, like Jesus, have to renounce their status for a season, and in this limited sense the expression "renunciation of status" might be appropriate. Jesus' followers were, however, assured, by the status reversal Jesus experienced at the hands of God in Philippians 2:9–11, that any status lost or renounced for the right reasons would ultimately be regained in manifold proportion.
19. Castelli (1991); Moore (1994).
20. Moore (1994, 114).

REFERENCES

Alcock, Susan E. (1993). *Graecia Capta: The Landscapes of Roman Greece.* Cambridge, Cambridge University Press.
— (1994). "Minding the Gap in Hellenistic and Roman Greece," in *Placing the Gods: Sanctuaries and Sacred Space in Ancient Greece*, ed. Susan E. Alcock and Robin Osborne. Oxford, Clarendon Press: 247–61.
Alexander, Loveday (1989). "Hellenistic Letter-Forms and the Structure of Philippians." *JSNT* 37: 87–101.
Arlandson, James Malcolm (1997). *Women, Class and Society in Early Christianity.* Peabody, MA, Hendrickson.
Ascough, Richard S. (1998). "Civic Pride at Philippi: The Text-Critical Problem of Acts 16.21." *NTS* 44: 93–103.
— (2003). *Paul's Macedonian Associations: The Social Context of Philippians and 1 Thessalonians.* Tübingen, Mohr-Siebeck.
Barrett, Anthony A. (2002). *Livia: First Lady of Imperial Rome.* New Haven, Yale University Press.
Bartchy, S. Scott (1991). "Community of Goods in Acts: Idealization or Social Reality?," in *The Future of Early Christianity: Essays in Honor of Helmut Koester*, ed. Birger Pearson. Minneapolis, Fortress: 309–18.
— (1992). "Slavery (Greco-Roman)," in *ABD*, ed. David Noel Freedman. New York, Doubleday: vol. VI, 65–73.
— (2003). "Who Should Be Called Father? Paul of Tarsus between the Jesus Tradition and Patria Potestas." *BTB* 33: 135–47.
Barton, Carlin A. (2001). *Roman Honor: The Fire in the Bones.* Berkeley, University of California Press.
Basevi, Claudio and Juan Chapa (1993). "Philippians 2:6–11: The Rhetorical Function of a Pauline 'Hymn,'" in *Rhetoric and the New Testament: Essays from the 1992 Heidelberg Conference*, ed. S. E. Porter and T. H. Olbricht. Sheffield, Sheffield Academic Press: 338–56.
Bauckam, Richard (1998). "The Worship of Jesus in Philippians 2:9–11," in Martin and Dodds (1998): 128–39.
Bauer, W., F. Danker, W. Arndt, and F. Gingrich, eds. (2000). *A Greek–English Lexicon of the New Testament and other Early Christian Literature.* Chicago, University of Chicago Press.
Beacham, Richard C. (1992). *The Roman Theater and Its Audience.* Cambridge, MA, Harvard University Press.
— (1999). *Spectacle Entertainments of Early Imperial Rome.* New Haven, Yale University Press.

Beard, Mary and John North, eds. (1990). *Pagan Priests: Religion and Power in the Ancient World.* Ithaca, Cornell University Press.

Beard, Mary, John North, and Simon Price (1998). *Religions of Rome: A History.* Cambridge, Cambridge University Press.

Beare, F. W. (1959). *A Commentary on the Epistle to the Philippians.* Peabody, MA, Hendrickson.

Beck, Robert (1996). "The Mysteries of Mithras," in Kloppenborg and Wilson (1996): 176–85.

Best, Ernest (1968). "Bishops and Deacons: Philippians 1,1." *SE* 4: 371–76.

Béteille, André (1985). "Stratification," in *The Social Science Encyclopedia,* ed. Adam Kuper and Jessica Kuper. London, Routledge & Kegan Paul: 831–34.

Betz, Otto (1977). "Paulus als Pharisäer nach dem Gesetz. Phil. 3.5–6 als Beitrag zur Frage des frühen Pharisäismus," in *Treue zur Thora. Beiträge zur Mitte des christlich-jüdischen Gesprächs. Festschrift für Günther Harder zum 75. Geburtstag,* ed. P. von der Osten-Sacken. Berlin, Institut Kirche und Judentum: 54–64.

Birley, Eric (1986). "The Flavian Colonia at Scupi." *ZPE* 64: 209–16.

Blass, F., A. Debrunner, and R. Funk (1961). *A Greek Grammar of the New Testament and Other Early Christian Literature.* Chicago, University of Chicago Press.

Bloomquist, L. Gregory (1993). *The Function of Suffering in Philippians.* Sheffield, Sheffield Academic Press.

Bockmuehl, Markus (1997). "The Form of God (Phil. 2.6): Variations on a Theme of Jewish Mysticism." *JTS* 48: 1–23.

  (1998). *The Epistle to the Philippians.* Peabody, MA, Hendrickson.

Bormann, Lukas (1995). *Philippi: Stadt und Christengemeinde zur Zeit des Paulus.* Leiden, Brill.

Bornhäuser, Karl. (1933). "Philipper 2,5–11." *NKZ* 44: 428–34, 453–62.

Bourdieu, Pierre (1977). *Outline of a Theory of Practice.* Cambridge, Cambridge University Press.

Breeze, David J. (1971). "Pay Grades and Ranks below the Centurionate." *JRS* 61: 130–35.

  (1974). "The Career Structure below the Centurionate during the Principate," in *ANRW* 2.1: 435–51.

Brown, Colin (1998). "Ernst Lohmeyer's Kyrios Jesus," in Martin and Dodds (1998): 6–42.

Bruce, Frederick F. (1990). *The Acts of the Apostles: Greek Text with Introduction and Commentary.* Grand Rapids, Eerdmans.

Brunt, P. A. (1971). *Italian Manpower 225 B.C.–A.D. 14.* Oxford, Clarendon Press.

  (1984). "The Role of the Senate in the Augustan Regime." *CQ* 34(2): 423–44.

Burnett, Andrew, Michael Amandry, and Père Pau Ripollès, eds. (1992). *Roman Provincial Coinage I: From the Death of Caesar to the Death of Vitellius (44 BC–AD 69).* London, British Museum Press.

Caird, G. B. (1976). "Paul's Letters from Prison: Ephesians, Philippians, Colossians, and Philemon." *New Clarendon Bible.* Oxford, Oxford University Press.

Calhoun, Craig (2002). "Stratification," in *Dictionary of the Social Sciences,* ed. Craig Calhoun. Oxford, Oxford University Press: 466–67.

Campbell, J. B. (1984). *The Emperor and the Roman Army, 31 BC–AD 235.* Oxford, Clarendon Press.

Campbell, R. Alistair (1994). *The Elders: Seniority within Earliest Christianity.* Edinburgh, T. & T. Clark.

Campenhausen, Hans von (1969). *Ecclesiastical Authority and Spiritual Power in the Early Church.* London, Black.

Castelli, Elizabeth A. (1991). *Imitating Paul: A Discourse of Power.* Louisville, Westminster and John Knox Press.

Cerfaux, Lucien (1959). *Christ in the Theology of St. Paul.* New York, Herder and Herder.

Clarke, Andrew (2000). *Serve the Community of the Church: Christians as Leaders and Ministers.* Grand Rapids, Eerdmans.

Collart, Paul (1928). "Le théâtre de Philippes." *BCH* 52: 74–124.

(1937). *Philippes, ville de Macédoine, depuis ses origines jusqu'à la fin de l'époque romaine.* Paris, E. de Boccard.

Conzelmann, Hans (1987). *Acts of the Apostles.* Philadelphia, Fortress.

Cotter, W. (1993). "'Our Politeuma Is in Heaven': The Meaning of Philippians 3:17–21," in *Origins and Method: Towards a New Understanding of Judaism and Christianity*, ed. B. H. McLean. Sheffield, JSOT Press: 92–104.

Creighton, Millie R. (1990). "Revisiting Shame and Guilt Cultures: A Forty-Year Pilgrimage." *Ethos* 18: 279–307.

Crossan, John Dominic (1998). *The Birth of Christianity.* San Francisco, HarperSanFrancisco.

Curchin, L. A. (1990). *The Local Magistrates of Roman Spain.* Toronto, University of Toronto Press.

Cushman, Philip (1990). "Why the Self Is Empty: Toward a Historically Situated Psychology." *AP* 45: 599–611.

(1995). *Constructing the Self, Constructing America: A Cultural History of Psychotherapy.* Reading, MA, Addison-Wesley Publishing Company.

Dalton, W. J. (1979). "The Integrity of Philippians." *Bib* 60(1): 97–102.

Davis, Kingsley (1953). "Reply." *ASR* 18: 394–97.

Davis, Kingsley and Wilbert E. Moore (1945). "Some Principles of Stratification." *ASR* 10: 242–49.

de Vos, Craig S. (1999a). *Church and Community Conflicts: The Relationships of the Thessalonian, Corinthian, and Philippian Churches with their Wider Communities.* Atlanta, Scholars.

(1999b). "Finding a Charge that Fits: The Accusation against Paul and Silas at Philippi (Acts 16.19–21)." *JSNT* 74: 51–63.

deSilva, David (1994). "No Confidence in the Flesh: The Meaning and Function of Philippians 3:2–21." *TrinJ* 15(1): 27–54.

(1999). *The Hope of Glory: Honor Discourse and New Testament Interpretation.* Collegeville, MN, Liturgical Press.

(2000). *Honor, Patronage, Kinship & Purity: Unlocking New Testament Culture.* Downers Grove, IL, InterVarsity.

Dobson, B. (1972). "Legionary Centurion or Equestrian Officer?" *AS* 3: 193–207.

Donahue, John F. (2003). "Toward a Typology of Roman Public Feasting." *AJP* 124(3): 423–41.

Dorcey, Peter F. (1992). *The Cult of Silvanus: A Study in Roman Folk Religion.* Leiden, Brill.

Downing, F. G. (1999). "'Honor' among Exegetes." *CBQ* 61: 53–73.
Dumont, Louis (1967). *Homo hierarchicus, essai sur le système des castes.* Paris, Gallimard.
Dunn, James D. G. (1980). *Christology in the Making.* Philadelphia, Westminster.
    (1998). "Christ, Adam, and Preexistence," in Martin and Dodds (1998): 74–83.
Edwards, Douglas R. (1996). *Religion and Power: Pagans, Jews, and Christians in the Greek East.* New York, Oxford.
Edwards, Mark J., ed. (1999). *Galatians, Ephesians, Philippians.* ACCS. Downers Grove, IL, InterVarsity.
Elliott, John H. (2002). "Jesus Was Not an Egalitarian. A Critique of an Anachronistic and Idealist Theory." *BTB* 32(2): 75–91.
    (2003). "Elders as Honored Household Heads and Not Holders of 'Office' in Earliest Christianity." *BTB* 33(2): 77–82.
Everitt, Anthony (2003). *Cicero: The Life and Times of Rome's Greatest Politician.* New York, Random House.
Fears, Rufus J. (1981a). "The Cult of Virtues and Roman Imperial Ideology," in *ANRW* 2.17.2: 827–948.
    (1981b). "The Theology of Victory at Rome: Approaches and Problems," in *ANRW* 2.17.2: 736–826.
Fee, Gordon D. (1992). "Philippians 2:5–11: Hymn or Exalted Prose?" *BBR* 2: 29–46.
    (1995). *Paul's Letter to the Philippians.* Grand Rapids, Eerdmans.
Feinberg, Paul D. (1980). "The Kenosis and Christology: An Exegetical-Theological Analysis of Phil 2:6–11." *TrinJ* 1: 21–46.
Fishwick, Duncan (1987). *The Imperial Cult in the Latin West: Studies in the Ruler Cult of the Western Provinces of the Roman Empire.* New York, E. J. Brill.
Fitzgerald, John T. (1992). "Philippians, Epistle to the," in *ABD*, ed. David Noel Freedman. New York, Doubleday: vol. V, 318–26.
Fitzmyer, Joseph A. (1988). "The Aramaic Background of Phil 2:6–11." *CBQ* 50: 470–83.
Flower, Harriet I. (1996). *Ancestor Masks and Aristocratic Power in Roman Culture.* Oxford, Clarendon Press.
Forbis, Elizabeth (1996). *Municipal Virtues in the Roman Empire: The Evidence of Italian Honorary Inscriptions.* Stuttgart and Leipzig, B. G. Teubner.
Fowl, Stephen E. (1990). *The Story of Christ in the Ethics of Paul: An Analysis of the Function of the Hymnic Material in the Pauline Corpus.* Sheffield, Sheffield Academic Press.
    (1998). "Christology and Ethics in Philippians 2: 5–11," in Martin and Dodds (1998): 140–53.
Frank, Robert H. (1985). *Choosing the Right Pond.* Oxford, Oxford University Press.
Fukuyama, Francis (1999). *The Great Disruption.* New York, The Free Press.
Fuller, R. H. (1965). *The Foundations of New Testament Christology.* London, Lutterworth.
Gaebler, Hugo (1929). "Die erste Colonialprägung in Philippi (Zur Münzekunde Makedoniens. X)." *ZN* 39: 260–69.
Gagé, Jean (1933). "La théologie de la Victoire impériale." *Revue historique* 171: 1–43.

Gardner, J. F. (1986). "Proofs of Status in the Roman World." *Bulletin of the Institute of Classical Studies of the University of London* 33: 1–14.

Garland, David E. (1985). "The Composition and Unity of Philippians: Some Neglected Literary Factors." *NovT* 27: 141–73.

Garnsey, Peter (1970). *Social Status and Legal Privilege in the Roman Empire.* Oxford, Oxford University Press.

(1996). *Ideas of Slavery from Aristotle to Augustine.* Cambridge, Cambridge University Press.

Garnsey, Peter and Richard Saller (1987). *The Roman Empire: Economy, Society and Culture.* Berkeley, University of California Press.

Geoffrion, T. C. (1993). *The Rhetorical Purpose and the Political and Military Character of Philippians: A Call to Stand Firm.* Lampeter, Mellen Biblical Press.

Glancy, Jennifer A. (2004). "Boasting of Beatings (2 Corinthians 11:23–25)." *JBL* 123(1): 99–135.

Glare, P. G. W., ed. (1985). *Oxford Latin Dictionary.* Oxford, Clarendon Press.

Gnilka, Joachim (1976). *Der Philipperbrief: Auslegung.* Freiburg, Herder.

Gradel, I. (2002). *Emperor Worship and Roman Religion.* Oxford, Oxford University Press.

Griffin, Miriam (1996). "Cynicism and the Romans: Attractions and Repulsions," in *The Cynics: The Cynic Movement in Antiquity and Its Legacy*, ed. R. Bracht Branham and Marie-Odile Goulet-Cazé. Berkeley, University of California Press: 190–204.

Gruen, Erich S. (1998). "Rome and the Myth of Alexander," in *Ancient History in a Modern University: The Ancient Near East, Greece and Rome*, ed. T. W. Hillard, R. A. Kearsley, C. E. V. Nixon, and A. M. Nobbs. Grand Rapids, Eerdmans: 178–91.

Grusky, David B., ed. (1994). *Social Stratification: Class, Race, and Gender in Sociological Perspective. Social Inequality Series.* Boulder, Westview Press.

Habermann, Jürgen (1990). *Präexistenzaussagen im Neuen Testament.* Frankfurt am Main, Peter Lang.

Haenchen, Ernst (1971). *The Acts of the Apostles.* Oxford, Basil Blackwell.

Halfmann, Helmut (1979). *Die Senatoren aus dem östlichen Teil des Imperium Romanum bis zum Ende des 2. Jahrhunderts n. Chr.* Göttingen, Vandenhoeck & Ruprecht.

Hamel, G. (1989). *Poverty and Charity in Roman Palestine, First Three Centuries C.E.* Berkeley, University of California Press.

Hawthorne, Gerald F. (1983). *Philippians.* Waco, TX, Word Books.

(1998). "In the Form of God and Equal with God (Philippians 2:6)," in Martin and Dodds (1998): 96–110.

Hemer, Colin (1989). *The Book of Acts in the Setting of Hellenistic History.* Tübingen, J. C. B. Mohr.

Hendrix, Holland L. (1992). "Philippi," in *ABD*, ed. David Noel Freedman. New York, Doubleday: vol. V, 315–17.

Hengel, Martin (1977). *Crucifixion in the Ancient World and the Folly of the Message of the Cross.* Philadelphia, Fortress.

(1991). *The Pre-Christian Paul.* Philadelphia, Trinity Press International.

Hofius, O. (1976). *Der Christushymnus Philipper 2:6–11.* Tübingen, J. C. B. Mohr.

Holloway, Paul A. (2001). *Consolation in Philippians: Philosophical Sources and Rhetorical Strategy.* Cambridge, Cambridge University Press.

Hooker, Morna D. (1978). "Philippians 2, 6–11," in *Jesus und Paulus: Festschrift für W. G. Kümmel*, ed. E. E. Ellis and Erich Grässer. Göttingen, Vandenhoeck & Ruprecht: 151–64.

Hoover, Roy W. (1971). "The HARPAGMOS Enigma: A Philological Solution." *HTR* 64: 95–119.

Hopkins, Keith (1965). "Elite Mobility in the Roman Empire." *Past & Present* 32: 12–26.

(1978). *Conquerors and Slaves.* Cambridge, Cambridge University Press.

Houston, George W. (1977). "Vespasian's Adlection of Men In Senatum." *AJP* 98(1): 35–63.

Howard, George (1978). "Phil 2:6–11 and the Human Christ." *CBQ* 40: 368–87.

Hurst, Lincoln D. (1998). "Christ, Adam, and Preexistence," in Martin and Dodds (1998): 84–95.

Hurtado, Larry W. (1984). "Jesus as Lordly Example in Philippians 2:5–11," in *From Jesus to Paul: Essays in Honour of Francis Wright Beare*, ed. P. Richardson and J. C. Hurd. Waterloo, Wilfrid Laurier University Press: 113–26.

(1993). "Lord," in *Dictionary of Paul and his Letters*, ed. Gerald F. Hawthorne, Ralph P. Martin, and Daniel G. Reid. Downers Grove, IL, InterVarsity: 560–69.

(2003). *Lord Jesus Christ: Devotion to Jesus in Earliest Christianity.* Grand Rapids, Eerdmans.

Jahn, J. (1984). "Zur Entwicklung römischer Soldzahlungen von Augustus bis auf Diokletian." *Studien zu den Fundmünzen der Antike.* 2: 53–74.

Jeremias, Joachim (1963). "Zu Phil. 2: ΕΑΥΤΟΝ ΕΚΕΝΩΣΕΝ." *NovT* 6: 182–88.

Johnson, Luke Timothy (1992). *The Acts of the Apostles.* Collegeville, MN, Michael Glazier.

Joshel, Sandra R. (1992). *Work, Identity, and Legal Status at Rome: A Study of the Occupational Inscriptions.* Norman, OK, University of Oklahoma Press.

Käsemann, Ernst (1950). "Kritische Analyse von Phil. 2, 5–11." *ZTK* 47: 313–60.

(1968). "A Critical Analysis of Philippians 2:5–11. God and Christ: Existence and Province." *Journal for Theology and the Church* 5: 45–88; English version of Käsemann (1950).

Kautsky, John H. (1982). *The Politics of Aristocratic Empires.* Chapel Hill, NC, University of North Carolina Press.

Keppie, Lawrence J. F. (1983). *Colonisation and Veteran Settlement in Italy, 47–14 B.C.* London, British School at Rome.

(1984). "Colonisation and Veteran Settlement in Italy in the First Century A.D." *Papers of the British School at Rome* 52: 77–114.

Kloppenborg, John S. (1996). "Collegia and Thiasoi," in Kloppenborg and Wilson (1996): 16–30.

Kloppenborg, John S. and Stephen G. Wilson, eds. (1996). *Voluntary Associations in the Graeco-Roman World.* London, Routledge.

Koester, Helmut (1976). "Philippians, Letter to the." *IDB Supplement.* Nashville, Abingdon: 665–66.

Kolendo, Jerzy (1981). "La répartition des places aux spectacles et la stratification sociale dans l'empire romain." *Ktema* 6: 301–16.

Koukouli-Chrysantaki, Chaido (1998). "Colonia Iulia Augusta Philippensis," in *Philippi at the Time of Paul and after His Death*, ed. Charalambos Bakirtzis and Helmut Koester. Harrisburg, PA, Trinity: 5–35.

Kreitzer, Larry J. (1998). "Where He at Last is First. Philippians 2:9–11 and the Exaltation of the Lord," in Martin and Dodds (1998): 111–27.

Krentz, E. M. (1993). "Military Language and Metaphors in Philippians," in *Origins and Method: Towards a New Understanding of Judaism and Christianity*, ed. B. H. McLean. Sheffield, JSOT Press: 105–27.

Larson, Jennifer (2004). "Paul's Masculinity." *JBL* 123(1): 85–97.

Lendon, Jon E. (1997). *Empire of Honour: The Art of Government in the Roman World*. Oxford, Clarendon Press.

Lenski, Gerhard E. (1966). *Power and Privilege: A Theory of Social Stratification*. New York, McGraw-Hill.

 (1994). "New Light on Old Issues: The Relevance of 'Really Existing Socialist Societies' for Stratification Theory," in *Social Stratification: Class, Race, and Gender in Sociological Perspective*, ed. David B. Grusky. Boulder, Westview Press: 77–84.

Lentz, J. C. (1993). *Luke's Portrait of Paul*. Cambridge, Cambridge University Press.

Levick, Barbara (1967). *Roman Colonies in Southern Asia Minor*. Oxford, Oxford University Press.

Lewis, Naphtali and Meyer Reinhold, eds. (1966). *Roman Civilization: Sourcebook II: The Empire*. New York, Harper Torchbooks.

Lipset, Seymour Martin, Reinhard Bendix, and Hans I. Zetterberg (1994). "Social Mobility in Industrial Society," in *Social Stratification: Class, Race, and Gender in Socological Perspective*, ed. David B. Grusky. Boulder, Westview Press: 309–18.

Littlejohn, James (1972). *Social Stratification*. London, George Allen & Unwin Ltd.

Lohmeyer, Ernst (1953). *Die Briefe an die Philipper, an die Kolosser und an Philemon*. Göttingen, Vandenhoeck & Ruprecht.

 (1961). *Kyrios Jesus: Eine Untersuchung zu Phil 2,5–11*. Heidelberg, Carl Winter Universitätsverlag.

MacMullen, Ramsay (1974). *Roman Social Relations: 50 B.C. to A.D. 284*. New Haven, Yale University Press.

 (1984). "The Legion as Society." *Historia* 33: 440–56 (reprinted in MacMullen, *Changes in the Roman Empire: Essays in the Ordinary* [Princeton: Princeton University Press, 1990] 225–35).

Malina, Bruce J. (1996). "Understanding New Testament Persons," in *The Social Sciences and New Testament Interpretation*, ed. Richard Rohrbaugh. Peabody, MA, Hendrikson: 41–61.

Malina, Bruce J. and Jerome H. Neyrey (1991). "Honor and Shame in Luke–Acts: Pivotal Values of the Mediterranean World," in *The Social World of Luke–Acts*, ed. Jerome H. Neyrey. Peabody, MA, Hendrikson: 25–65.

Malina, Bruce J. and Richard L. Rohrbaugh, eds. (1992). *Social Science Commentary on the Synoptic Gospels*. Minneapolis, Fortress.

Marshall, I. Howard (1980). *Acts*. Leicester, Inter-Varsity.

Marshall, Thomas H. (1950). *Citizenship and Social Class*. Cambridge, Cambridge University Press.

Martin, Dale B. (1990). *Slavery as Salvation: The Metaphor of Slavery in Pauline Christianity.* New Haven, Yale University Press.
Martin, Ralph P. (1976). *Philippians.* Grand Rapids, Eerdmans.
 (1983). *Carmen Christi: Philippians 2:5–11 in Recent Interpretation and in the Setting of Early Christian Worship.* Grand Rapids, Eerdmans.
 (1998). "Carmen Christi Revisited," in Martin and Dodds (1998): 1–5.
Martin, Ralph P. and B. Dodds, eds. (1998). *When Christology Began: Essays on Philippians 2.* Louisville, TN, Westminster/John Knox.
Maxfield, V. A. (1981). *The Military Decorations of the Roman Army.* Berkeley, University of California Press.
McLean, B. Hudson (1996). "The Place of Cult in Voluntary Associations and Christian Churches on Delos," in Kloppenborg and Wilson (1996): 186–225.
Merk, Otto (1968). *Handeln aus Glauben. Die Motivierungen der paulinischen Ethik.* Marburg, N. G. Elwert.
Meyer, H. A. W. (1875). *Critical and Exegetical Handbook to the Epistles of Philippians and Colossians.* Edinburgh, T. & T. Clark.
Millar, Fergus (1990). "The Roman Coloniae of the Near East: A Study in Cultural Relations," in *Roman Eastern Policy and Other Studies in Roman History*, ed. Heikki Solin and Mika Kajava. Helsinki, Societas Scientiarum Fennica 91: 7–58.
Minnen, Peter van (1994). "Paul the Roman Citizen." *JSNT* 56: 43–53.
Moore, Stephen D. (1994). *Poststructuralism and the New Testament: Derrida and Foucault at the Foot of the Cross.* Minneapolis, Fortress Press.
Morgan, Robert (1998). "Incarnation, Myth, and Theology. Ernst Käsemann's Interpretation of Philippians 2:5–11," in Martin and Dodds (1998): 43–73.
Moule, C. D. F. (1970). "Further Reflexions on Philippians 2.5–11," in *Apostolic History and the Gospel. Biblical and Historical Essays Presented to F. F. Bruce*, ed. Ward. W. Gasque and Ralph P. Martin. Exeter, Paternoster: 264–76.
Moxnes, Halvor (1991). "Patron–Client Relations and the New Community in Luke–Acts," in *The Social World of Luke–Acts*, ed. Jerome Neyrey. Peabody, MA, Hendrickson: 241–68.
 (1993). "Honor and Shame: A Reader's Guide." *BTB* 23: 167–76.
 (1996). "Honor and Shame," in *The Social Sciences and New Testament Interpretation*, ed. Richard Rohrbaugh. Peabody, MA, Hendrickson: 19–40.
Murphy-O'Connor, Jerome (1976). "Christological Anthropology in Phil. II, 6–11." *RB* 83: 25–50.
Neyrey, Jerome H. (2002). "Spaces and Places, Whence and Whither." *BTB* 32(2): 60–74.
Nicols, J. (1980). "Pliny and the Patronage of Communities." *Hermes – Zeitschrift für Klassische Philologie* 108: 365–85.
O'Brien, Peter T. (1991). *The Epistle to the Philippians.* Grand Rapids, Eerdmans.
O'Neill, J. C. (1988). "Hoover on Harpagmos Reviewed, with a Modest Proposal Concerning Philippians 2:6." *HTR* 81: 445–49.
Oakes, Peter (2001). *Philippians: From People to Letter.* Cambridge, Cambridge University Press.
Ollrog, Wolf-Henning (1979). *Paulus und seine Mitarbeiter.* Neukirchen-Vluyn, Neukirchener.

Ostrow, S. E. (1990). "The Augustales in the Augustan Scheme," in *Between Empire and Republic: Interpretations of Augustus and His Principate*, ed. Kurt A. Raaflaub and Mark Toher. Berkeley, University of California Press: 364–79.

Papazoglou, Fanoula (1982). "Le territoire de la colonie de Philippes." *BCH* 106: 89–106.

Peterman, G. W. (1997). *Paul's Gift from Philippi*. Cambridge, Cambridge University Press.

Pilch, John J. (1993). "Honor/Shame," in *Biblical Social Values and Their Meaning*, ed. John J. Pilch and Bruce J. Malina. Peabody, MA, Hendrickson: 95–104.

Pilhofer, Peter (1995). *Philippi. Band 1: Die erste christliche Gemeinde Europas.* Tübingen, J. C. B. Mohr.

  (2000). *Philippi. Band 2: Katalog der Inschriften von Philippi.* Tübingen, J. C. B. Mohr.

Pitt-Rivers, J. A. (1966). "Honour and Social Status," in *Honour and Shame: The Values of Mediterranean Society*, ed. J. G. Peristiany. Chicago, University of Chicago Press: 21–77.

Portefaix, Lilian (1988). *Sisters Rejoice. Paul's Letter to the Philippians and Luke–Acts as Seen by First-Century Philippian Women.* Stockholm, Almqvist & Wiksell International.

Pretorius, Emil (1998). "Role Models for a Model Church. Typifying Paul's Letter to the Philippians." *Neotestamentica* 32(2): 547–71.

Price, S. R. F. (1984). *Rituals and Power: The Roman Imperial Cult in Asia Minor.* Cambridge, Cambridge University Press.

Purcell, Nicholas (1983). "The Apparitores: A Study in Social Mobility." *Papers of the British School at Rome* 51: 125–73.

Raleigh, M., M. McGuire, W. Melega, S. Cherry, S.-C. Huang, and M. Phelps (1996). "Neural Mechanisms Supporting Successful Social Decisions in Simians," in *Neurobiology of Decision-Making*, ed. Antonio Damasio. New York, Springer: 68–71.

Rapske, Brian M. (1994). *The Book of Acts and Paul in Roman Custody.* Grand Rapids, Eerdmans.

Rawson, E. D. (1987). "Discrimina ordinum: The Lex Iulia Theatralis." *Papers of the British School at Rome* 55: 83–114.

Reinhold, Meyer (1970). *History of Purple as a Status Symbol in Antiquity.* Brussels, Latomus.

  (1971). "Usurpation of Status and Status Symbols in the Roman Empire." *Historia* 20(1): 275–302.

Reumann, John (1996). "Philippians, Especially Chapter 4, as a 'Letter of Friendship': Observations on a Checkered History of Scholarship," in *Friendship, Flattery, and Frankness of Speech: Studies on Friendship in the New Testament World*, ed. John T. Fitzgerald. Leiden, Brill: 83–106.

Richardson, Cyril C., ed. (1970). *Early Christian Fathers.* New York, Macmillan.

Robbins, Charles J. (1980). "Rhetorical Structure of Philippians 2:6–11." *CBQ* 42: 73–82.

Robinson, H. Wheeler (1955). *The Cross in the Old Testament.* Philadelphia, Westminster.

References

Rohrbaugh, Richard (2002). "Ethnocentrism and Historical Questions about Jesus," in *The Social Setting of Jesus and the Gospels*, ed. Wolfgang Stegemann, Bruce J. Malina, and Gerd Theissen. Minneapolis, Fortress: 27–43.

Runcimann, W. G. (1968). "Class, Status, and Power," in *Social Stratification*, ed. John A. Jackson. New York, Cambridge: 25–61.

Sack, Robert D. (1986). *Human Territoriality. Its Theory and History.* Cambridge, Cambridge University Press.

Saller, Richard P. (1982). *Personal Patronage under the Early Empire.* Cambridge, Cambridge University Press.

(1994). *Patriarchy, Property and Death in the Roman Family.* Cambridge, Cambridge University Press.

(2000). "Status and Patronage," in *The Cambridge Ancient History*, ed. Alan K. Bowman, Peter Garnsey, and Dominic Rathbone. Cambridge, Cambridge University Press: vol. XI, 817–54.

Salmon, Edward T. (1969). *Roman Colonization under the Republic.* London, Thames & Hudson.

Sanders, E. P. (1986). "Paul on the Law, His Opponents, the Jewish People in Philippians 3 and 2 Corinthians 11," in *Anti-Judaism in Early Christianity. Paul and the Gospels*, ed. Peter Richardson and David Granskou. Waterloo, Ontario, Canada, Wilfrid Laurier University Press: vol. I, 80–84.

Sass, G. (1941). "Zur Bedeutung von δοῦλος bei Paulus." *ZNW* 40: 24–32.

Scheid, John (1997). "Augustales," in *Der Neue Pauly. Enzyklopädie der Antike*, ed. Hubert Cancik and Helmuth Schneider. Stuttgart: vol. II, cols. 291–92.

Schenk, Wolfgang (1984). *Die Philipperbrief des Paulus: Kommentar.* Stuttgart, W. Kohlhammer.

Schneider, J. (1971). "σταυρός κτλ.," in *TDNT*, ed. Gerhard Kittel. Grand Rapids, Eerdmans: vol. VII, 572–80.

Schumpeter, Joseph (1953). *Aufsätze zur Soziologie.* Tübingen, Mohr-Siebeck.

Schwartz, Daniel R. (1984). "The Accusation and the Accusers at Philippi (Acts 16.20–21)." *Bib* 65: 357–63.

Schweizer, Eduard (1955). *Erniedrigung und Erhöhung bei Jesus und seinen Nachfolgern.* Zurich, Zwingli.

(1961). *Church Order in the New Testament.* Naperville, IL, A. R. Allenson.

Seeley, David (1994). "The Background of the Philippians Hymn (2:6–11)." *Journal of Higher Criticism* 1: 49–72.

Sève, Michel (1989–90). *Recherches sur les Places Publiques dans le monde Grec du Premier au Septième Siècle de Notre Ere.* Lille: Lille-Thèses.

(1996). "Nouveautés épigraphiques au forum de Philippes: Questions de méthode," in *Inscriptions of Macedonia. Third International Symposium on Macedonia.* Thessaloniki, Aristotle University of Thessaloniki: 173–83.

Sève, Michel and P. Weber (1988). "Un Monument Honorifique au Forum de Philippes." *BCH* 112: 477–79.

Shelton, Jo-Ann (1988). *As the Romans Did: A Sourcebook in Roman Social History.* New York, Oxford University Press.

Sherwin-White, A. N. (1992). *Roman Law and Roman Society in the New Testament.* Grand Rapids, Baker Book House.

Silva, Moisés (1992). *Philippians.* Grand Rapids, Baker Book House.

Spawforth, A. J. S. (1996). "Roman Corinth: The Formation of a Colonial Elite," in *Roman Onomastics in the Greek East: Social and Political Aspects*, ed.

A. D. Rizakis. Athens, Kentron Hellenikes kai Romaikes Archaiotetos. 21: 167–82.
Speidel, M. A. (1970). "The Captor of Decebalus: A New Inscription from Philippi." *JRS* 60: 142–53.
 (1992). "Roman Army Pay Scales." *JRS* 82: 87–106.
Staley, Jeffrey L. (1999). "Changing Woman: Postcolonial Reflections on Acts 16.6–40." *JSNT* 73: 113–35.
Stanley, Christopher D. (1999). "'Pearls Before Swine': Did Paul's Audiences Understand His Biblical Quotations?" *NovT* 41: 124–44.
Stanton, Graham N. (1974). *Jesus of Nazareth in New Testament Preaching.* Cambridge, Cambridge University Press.
Stegemann, W. Ekkehard and Wolfgang Stegemann (1999). *The Jesus Movement: A Social History of Its First Century.* Minneapolis, Fortress.
Stegemann, Wolfgang (1987). "War der Apostel Paulus ein römischer Bürger?" *ZNW* 78: 200–29.
Stowers, Stanley K. (1991). "Friends and Enemies in the Politics of Heaven: Reading Theology in Philippians," in *Pauline Theology,* ed. J. M. Bassler. Minneapolis, Fortress: vol. I, 105–21.
Strimple, R. B. (1979). "Philippians 2.5–11 in Recent Studies: Some Exegetical Conclusions." *WTJ* 41(2): 247–68.
Sumi, Geoffrey S. (2002). "Impersonating the Dead." *AJP* 123(4): 559–85.
Syme, Ronald (1939). *The Roman Revolution.* Oxford, Oxford University Press.
Talbert, C. H. (1967). "The Problem of Pre-Existence in Philippians 2:6–11." *JBL* 86: 141–53.
Taylor, Lily R. (1931). *The Divinity of the Roman Emperor.* Middletown, CT, American Philological Association.
Taylor, Ralph B. (1988). *Human Territorial Functioning: An Empirical Evolutionary Perspective on Individual and Small Group Territorial Cognitions, Behaviors and Consequences.* Cambridge, Cambridge University Press.
Tellbe, Mikael (1994). "The Sociological Factors behind Philippians 3.1–11 and the Conflict at Philippi." *JSNT* 55: 97–121.
 (2001). *Paul between Synagogue and State.* Stockholm, Almqvist & Wiksell International.
Theissen, Gerd (1999). *The Religion of the Earliest Churches: Creating a Symbolic World.* Minneapolis, Fortress Press.
Treggiari, Susan (1996). "Social Status and Social Legislation," in *The Cambridge Ancient History,* ed. Alan K. Bowman, Peter Garnsey, and Dominic Rathbone. Cambridge, Cambridge University Press: vol. X, 873–82.
Tumin, Melvin M. (1953). "Some Principles of Stratification: A Critical Analysis." *ASR* 18: 378–94.
Udoh, Fabian E. (2000). "Paul's View on the Law: Questions about Origin (Gal. 1:6–2:21; Phil. 3:2–11)." *NovT* 42(3): 214–37.
Vermes, Geza (1995). *The Dead Sea Scrolls in English.* London, Penguin Books.
Vollenweider, Samuel (1999). "Der 'Raub' der Gottgleichheit. Ein religionsgeschichtlicher Vorschlag zu Phil 2.6(–11)." *NTS* 45(3): 413–33.
Walker-Ramisch, Sandra Walker (1996). "Graeco-Roman Voluntary Associations and the Damascus Document: A Sociological Analysis," in Kloppenborg and Wilson (1996): 128–45.

Wallace-Hadrill, A. (1990). "Roman Arches and Greek Honours: The Language of Power at Rome." *Proceedings of the Cambridge Philological Society* 36: 143–81.

Watkins, Thomas H. (1979). "Roman Citizen Colonies and Italic Right," in *Studies in Latin Literature and Roman History.* Deroux, C. Brussels, Latomus. CollLat 164: 59–99.

  (1983). "Coloniae and Ius Italicum in the Early Empire." *CJ* 78(4): 319–336.

Watson, Duane F. (1988). "A Rhetorical Analysis of Philippians and Its Implications for the Unity Question." *NovT* 30: 57–88.

Weaver, P. R. C. (1967). "Social Mobility in the Early Roman Empire: The Evidence of the Imperial Freedmen and Slaves." *Past & Present* 37: 3–20.

Webster, Graham (1969). *The Roman Imperial Army of the First and Second Centuries A.D.* London, Black.

Weiss, Johannes (1959). *Earliest Christianity.* New York, Harper & Bros.

White, L. Michael (1990). "Morality between Two Worlds: A Paradigm of Friendship in Philippians," in *Greeks, Romans and Christians: Essays in Honor of Abraham J. Malherbe,* ed. David L. Balch, Everett Ferguson, and Wayne A. Meeks. Minneapolis, Fortress: 201–15.

  (1995). "Visualizing the 'Real' World of Acts 16. Toward Construction of a Social Index," in *The Social World of the First Christians: Essays in Honor of W. A. Meeks,* ed. L. M. White and O. L. Yarbrough. Minneapolis, Fortress: 234–61.

Whittaker, Charles R. (1997). "Imperialism and Roman Culture: The Roman Initiative," in *Dialogues in Roman Imperialism: Power, Discourse, and Discrepant Experience in the Roman Empire,* ed. D. J. Mattingly. Portsmouth, RI, Journal of Roman Archaeology: vol. XXIII, 143–63.

Wick, Peter (1994). *Der Philipperbrief. Der Formale Aufbau des Briefs als Schlüssel zum Verständnis seines Inhalts.* Stuttgart, W. Kohlhammer.

Williams, Demetrius K. (2002). *Enemies of the Cross of Christ: The Terminology of the Cross and Conflict in Philippians.* London, Sheffield Academic Press.

Winter, Bruce (1994). *Seek the Welfare of the City: Christians as Benefactors and Citizens.* Grand Rapids, Eerdmans.

Witherington III, Ben (1998). *The Acts of the Apostles: A Socio-Rhetorical Commentary.* Grand Rapids, Eerdmans.

Wolf, Charlotte (1985). "Status," in *The Social Science Encyclopedia,* ed. Adam Kuper and Jessica Kuper. London, Routledge & Kegan Paul: 825–27.

Wright, N. Thomas (1986). "ἁρπαγμός and the Meaning of Philippians 2:5–11." *JTS* 37: 321–52.

  (2000). "Paul's Gospel and Caesar's Empire," in *Paul and Politics,* ed. Richard A. Horsley. Harrisburg, PA, Trinity Press International: 160–83.

  (2001). "A Fresh Perspective on Paul?" *BJRL* 83(1): 21–40.

  (2003). *The Resurrection of the Son of God.* Minneapolis, Fortress.

Zahrnt, Michael (1988). "Vermeintliche Kolonien des Kaisers Hadrian." *ZPE* 71: 229–49.

Zanker, Paul (1988). *The Power of Images in the Age of Augustus.* Ann Arbor, The University of Michigan Press.

INDEX OF ANCIENT SOURCES

Old Testament

Genesis
  1:26   204
Joshua
  24:29   120
2 Kings
  14:25   120
Nehemiah
  10:29   120
Job
  40:10   133
Psalms
  88:21 [LXX]   120
Isaiah
  42–53   136, 206
  42:1 [LXX]   136
  45   152
  52–53   206
2 Maccabees
  9:12   133
Sirach
  8:1–2   8
  13:2–3   8

New Testament

Matthew
  6:29   133
  23:12   157
Mark
  10:35–37   25, 28
Luke
  7:25   132, 133
  12:27   133
  14:8–10   175
Acts
  2:10   195
  2:44–45   176
  4:32–37   176
  13:14   195
  13:50   112
  13:51   195
  14:1   195
  14:1–7   195
  14:5   195
  14:6   195
  14:8   195
  14:19   195
  14:19–20   195
  14:21   195
  14:23   121
  16   110–15, 116, 193, 194
  16:1–2   195
  16:2   195
  16:8   195
  16:11   195
  16:11–40   161–62
  16:12   110–11, 195
  16:12–40   111
  16:13   87
  16:19   112
  16:20   111, 112
  16:20–21   111, 195
  16:20b–21   110
  16:22   111, 112
  16:23   111
  16:27   111
  16:35   111, 112
  16:36   111, 112
  16:37–39   112–13, 196
  16:38   111, 112
  16:38–39   116
  18:1   195
  19:1   195
  20:2   195
  20:5–6   195
  20:17   121
  20:28   121
  21:7   195

Index of ancient sources

28:12 195
28:13 195
Romans
  1:1 117, 118, 119
  1:7 117
  8:3 204
  11:1 126
1 Corinthians 158
  1:1–2 117, 119
  1:26–29 158
  6:1–11 176
2 Corinthians
  1:1 117, 119
  8:9 204
  11 126–27, 201
  11:21b–23 201
  11:22–29 124
  11:23–12:12 121
Galatians
  1 126–27
  1:1–2 117
  1:13 201
  1:13–14 124, 125–27
  1:13–2:14 121
  4:3–5 136
Ephesians
  1:1 117, 119
Philippians 72, 186, 197, 199–200
  1:1 117–21, 162, 197
  1:2 210
  1:3 197
  1:27 117
  1:27–30 154, 211
  2 1, 142, 144, 162–63, 165–66, 202
  2:1–4 154
  2:1–5 211
  2:1–11 211
  2:3 120, 129, 162, 198
  2:5 121, 135, 144, 202, 211
  2:5–11 154
  2:6 116, 131–32, 134–35, 148, 152, 153, 204
  2:6–7c 204
  2:6–8 2, 118, 121, 129–36, 153, 154, 163, 203–4, 209, 213
  2:6–11 110, 116, 128, 129, 132, 153–54, 155–56, 176, 196, 202–3
  2:7 131, 132, 135–36, 139, 141, 142, 143, 163, 196, 197
  2:7–8 135
  2:7d–8 204
  2:8 131, 143–48, 163
  2:9 131, 149, 150, 151, 209
  2:9–10 151
  2:9–11 2, 56, 151–56, 163, 196, 203, 206, 210, 213
  2:10 136, 151
  2:10–11 151, 210
  2:11 133, 151
  2:12–18 154
  2:14–15 199
  2:19 210
  2:19–24 197
  2:22 197
  2:24 210
  3 123, 124, 126–27, 201
  3:1 210
  3:2–3 124, 199–200, 201
  3:2–4 122–23
  3:2–7 121–22
  3:2–9 200
  3:2–11 202
  3:3 122
  3:3–4 200
  3:4 122, 123, 126
  3:4–6 125–27, 162
  3:4–16 127
  3:5 200, 201
  3:5–6 117, 121–28, 196–97, 201
  3:7 123
  3:7–11 124
  3:8 123, 126, 210
  3:9 123
  3:15–17 127
  3:20–21 210
  4:1 210
  4:10 210
  4:23 210
Colossians
  1:1–2 118, 119
1 Thessalonians
  1:1 118, 119
2 Thessalonians
  1:1 118, 119
1 Timothy
  3:2 121
Titus
  1:5 121
  1:7 121
Hebrews
  12:2 145
James
  2:1–4 9, 19
  2:5–6 9
  5:14 121
1 Peter
  5:1 121

228 Index of ancient sources

Revelation
  13:16 9

Dead Sea Scrolls

1QS
  6.9–10 27

Christian literature

Ambrosiaster
  Epistle to the Philippians
  2.8.1–2 202
Augustine
  On Faith and Creed
  11 208
Eusebius
  Historia ecclesiastica
  5.1.47 31
John Chrysostom
  Homily on Philippians
  2.1.1–2 197
  8.2.5–11 145
Justin Martyr
  1 Apology
  1.13.4 145
Lactantius
  Institutiones
  4.26.29 145
Marius Victorinus
  Epistle to the Philippians
  2.67 202–3
Melito of Sardis
  Homily on the Passion
  96 145
Minucius Felix
  Octavius
  9.4 146
Novatian
  De Trinitate
  22.8–9 205
Origen
  Contra Celsum
  6.10 145
Theodore of Mopsuestia
  Epistle to the Philippians
  2.2 205

Greco-Roman

Aelius Aristides
  Orationes
  24.34 7
  26.71 60

Appian
  Bella civilia
  1.116 146
  1.120 209
  2.148 133
  4.105 65, 183
  4.105–38 183
  4.115 185
Apuleius
  Metamorphoses
  1.24–25 17
  3.12 42–43
  9.12 136–37, 138
  11.8–17 190
Aristotle
  Rhetorica
  2.6.26 50
Artemidorus Daldianus
  2.3 62
  3.52 62
Augustus
  Res gestae
  2 67
Aulus Gellius
  Noctes Atticae
  4.14 15–16
  16.13.8–9 66, 160
Caesar
  Bellum Gallicum
  5.44 76
  7.80 76
Cicero
  De domo sua
  1 189
  De legibus
  3.3.6–9 179
  De officiis 179
  1.42 19–20
  2.13 76
  2.25 20
  De republica
  1.12 44
  5.4 50
  Pro Archia
  26 44–45
  Pro Plancio
  15 3, 158
  60 178
  Pro Sestio
  45.96–97 11
  Pro Sulla
  48 140
  In Verrem
  2.5.12 146, 209

Index of ancient sources

2.5.167   114
2(5)162   147–48, 209
2(5)168–70   147–48, 209
Epistulae ad familiares
13.10.1   208
13.57.2   30
Orationes Philippicae
1.34   34
2.44   172
Partitiones oratoriae
26.91–92   44
Tusculanae disputationes
2.24.58   35
Claudian
In Eutropium
1.29–31   59
Digest
1.2.16–28 (Pomponius)
   179
Codex Theodosius 7.1.10
   [367]   76
Dio Cassius
47.35–49   183
49.12.4   209
51.4.6   187
52.19.1   178
54.3.7   209
55.22.4   172
55.31.2   32
56.42.2   187
69.19.1   73
Dio Chrysostom
Orationes
4.95   210
12.11   49
14.1   139
14.4   139
14.19   191
15.31–32   207–8
16.3   37–38
29.21   34
30.26   88
30.29–30   28
31.17   36–37
31.20   36–37, 89
31.22   40–41, 88–89
34.29   98
34.51   59
46.3   177
52.8.5   140
66.2   40
66.8   40
66.12   44
66.15   114

66.18   34
66.18–19   42
72.1–2   18
77/78.24   40–41
Diodorus Siculus
5.38.1   137, 138
16.3.7   65
16.8.6–7   65
31.25.2   16, 171
Dionysius of Halicarnassus
Antiquitates Romanae
5.51.2   209
7.69.1   209
Epictetus
Dissertationes
3.24.99   7
4.1.55   208
FIRA 2
Paulus, *Opinions*
5.19–19a   31
5.22.1–2   174
Fronto
Epistulae ad amicos
1.20   30
Epistulae ad Pium
1.10   51
Gaius
Institutiones
1.3.9   136, 206
Horace
Epistulae
2.1.197–98   171
Satirae
1.5.34–36   10
1.6.23–24   44
1.6.92   141
1.8.32   209
Isocrates
Ad Demonicum   50
Josephus
Antiquitates Judaicae
19.86   173
Bellum Judaicum
3.87   73
5.503   77
7.11   77
Juvenal
Satirae
1.01   179
4.1   207
5.12–25   26–27
5.67–71   26–27
6.490–93   207
6.84   207

Livy
  10.9.6   179
  22.33.2   209
  29.18.14   209
  33.36.3   209
  34.44.54   172
  42.34   13
Lucian
  Demonax
  58   44
  63   44
  Peregrinus
  18   44
  Saturnalia
  19   6, 157
  20   7
Lucretius
  De rerum natura
  1.922–23   45
  3.59–78   45
  4.4   45
  5.1120–35   45
Martial
  Epigrammaton libri
  3.94   207
  5.8   170
  5.14   170
  5.23   170
  5.25   170
  10.49   26
Orosius
  5.9.4   209
Petronius
  Satyricon   207
  32.1–3   14
  53.3   209
  117.11–12   139
Phaedrus
  3, *prologus* 34–36   140
Philo
  In Flaccum
  78   31
  Legatio ad Gaium
  110   204
Plautus
  Aulularia
  505–22   20–21, 171
  Bacchides
  362   146
  Miles gloriosus
  372   146
Pliny the Elder
  Naturalis historia
  33.6   170

  33.23   170
  33.32   14
Pliny the Younger
  Epistulae
  1.8   176–77
  1.14.5   46–47
  1.14.8   48
  1.19   10
  2.6   26
  3.2.6   51
  3.6   39
  3.20   55
  3.20.8–9   50
  4.15.9   208
  4.17.3   56
  7.29.3   180
  7.31.4   56
  8.6   180
  8.16.1–2   137–38, 206
  8.16.2–3   59
  8.24.9   149
  9.3   36
  9.5   31–32
  9.6.3   7
  10.12.2   55
  10.29–30   208
  10.96   31
Plutarch
  Agesilaus
  1   46
  Antonius
  22   183
  Brutus
  38–53   183
  46   70
  Cato Maior
  16.1–2   179
  18.4   39
  Cato Minor
  1.1   178
  16.4   178
  Cicero
  8.1   177
  13   172
  Crassus
  8   146
  Dion
  3–4   46
  Eumenes
  4.3   177
  Pelopidas
  3   46
  Phocion
  31.2   177

Index of ancient sources

Pompeius
21   146
Tiberius Gracchus
12   43
Quaestiones conviviales
616b–c   26
Polybius
6.12.1–9   179
6.23   72
6.39   72
6.53   16
Porphyry
De abstinentia
4.16   57
Quintilian
Institutio oratoria
3.8.1   37
6.3.63   22
9.3.56   49
Sallust
Bellum Catilinae
7.6   76
54   49
Bellum Iugurthinum
1.3   178
Scriptores Historiae Augustae
Commodus
3.3   180
Hadrian
18.7–11   207
Seneca
Ad Helviam
7.7   64
De clementia
1.26.1   146
De beneficiis
4.16.2   37
Epistulae
47.16   18
Strabo
Geographia
7, fr. 34   65
7, fr. 41   183, 186
Suetonius
Divus Augustus
1–6   46
2   5, 140
13   69
14   22
25   142
35   15, 54
38   15, 32
40   13, 22, 85, 172, 209

44   23, 24, 170, 173
49   72
74   27
94   13
Gaius Caligula
1   46
22   210
26   173
52   14
Divus Claudius
1–2   46
15   13
17   15
21   23
24   11, 180–81
25   178, 196, 207
26   210
28   180
29   210
34–37   210
Domitianus
8   170
Galba
14   14
Divus Iulius
33   14
39   14
43   170
45   170
48   27
76   53–54, 170
80   54
Nero
4   179
11   23
26–29   210
33–39   210
53   210
Tiberius
1–4   46
13   13
14   187
25   73
42   179
Symmachus
Epistulae
9   149
Tacitus
Annales
1.17   186
2.12   140
2.36   180
2.9   75
3.36   7, 8

Tacitus (*cont.*)
  4.6 55
  4.38 179
  6.3 23–24
  11.21 47
  11.23–25 54–55
  12.41 169
  12.52 10
  12.53 180
  12.64 52
  13.34 169
  13.46 140
  13.54 21–22
  14.31 70
  14.45 141
  14.59 210
  14.64–65 210
  15.44.3 146, 208
  15.60 210
  Historiae
  2.72 209
  4.6 45
  4.11 209
Valerius Maximus
  1.6.13 188
  1.8.8 188
  2.7.12 147
  3–6 178
  5.8.3 47
  5.8.4 76–77
  6.2.8 140–41
  6.5.6 29
  7.2.14 ext. 32
  7.6.1a 141–42
  8.4.1 208
  8.5.5 178
  8.5.6 28–29
  8.6.2 18
  8.14 60
  8.14, ext. 3 177
  9.14.1–2 7–8
  9.15.1 48
Varro
  De lingua Latina
  5.14.80–82 179
  De re rustica
  1.17.7 207
Velleius Paterculus
  1.15.5 185
  2.104.4 77
Vitruvius
  De architectura
  6.5.1–2 171

Inscriptions

CIL
  1.593 173
  1.594 173
  2.1963 57–58
  2.5439 173
  6.10234 57
  9.4815 39
  9.5074 173
  11.6167 173
  12.6038 189
  12.6039 173
  14.2112 58–59
  14.2979 173
ILS
  1909 175
  2117 59
PILHOFER
  001/L027 82, 98–99, 189, 192
  002/L028 83, 189
  004/L030 98, 192
  022/G220 106, 194
  026/L123 99–100, 193
  031/L121 98, 192
  037/L037 83–84, 190
  040/G040 109, 194
  057/L046 105, 193
  058/L047 79, 187
  061/L050 94, 192
  071/G437 127, 202
  077/G067 127, 202
  087/L265 96, 192
  120/L618 98, 192
  132/L303 106, 194
  133/G441 101, 193
  142/G562 105, 193
  143/G563 105, 193
  144/G298 105, 193
  148/L682 101, 193
  163/L002 101, 102, 103, 193
  164/L001 101, 102, 103, 193
  165/L003 101, 193
  166/L004 101, 102, 103–4, 193
  175/L012 106, 194
  177/L014 105, 193
  198/L307 91, 192
  201/L305 68, 185
  202/L313 78–79, 187
  203/L314 68, 185
  208/L461 68, 185
  213/L347 89–90, 103, 104, 191, 193

Index of ancient sources

214/L349	90, 125–26, 191, 201
215/L350	90, 191
217/L348	90, 191
218/L352	90–91, 125–26, 192, 201
219/L353	79, 90–91, 188, 192
226/L344	83, 189
228/L331	92, 192
229/L342	92–93, 192
230/L334	93
231/L341	192
232/L336	93, 115, 192, 196
233/L332	92, 192
235a/L804	192
240/L465	93–94, 150, 192, 209
249/L373	94, 100, 192, 193
252/L467	94–95, 101, 192, 193
254/L442	68, 185
257/L445	95, 192
270/L387	107, 108, 194
281/L371	185
282/L370	68, 185
287/L378	194
307/G410	101, 193
321/L377	100, 101, 105, 107, 108, 193, 194
322/L379	194
333/L268	106, 194
340/L589	100, 101, 193
344/L449	106, 194
348/G356	183
350/L448	100, 101, 106, 193, 194
386a/L839	96–97, 192
392/L6242	108, 194
394/L779	107, 194
395/L780	97, 125–26, 192, 201
396/L781	97, 192
416/L166	107, 108, 194
418/L266	74–75, 183, 185, 187
432/L163	106, 194
438/L077	98, 192
451/L158	105–6, 193, 194
452/L164	68, 185
455/L083	83–84, 190
476/L092	106–7, 108, 184, 194
492/L110	99, 192
493/L113	99, 193
502/L247	193
519/L245	105, 193
522/L210	79, 149, 188, 209
524/L103	101, 193
525/L104	101, 106, 193, 194
529/L106	105, 193
535/G207	105, 193
558/L408	194
581/L239	106, 194
588/L236	105, 193
597/G221	101, 193
600/L229	114, 196
700/L738	82, 189

SIG
2.814.30–31, 55   152

Papyri and Ostraca

Heidelberg Papyri
1716.5   133
Oxyrhynchus Papyri
1.37.5–6   152
Ostraca
1038 (from Thebes)   152

INDEX OF MODERN AUTHORS

Alcock, S., 71
Arlandson, J., 138

Bartchy, S., 138
Barton, C., 35, 159, 164
Bormann, L., 71, 75, 80, 84
Bourdieu, P., 48

Castelli, E., 166
Collart, P., 83

Dorcey, P., 86, 101
Dumont, L., 163

Elliott, J., 164-65
Everitt, A., 85

Fee, G., 119, 120, 123, 135
Flower, H., 16-17
Forbis, E., 95
Fowl, S., 131, 154
Fukuyama, F., 164

Garnsey, P., 60, 81, 112

Hengel, M., 144-45
Hoover, R., 133-34
Hopkins, K., 4-5

Kloppenborg, J. S., 58
Koukouli-Chrysantaki, C., 80
Kreitzer, L., 153

Lendering, J., 52
Lendon, J., 34-36, 41-53, 60-62, 76-78, 151
Lenski, G., 3-4, 37-38, 40, 138, 212
Littlejohn, J., 1, 31
Lohmeyer, E., 129

MacMullen, R., 38, 40, 60, 105, 141
Malina, B., 41, 49-50
Martin, D., 107-8, 139
Merk, O., 143
Moore, S., 166
Moxnes, H., 35-36, 41, 175

Neyrey, J., 41, 85

Oakes, P., 71, 106, 113-14, 127
O'Brien, P., 119, 120, 123-24, 132, 145

Papazoglou, F., 115
Pascal, B., 32
Pilhofer, P., 67, 71, 84-85, 111-12, 121, 126, 194, 195
Price, S. R. F., 81

Rapske, B., 113, 116
Reinhold, M., 63

Sack, R., 85
Saller, R., 22, 25, 32, 60, 81, 182
Salmon, E. T., 70
Schweizer, E., 131
Sève, M., 92
Speidel, M. A., 73
Stegemann, E., 9, 139
Stegemann, W., 9, 139, 140

Tellbe, M., 133, 152-53
Theissen, G., 157

Walker-Ramisch, S., 61
Whittaker, C., 87
Witherington, B., 110-11
Wright, N. T., 152

SUBJECT INDEX

adlectio, 192
aediles, 52, 97
  in Silvanus cult, 102–3
agrarian society, 4
Alexander the Great, 80, 188
ancestor masks (*imagines*), 16–17
ancestry, *see* birth status
Antioch, 66, 112
Antony, Mark, 5–6, 140
  and Philippi, 67, 69–70, 74
Aphrodisias, 184–85
Aramaic, 152, 203
army
  competition for honors in, 75–78
  cursus, 59, 78–80
  slaves in, 141–42
  and social mobility, 60–61, 182
  social stratification in, 59, 72–75, 159–60
attire, 12–19
  in the army, 72
  glory and, 132–33
  occupations and, 18–19
  in scheme of values, 48
  status system, 12–19, 85, 201;
    attempts to usurp, 14–15, 170;
    objections to, 18–19
Augustales, see *sexviri Augustales*
Augustus (Octavian), 5–6, 15, 54, 67, 85, 140, 170–71, 185
  and the army, 72–73
  and the goddess Victoria, 67–68, 185, 188
  and Philippi, 65–66, 67–70, 80, 185, 187, 209

Bacchus, cult of, 100
banquets, seating at, 25–28
benefaction, 38, 77, 91–92, 93, 94–95, 99–100, 177
  in Silvanus cult, 103–4

birth status, 46–48
  attempts to falsify, 47–48
  see also status
"bishops and deacons," 118, 120–21, 198–99
body, status and, 48–49

Caesar, Julius, 53–54, 170, 177
cap of liberty (*pilleus*), 17–18
children, 99
Christianity
  and citizenship, 197
  early ethics, 157, 211
  and honor/status, 145–46, 157, 164–66, 213
  and individualism, 81
  metaphor of family, 176
  and Philippian culture, 127–28
  and political order/politics, 189
  ruler cult and, 150, 151–53
  Silvanus cult and, 101–2
  and social organization, 120–21
  and social stratification, 9, 62, 164–65
  and status, *see under* honor *in this entry*
  and status system of attire, 19
Christology, 129, 211
church leaders
  terminology for, 118, 120–21, 198–99
  and voluntary associations/groups, 198
circumcision, 122–23, 124, 200, 201
citizenship, 31, 114, 209
  attire and, 13–14
  Christians and, 197
  crucifixion and, 147–48
  and the flaminate, 82
  Paul and, in relation to Philippi, 112–14, 126
  see also Roman citizenship *under* Philippi

235

city prefects, 52
class, 6, 61, 186
  see also social stratification
Claudius, 54–55, 66, 180–81
clothing, see attire
collectivism, 41, 49–50, 177–78
  see also communism and community
colonization, see Roman colonization
communism, 163, 212
community, 41, 154, 155–56, 165, 177–78, 211
  see also collectivism
conflict theory, 163, 212
consciousness, social stratification and, 28, 32–33, 62, 63, 163–65
consuls, 52
Corinth, 184
countercultural groups, 61–62
crucifixion, 21, 131, 144–48, 165–66
  slavery and, 146–48
Cupid, cult of, 100
cursus honorum, 51–52, 55–56, 158–59
  Jesus and, 56
  Paul and, 123–28
  provincial, 57–58, 159
  replication in non-elite settings, 56–62
  in Rome, 51–56
  in scheme of values, 48
  violation of, 53–55
  see also public office and under Philippi
cursus pudorum, 129–48, 162–63
Cybele, cult of, 100, 191

deconstruction, 165
decurions, 9–11
Dio Chrysostom, 28, 36–37, 42, 88–89, 207–8
Dionysus, cult of, 86–87, 101
doctrine, ethics and, 129, 202
dreams, interpretation of, 62
dress, see attire

education, 46, 178
emperors, 133, 152–53
  see also ruler cult
equestrians, 9–11
  rings, 14–15, 17
ethics, 166
  doctrine and, 129, 202
  early Christian, 157, 211
exemplars
  inscriptions and, 95, 203
  Jesus as, 144, 203

family
  birth status, 46–48
  metaphor of, 176
  fathers, 47
  see also patriarchy
festivals
  of ruler cult, 81, 83, 84
  see also rituals
flamines, 82–84, 189
flogging, 196
food distribution, 32, 175
freedpersons, 140–41, 158, 207
  cap of liberty (pilleus), 17–18
  and positions of honor, 181
  recording status, 107–8
  social mobility, 60–61, 182
  and the toga, 12
functionalism, 163–65, 212
funerals, 16–17

games, seating at, 15
gender issues, 101, 212–13
gold rings, 14–15, 17
Greek cities, 184–85
Greek culture, 46, 191
  Philippi and, 66, 71–72, 184–85
guilt, 49–50

Hellenic culture, see Greek culture
hierarchy
  in cults/religions, 56–57, 58, 182
  among slaves, 59–60
  in voluntary groups, 57–59, 181
  see also cursus honorum and social stratification
historical accuracy, 4–6
honor, 11, 34–39
  ascribed/acquired, 124–26
  and birth status, 46–48, 124–26
  centrality as value, 35–40, 175–76
  Christianity and, 164–66
  conferring, 52–55, 149–50, 209
  guilt and, 49–50
  obedience and, 143–44
  Paul and, 120–21
  as public commodity, 35, 38–45
  public office and, 51
  reconstruction/reversal, 116, 121, 135, 148–49, 154–55, 166, 196
  wealth and, 37–40
  see also cursus honorum and under Philippi
Horace, 141
household conversion, 102, 193

Subject index

household slaves, 137–38, 207
housing, 48, 171
humility/humilification, 143

Iconium, 66
imagines (masks), 16–17
imperial cult, *see* ruler cult
individualism, 49–50, 177–78
  religion and, 81
  see also collectivism
inscriptions, 182–83
  function, 95, 203
  see also under Philippi, honor/status in
Isis, cult of, 94–95, 101, 190, 191

Jewish Messianists, 122
Jewish worship, 87
judges, 52
  see also magistrates
justice, *see* legal system

land allotment, ritual for, 74
latus clavus, 14, 15, 150
legal status, *see under* status
legal system, 15–16, 28–32, 112–13, 147–48
Livia, 80, 82
  priestesses of, 82, 83
living in public, 159, 179
Luke, and Philippi, 110–11, 161–62, 194, 195

Macedonia, 110–11, 194, 195
  voluntary associations/groups, 181
Macedonian churches, 119, 198
magistrates/magistracies, 52, 53, 58, 179–80, 192
mantle, Greek, 13–14
manual work, attitudes to, 20–21, 45
manumission, 17
  see also freedpersons
masks (*imagines*), 16–17
meals, seating at, 25–28
Messianists, Jewish, 122
military, *see* army
Mithraism, 56–57, 182
morality, 49–50
motivation, 49–50, 163, 203, 212

names, 151
natal origin, *see* birth status

obedience, 143–44
occupations, 19–21, 60
  and attire, 18–19
  see also social mobility
Octavian, *see* Augustus
ontological questions, 129
orchestra, 23, 24

paganism, *see* religion
parades, 32
patres, in Silvanus cult, 103
patriarchy, 212–13
  see also fathers
patronage, 38, 177
Paul of Tarsus, 62
  actions in Philippi compared to Jesus, 116, 196
  authorship questions concerning, 130, 155–56, 199–200, 202–3
  citizenship and status, 195–96
  "opponents" in Philippi, 122, 200, 201
  and Philippi, 79, 87, 127–28, 188, 191
  relationships with different churches, 119
  self-descriptions analyzed with regard to status, 117–20, 121–28, 162
  ways of addressing recipients of letters, 118, 120–21
Philip II, 80
Philippi, 46, 63, 160–61
  Antony and, *see under* Antony
  Augustus and, *see under* Augustus
  baths, 99–100
  Christians in, 206
  colonization of, 65–72, 160
  cursus, 88, 97, 192
  and emperors (*see also* ruler cult *in this entry*), 68–69
  forum, 66, 86, 89–94, 160
  and Greek culture, 66, 71–72, 184–85, 191
  history, 64–66, 67–68, 70–1
  honor/status in, concern with, and expressions of, 89–109, 116, 142, 160–61; Paul and, 125–26
  inscriptions from, 182–83
  Jewish worship in, 87
  languages used in, 66, 183–84, 191
  Luke and, 110–11, 194, 195
  marketplace, 94–96
  military orientation, 69, 74–75, 187
  population, 70, 185–86
  power in, 70, 71–72, 160
  public offices/honors in, 66, 89–109

238   Subject index

Philippi (*cont.*)
  religion in (*see also* ruler cult *in this entry*), 66, 80, 86–87, 161
  Roman citizenship in, 113–16
  Romanness, 66–69, 70, 71–72, 116, 120–21, 183–84, 190
  ruler cult in, 78, 80–84, 86, 87, 160, 188
  theater, 66, 106–7, 184, 190, 194
  and Thracian culture, 84–85, 191
philosophers, 44–45
pilleus (cap of liberty), 17–18
postmodernism, 165
posture, 48–49
praetors, 52
prefects, city, 52
priorities, 37–40
privacy issues, 159, 179
  religion and, 81, 189
provinces
  replicating Roman social structures, 24–25
  see also under cursus honorum
public, living in, 159, 179
public events, seating at, *see* seating at public events
public gods, 81
public office
  honor and, 51
  in Philippi, 66
  and status of person bestowing it, 56
  see also cursus honorum
punishments, 24, 31, 47, 179
  status and, 196
  see also under slavery

quaestors, 52, 97
Qumran communities, 27

recognition, desire for, 34
  see also honor
relational issues, 154, 155–56, 211
  see also community *and* social stratification
religion, 81–84, 189, 191
  and honor/status, 100–6
  household conversion, 102, 193
  individual/public, 81–84
  in Philippi, *see under* Philippi
  pluralism, 80, 190–91
  and political order/politics, 189
  territoriality, 85–87
  see also Christianity, ruler cult, *and* Silvanus, cult of

religious groups, hierarchy in, 56–57, 58, 182
resistance, 14–15, 55, 170–71
retinues, 46
rings, 14–15, 17
rites of passage, 201
rituals
  for foundation of Roman cities, 67
  for land allotment, 74
  of ruler cult, 81
  see also festivals
Roman cities, foundation rituals, 67
Roman citizenship, *see* citizenship
Roman colonization, 65–72, 159–60, 183
  and Greek culture, 184–85
  see also under Philippi
Roman society/social organization, 6–11, 157–60
  see also cursus honorum and status
Rome, forum, 85
Rufus, Quintus Paquius, 74
ruler cult, 80–84, 86, 160, 188
  Paul and, 150, 151–53
  see also under Philippi

sacerdotes, in Silvanus cult, 102
sacerdotes divae Augustae, 82
sacred/secular dichotomy, 189
salutatio, 46, 73, 174
seating
  at private banquets, 25–28
  at public events, 15, 21–25, 190
senators, 9–11
Seneca, 18–19
Serapis, cult of, 101
servants, *see* slavery/servanthood
sexviri Augustales, 82–84, 189–90
shame
  guilt and, 49–50
  see also honor
Silvanus, cult of, 66, 86, 101–5, 161, 193
slavery, 131, 136–42
  crucifixion and, 146–48
  and human nature, 205
  in Philippi, 206
  and punishments, 196, 208
  see also slaves
slavery/servanthood, terminology of, 119–20, 135–36, 139, 206
slaves
  in the army, 141–42
  freed, *see* freedpersons
  hierarchy among, 59–60

Subject index

recording status, 107–8
resources, 206
treatment of, 137–38, 207
see also slavery
social class, *see* class
social leveling, attempts at, 163, 170–71, 212
social mobility, 47–48, 60–61, 158
social replication, *see* value replication
social status, *see* status
social stratification
  acceptance of, 31–32
  in the army, *see under* army
  biology and, 212
  Christianity and, *see under* Christianity
  consciousness and, 28, 32–33, 62, 63, 163–65
  defined, 3–4
  functionality, 163–65
  Jewish, 8
  modern western society and, 30, 164, 174
  public expressions of, 11–33, 63
  Roman, 6–11, 157–60
  ruler cult and, 81–84
  two-strata perspective, 6–9, 157–58
  ubiquity, 30, 163–65
  see also honor
social upheaval, 55, 170
socialism, 163, 212
societies, types, 3–4
soldiers, *see* army
sources, 4–6
  limitations, 32–33
space, territoriality, 85–87
status, 138–42
  Christianity and, *see* honor/status *under* Christianity
  legal, 48
  names and, 151

see also birth status, citizenship, honor, slavery, *and* social stratification
stigma, 141–42, 144–48, 158
suffering, 154, 211
Suregethes, cult of, 101
symbols, 165–66

tables, seating at, 25–28
territoriality, 85–87
theaters, 24–25, 172
  in Philippi, 66, 106–7, 184, 190, 194
  see also seating at public events
Thracian culture, 84–85, 191
Thracian Horseman, cult of, 86–87, 191
toga, 12–14, 85, 201
trade unions, 61–62
tribes, 114–16, 126, 162, 197, 201
truth, sources and, 4–6
two-strata perspective, 6–9, 157–58

urban patronage, 38, 177

value replication, 46, 71–72, 186
values, 37–40, 48–50
  see also honor
Victoria (goddess), 67–68, 185, 188
virtue, 49–50
voluntary associations/groups, 57–59, 61–62, 100–9, 161, 181
  Paul and, 127–28, 198

wealth, 48
  honor and, 37–40
  and social mobility, 60
whipping, 196
women, 101, 212–13
work
  attitudes to, 20–21, 45
  see also occupations